Power Lines

Other titles in the series

Voices and Visions:
New Thinking for the New Century

About the series:

As the dawn of the 21st century approaches, the search for new answers and new solutions to both longstanding and escalating new crises has become more difficult. The end of the Cold War has not led to a new era of peace and egalitarian justice, or even an end to war, virulent nationalisms or generation-slaying famines.

This new series is designed to bring together some of the most innovative thinkers of the 20-21st century, as they take on these challenges. It will include groundbreaking works in philosophy, politics, economics, history and historiography, cultural criticism, women's studies and analysis of current affairs, as they intersect and cross-fertilize and bring new approaches to each other.

Titles published:

Visions and Revisions: Reflections on Culture and Democracy at the End of the Century
by Marcus Raskin

Calling the Shots: How Washington Dominates Today's UN
by Phyllis Bennis, foreword by Erskine Childers

To order a complete catalog or request additional information, please call **1-800-238-LINK** or write to:

Interlink Publishing
46 Crosby Street
Northampton, MA 01060
Tel: (413)582-7054 Fax: (413)582-7057
e-mail: interpg@aol.com

Power Lines

U.S. Domination in the New Global Order

ALEJANDRO BENDAÑA

OLIVE
BRANCH
PRESS

An imprint of Interlink Publishing Group, Inc.
New York

First published in 1996 by

Olive Branch Press
An imprint of Interlink Publishing Group, Inc.
99 Seventh Avenue, Brooklyn, New York 11215

Library of Congress Cataloging-in-Publication Data

Bendaña, Alejandro.
Power lines: U.S. domination in the new global order / Alejandro Bendaña
p. cm.
Includes bibliographical references and index.
ISBN 1-56656-167-1 (hardback) ISBN 1-56656-168-X (paperback)
1. International economic relations. 2. International economic integration.
3. United States — Foreign economic relations — Developing countries.
4. Developing countries — Foreign economic relations — United States.
5. International business enterprises — United States. I. Title.
HF 1359.B434 1996
337 — dc20

96-4559
CIP

Printed and bound in the United States of America
10 9 8 7 6 5 4 3 2 1

For Zoilamérica

I do not believe in any effort called peace education,
if instead of revealing the world of injustice,
tends to cloud it and blind its victims ...
Reflection, if it is true reflection, leads to practice ...

— *Paulo Freire*

CONTENTS

INTRODUCTION

This book is intended to assess some of the sweeping changes of the past few years as they may affect the South. Because these changes have been less significant in the South, we write chiefly about the North. If we are to advance in the path of humanist development, it is critical that we seek to understand the global context in which we operate and to think through its implications. We in the South must be especially mindful of the role of such analysis to sustain and inform the necessary refocusing of many of our strategies for transformation.

We do not address all of the many international issues that occupy headlines. Some episodes are examined on account of what they tell us of the nature of the global power system and the role of the United States in it. Such a concern, of course, is not exclusive to any region or social sector, particularly those who believe that the power structure itself poses a threat to the survival of humanity, and that a selected few do not have the right to determine the conditions of life and death for the many.

A strenuous effort must be made to come to terms, coldly but from a standpoint of principle, with the dramatic changes of the past few years. One must start with the recognition that history did not begin or end with the collapse of the Soviet bloc. Many momentous shifts were already underway on the world stage, some of which contributed to political change in Eastern Europe and in the world balance of forces. Changes in this part of the world are linked to equally momentous surges in the transnationalization of capital and markets. The combination of political and economic turmoil forces us to re-evaluate concepts and modalities of transformation that carry over into rethinking the way we analyze world dynamics and United States global engagement.

When things are confusing, magical interpretations always appear as a ready substitute for hard thinking and action. Some interpretations of change and power focus on the dizzying expansion of technology misleading termed "revolutionary." Technological changes, however, should not be measured outside the remarkably resilient structure of Western power and domination inherited from the past. The transformative potential of science is by and large shaped, controlled, and circumscribed by the same forces that circumscribe democratic transformation itself. This, of course, is not a simple relationship, nor a harmonious one, but before the vision of billions of information-driven human beings carrying laptop computers can materialize, questions have to be posed about power and the contradiction between concentrated wealth and massified poverty.

Cybernetics notwithstanding, one could claim that little has changed for most people in the South, that the end of the Cold War signifies little more than ideological confusion: the long and violent economic war against the South continues and in many senses is intensified. Some in the North now appear shocked at the magnitude and depth of social forces exploding in the South, at the shifting configuration of nations and the degree of violence employed. But what is new to some has been daily fare for others. What does seem novel is the post-Cold War compulsion in the North to "do" something about it, sometimes by applying conflict-resolution techniques, other times by simply intervening in the best tradition of upholding the white man's burden.

Others tell us that because the entire global environment has changed, and because this is the new permanent reality, we therefore must also adapt all thought and action to the new fashion or reality. It is further said that in the absence of a socialist bloc in the world system, no longer can strategic programs of liberation movements in the South afford to remain the same as when imperialism faced a military, political, and economic counterweight.

Privileged elites in the South join in the "realist" chorus coming from the North. Like their Northern counterparts, they replace the Cold War prism through which they viewed the world with a new one labeled "globalization." All of a sudden we have a new all explaining and all enveloping invincible notion of techno-scientific proof: "global market forces" are at once premise, cause, manifestation, and consequence of practically all that is new or presented as new in the fields of culture, production, information, institutions, consumption, organization, marketing, finance, and values.

In truth, the tendency to elevate the market to the rank of universal law or even liberation force is endemic to capitalism itself. State and market reinforce each other in order to project globalization. Modern pundits would do well to recall Karl Polanyi's carefully documented findings of 1944 of how the market is the result of a conscious and often violent intervention by political forces, and that the consideration of market forces outside its political and social context not only distorts our view of human beings and society, but becomes a serious impediment to addressing the problems of humankind. Yet to this day, attempts to question the validity of the free market and of free enterprise as a basis of development and democracy in the South provoke violent ideological and political responses.

Worse perhaps, market values are universalized so as to invade ways of thinking, or perhaps non-thinking; that is to say, to affect patterns of action and non-action. We are told the market does not require much guidance. United States or International Monetary Fund intervention in sovereign countries is not seen as such, but rather as part of giving nature a helping hand in the unstoppable march of the expanding marketplace.

It follows that there is no room for protest against the natural order of things. Imperialism and ruling elites have ceased to exist, or even become identifiable, because the force is the "invisible hand" of the market, which corrects all political, economic, and ideological distortions and imposes solid behavior. Capital is the new global deity for whom borders and nationalist ideologies are relics from the past.

Apparently nations in the South are damned if they accept globalism and damned if they don't. And which form of domination may not even be a matter of choice. Countries in the South are inextricably parts of a broader international system. World power structures and global economics have significantly diminished the possibilities for autonomous development. There is a corresponding temptation to dispense with political mobilization.

The post-Cold War presumption is that the West, now victorious over the evil empire, can marshall the same combination of political, economic, and military power to inaugurate a new period in world history; again, of course, under the unchallenged tutelage of the United States. The repercussions of this phenomenon are more apparent in the South (especially with the disappearance of support for nationalist or anti-capitalist movements and states), but we argue that patterns of North-North conflicts are important indicators of how globalization in general and the U.S. in particular are laying down world ground rules for rich and poor to follow. Washington remains determined to prevent the rise of military competitors and to rein in economic ones.

At the same time, corporations spin worldwide webs to seek out the cheapest labor, franchising activities wherever capital can secure the highest profit. How do they interact with each other, with their governments, with bankers and financial markets? Some hypotheses are raised.

We have tried to neither mystify nor deify the nation-state. This is not an easy effort in this day and age of a United States reasserting and exercising its "right" to intervene unilaterally on the one hand, and of transnationalized capital and cross-national production on the other. Perhaps the classical notions of pure "national" corporate capital or ruling elites are losing meaning, but we have not yet arrived at a transnationalized international operating system capable of insuring open markets in both the North and South. While the rich governments have no major disagreement in mandating the World Bank and the IMF to push for the free global movement of capital and to pressure the South to increase capital-friendly inducements, these same institutions are unable to turn on their masters and demand concessions inside the rich countries themselves.

Corporate capital, national or transnational, is inherently incapable of managing the pace and consequences of its own expansion. This has always been the case. Without ground rules, the system remains vulnerable to the triple threats of socialistic or nationalistic state-managed economies, anarchy brought on by cut-throat national capitalist rivalries, or market breakdowns provoked by out of control speculators. Government, therefore, is as much a burden as a necessity, to get capital into markets and out of trouble, but otherwise, to get out of the way. The problem is the multiplicity of governments with different rules of engagement and favoritism.

Some claim that globalization has already subverted United States politics, transforming its government into a world political center, pulled away from domestic concerns by a network of global linkages and responsibilities. This may be an exaggeration, although it is true that the assumption of "internationalist" duties — imperialist in the case of the U.S. — entails diminishing national democracy and public accountability. By the same token, greater democracy may curtail Washington's hand in seeking to control economic, political, and socio-cultural world makeovers in order to make the world safe for U.S. corporations and capitalist expansion.

One retains the hope of being proven totally wrong in regard to the projection of unipolarity here presented. At the same time, citizens of the South must also understand that the privileged North-oriented minorities in their own countries form part of that U.S.-dominated system that challenges human dignity and social justice in both North and South. The division of labor respects no borders as it creates new disparities of well-being within and across nations. And in the context of free market competitiveness, so too does the power structure reduce its willingness and capacity to reverse the devastating social effects of inequality. U.S. power and corporations will only grow more distant from their own citizens as transnational ties are forged with isolated local elites and capital around the world.

1

Global Structural Adjustment

In the United Nations Charter, the founding governments pledged to "employ international machinery for the promotion of the economic and social advancement of all peoples," also committing themselves to promote "higher standards of living, full employment, and conditions of economic and social progress and development with a view to the creation of conditions of stability and well-being." International cooperation would be the instrument to "solving international problems of an economic, cultural, or humanitarian character." And the United Nations would constitute "a center for harmonizing the actions of nations" in reaching such common ends.

Fifty years later, the global social picture indicates a massive failure to achieve this primordial legal and moral obligation. Rising unemployment, poverty, and crime are virtually endemic. Inter-ethnic violence and civil war are on the rise in many parts of the world. Material progress achieved in some areas over the last half century is now eroding in the face of social and economic crisis. Instead of accelerating socioeconomic progress, the end of the Cold War had a destabilizing effect in many quarters, as old conflicts returned with new vengeance and new social tensions refused to be confined to national borders.

The East-West conflict was in many senses simply a useful interpretative framework for the long-standing conflict occasioned by the global maldistribution of wealth and power. The United Nations *Human Development Report 1992* found that 20 percent of humanity, almost all of it in a few rich countries in the North, accounted for 82.7 percent of world gross national product; 81.2 percent of world trade; 94.6 percent of all commercial lending; 80.6 percent of all domestic savings; and 80.5 percent of all research and development. At the other extreme, the poorest 20 percent, virtually all in the South, accounted for 1.4 percent of world gross national product; 1 percent of world trade; 0.2 percent of all commercial lending; 1 percent of domestic savings; and 1.3 percent of domestic investment. In 1960, the wealthiest fifth of the world's nations were 30 times richer than the poorest fifth. By 1990, they were 60 times richer.[1]

And what about "order" in this new globalized world of ours? According to one study, "The global number of conflicts, which had declined between 1987 and 1990, rose rapidly in 1991 and 1992, setting an all-time record of 29 major wars underway in a single year .... War deaths were the highest in 17 years, extending a pattern of growing violence and human suffering in local wars." According to the International Peace Research Institute, in December 1993, 52 wars were being fought across the globe, and another 37 countries were experiencing systemic violence.[2]

These aspects of the post-Cold War order are evident, but the causes of those manifestations demand further discussion. Few would disagree that many of the features of the massive changes in the international political terrain that became visible in the late 1980s actually emerged before then, and have continued to develop since. And the question must be posed whether the violent breakdown of certain states, from the former Yugoslavia to Rwanda to Somalia, is related to the economic dislocation caused by national or regional elites seeking to increase their own market efficiency by "de-linking" themselves from nearby, but less "efficient" regions, policies, or cultures.

Is it true that what has come to be called the North-South conflict, the battle between haves and have-nots, was already present, although somewhat obscured from the perspective of the Western media, during the Cold War? What does the collapse of the Soviet Union and state socialism in Eastern Europe entail for that conflict? How does the absence of a substantive military and diplomatic counterweight to "Western" colonialism affect current North-South relations?

A further question stems from what is now termed "globalization" — a multi-faceted process that increasingly interlocks different regions of the world while attempting to homogenize popular perceptions of vastly disparate social realities, and sometimes even the reality itself. Some would claim that the collapse of the Eastern European states was attributable to globalization, at least its economic components. Although some features of a "world economy" can be dated back to the seventeenth century, never before have external "global" factors weighed so heavily on so many nations, inverting in many senses the previous general balance between the "national" and the "external," particularly in the most powerful and influential (and most developed capitalist) core economies themselves.

The predominance of the external over the internal is certainly as old as colonialism itself, but even in the old-style colonies there were pockets, and sometimes entire sectors, that maintained some degree of autonomy — if not in economic life, then in other spheres of social interaction. Today's national economies in effect are tied together not only by trade in goods, but also through trade in services, financial and multinational production, and images.

But "globalization," like the market itself, is not some impersonal natural system like the tide or the weather. As with the technology that catapults the integration, globalization and the market reflect and uphold the prejudices and material interests of the large investors. Their urge to consolidate and institutionalize the inherently unbalanced integration process is also shared by powerful governments and the international economic institutions. Frameworks such as the communications or information revolution, while underscoring the dramatic pace of contemporary technological change, do not themselves advance our understanding of social changes or shifts in the distributions of wealth and power.

Global changes pose important theoretical and analytical challenges. Without presuming the capacity to predict the future, we must seek to interpret the present. How should we conceive and analyze political and economic forces driving new forms of transnationalization, while still responding to established profit-driven motivations capable of generating and broadening lines of power, and political and ideological self-defense? The system itself, of course, denies its colonialist nature and presents its expansion as the spontaneous and natural action of "the market." That is, market reality is presented as the only influence on the economy, denying the authoritarian role played by big capital and its partners in governments and the multilateral financial and trade organizations.

Humanist value judgments do not form part of that "reality." Nor can purely economic motivation explain governmental decision-making, as states will continue to be guided by risk assessments and perceptions often alien to liberal capitalist theory, which is perhaps why nation-states continue to go to war when it is clear that in economic terms more tends to be lost than won. This is also why states have failed to effectively regulate and stabilize an international financial system which, most experts agree, requires regulation in order to function and generate profits.[3]

Nagging doubts were cast aside when pundits and politicians rushed to theorize about the meaning of the "victory" of the West in the Cold War. Generalization once again overtook discussions about the role and policies of specific states — both East and West — in order to posit the victory of one "system" over another. We witnessed the proclamation of the end of theory and history as part of an ideological triumphalist declaration that with the collapse of the Eastern European socialist regimes, capitalism was now proclaimed the winner and "only" path for the rest of the world to follow. The difficulties faced by the remaining non-capitalist states, especially in the South, and their incapacity to build effective Third World blocs, only reinforced this interpretation. Fewer and fewer governments, regional state organizations, or intergovernmental bodies, including the UN, had the will and capacity to contest the dictates of corporate capital.

But renewed elite confidence in capitalism has not translated into a new capacity of that system to solve basic social and economic problems, particularly in the South. Nor has it promised a more equitable relationship between rich and poor. What the new ideological zeal and new geopolitical terrain does entail is a greater possibility of cooptation of elites and middle sectors in the South. Power and greed combine therefore to permit the North to dictate terms of trade, investment, and political development on the peoples of the South more easily, while at the same time claiming that it is nothing more than a proven universalist market conception of democracy and economic growth that is inexorably at work.

If there is anything new and universal about the new world order, it is the spread and level of violence. Neo-liberal governments in the South, made financially and politically powerless by the control of the North, the debt crisis, and the collapse in commodity prices, have few options save repression to answer growing social unrest. We cannot expect "orderly" behavior and "proper" adherence to Gladstonian liberal principles from the governments of a world in which 1 billion people lack basic health care, in a world which spends over $600 billion a year on military programs but in which one adult in four is unable to read and write, and a world in which one-fifth of the population goes hungry every day, where over two billion suffer from hidden hunger or nutrient deficiency, most of them women and children, and a world populated largely by victims of the growing disparity in access to basic resources and fundamental human rights.[4]

So how and where to resist the continued concentration of power centered in the United States and its allies and instruments, the Group of Seven, the international financial institutions, and the large transnational corporations? How to challenge their intolerable capacity to effectively set the parameters and limitations of economic, social, and political development, North and South, based on an ideological superstructure that would have us believe that if we work and toil just a little bit longer, no matter how bad our conditions, salvation will materialize. It is a question also posed by unions and workers in the North whose political influence has been steadily diminished. Unions have watched as social programs are dismantled, as money and power continue to shift to employers and corporations. At the same time the State itself, while leaving untouched skyrocketing military budgets, becomes an instrument of privatization, helping the economically powerful to reduce what industrialists call "the social costs" that affect their competitiveness and profits.

In the United States, where one out of seven persons lives in poverty, the B-2 Stealth bomber, the most expensive combat plane in history, is scheduled to cost $2.3 billion per plane, or about three times its weight in gold.[5] Corporate profits in the U.S. and the UK are at a 30-year record level. It is no surprise that that rate should coincide with the ferocious attacks launched by President Reagan and Prime Minister Thatcher against poor people and labor. The only surprise is that even the business-revered weekly the *Economist* once spoke so plainly, terming the lucre "profits without honor," concluding that the revival has clearly been at the expense of workers, particularly the unskilled.[6]

The question remains, though, whether Washington's superpower standing and primacy among competitors translates into U.S. capacity to impose its own dominance as a new "order" on the capitalist system as a whole. When the periods of boom peter out, the limits and contradictions of hegemony in the real world reveal themselves, as illusions of "free" trade and universal economic complementarity become their first victims.

WINNERS AND LOSERS

Undeniably, the divide between "North" and "South" is widening and deepening. One need only point to deteriorating terms of trade, the instability in prices for most traditional exports from the South, and the overall net flows of capital from South to North generated by debt servicing to see the clear divide between nation-states in the two economic realms of the world.

Structural adjustment programs largely drawn up in the North further accentuate the divide by undermining the already weak capacity of governments in the "Third World" to adopt policies that would mitigate the effects of "free trade" in markets dominated by huge corporate conglomerations. These programs, or SAPs, are primarily the creation of such international financial institutions as the International Monetary Fund and the World Bank. Designed for usually impoverished developing countries as the conditions for receiving IMF or World Bank loans, they restructure economic relations in the country by redefining the social contract between the government, the wealthy few, and the rest. "The rest" are the ones who pay the price — through often dramatic reductions in state expenditures on social programs. This means selling public sector enterprises, eliminating subsidies, devaluing currencies, charging fees for basic services such as education and health care, dropping tariffs aimed at protecting local production, etc.

But the nature of the system and the depth of the crisis is such that elements of both "North" and "South" overlap and coexist almost everywhere on the planet. Industrial societies of the North have their internal "South" — usually immigrants and minorities — while the "Third World" maintains its own enclaves of the North, in the form of local capitalists who profit from globalization and their nation's own poverty. Some additional facts underscore the appearance of a globally bifurcated society, as the poorest of the poorer countries tend to be the hardest hit, and the richest in parts of the South now figure among the richest in the world, and their countries suffer the planet's most disproportionate distribution of income.

In 1988 the secretary-general of the United Nations concluded that "the most vulnerable population groups, in particular women, youth, the disabled and the aged, have been severely and adversely affected."[7] According to one expert, "At least six million children under five years of age have died each year since 1982 in Africa, Asia and Latin America because of SAPs."[8] *Forbes* magazine, meanwhile, calculates that the number of billionaires in the world has increased from 145 in 1987 to 358 in 1994. Together they control a capital of $761.9 billion, about the equivalent to the annual per-capita income of 45 percent of the world's population.[9]

The critical dividing line to be made within the South is not between Africa and East Asia, including the so-called Tigers of East Asia, but between the governing capitalist elites throughout the South and most of its national populations. True, income disparity between the wealthiest fifth of the world's nations and the poorest fifth doubled between 1960 and 1990. But according to the UN, the skewed distribution of income *within* countries grew at a far higher level, as the richest 20 percent of the world's peoples became at least 150 times richer than the bottom 20 percent.[10] There are no figures showing income disparity within the South, but *Forbes'* recap does indicate that the reproduction rate for billionaires has been higher in the South: in Latin America, from 12 in 1987 to 47 in 1994 — of whom 24 were Mexican with total assets of $44.1 billion. That extraordinary billionaire breeding program may have been part of the reason Mexico was long viewed as a model of successful structural adjustment and advantageous integration — at least until the indigenous uprising in Chiapas which began the very day the North American Free Trade Agreement took effect, followed by the 1994 collapse of the Mexican economy.

In such a collaborative mutually-rewarding effort between companionable elites of the North and South, new infusions of Northern (often multilateral) cash to their Southern counterparts serve to buttress their ideological neo-liberal convictions as well as providing immediate financial gain. The result is to leave the ruling classes in the South largely unaffected personally by the devastating austerity policies they willfully negotiate with the IMF, the World Bank, and institutions such as USAID. On the contrary, bureaucratic elites that run the state apparatuses of the South become entrepreneurial ones to reap the benefits of privatization and free global movement of capital and trade, to create new business opportunities from increased incentives to attract private capital, and partnerships with incoming foreign capital, thereby further concentrating wealth in their own countries. Thus, while it is true that the profit-oriented world economy accentuates the differences between rich and poor countries and people, it also strengthens the bond between elites in the South and their counterparts in the North, divorcing both of them further from the poor in each latitude.

True, regional intergovernmental bodies and governments in the South, including well meaning ones, as well as the UN, may ritualistically denounce the unjust nature of the present global order. They have been doing so for some time. Of late, however, the intensity of that criticism has lessened, a result no doubt of the increased influence of neo-liberal ideologies in those diplomatic circles combined with growing fear of the consequences of opposing the dominant economic powers, while also expressing the indigenous economic stakes in the same North-controlled structures of exploitation.

If there are no substantive ideological or prescriptive differences between elites of North or South over how to attain (or, perhaps more significantly, define) "development," then it is illogical to argue that the structural reform programs are imposed on unwilling governments. More often than not, the governing powers in the South will anticipate the "free market" requirements of the multilateral institutions on their own when drawing up their own social policies. The terms are then negotiated, but it is schedules or specific percentages that are subject to bargaining, not the nature of the programs themselves, nor the moral or even economic viability of the social implications. In reality, most governments in the South and in the East feel they have no available options, politically or economically, to pay the price for resisting the free market formulas. But feeling incapable is one thing, and being unwilling even to try is another. And the difference can be explained in terms of class alliances that transcend borders and hemispheres, with all their respective financial underpinnings and ideological affinities.

It is too easy therefore to denounce the "imposition" of IMF and World Bank programs without looking at the fundamental make-up of the governing classes in the South on the one hand, and the economic forces and geopolitical interests represented by the Bretton Woods institutions on the other. Analyses that dispense with the treatment of colonialism tend to point to the World Bank and the IMF as the supreme authoritarian bodies responsible for global poverty. But colonialism is a social force at work in nations both North and South, with winners and losers in each. The difference, however, is that the very process of colonization imposes strict, and growing, limitations on how and to what degree the colonized can imitate and acquire the privileges of the colonizer.

The same structural adjustment terms stand as an impediment to regional cooperation for development based even on the elites' own regional interests, which might include the negotiation of preferential or free trade or protection agreements between member countries and around a region as a whole, independently of the North. The World Bank, however, under orders from its chief Northern stockholders, is dead set against the creation of regional development blocs "discriminating against third parties," that is to say outside of the global framework of neo-liberalism. Groupings will either adhere to common North-dominated liberalization measures, or they shall not group at all. For example, the hope that the new South Africa can bring enough clout to counter the Northern agenda for southern Africa is undermined by active campaigns by the United States to bring this nation under effective IMF/World Bank influence, encouraging it to borrow heavily.[11] But in essence the same debate is repeated in Europe and the United States when the question is posed whether further regional integration within a liberal capital-oriented framework will yield prosperity for corporations despite its dislocation of people.

Far from representing a "failure" of the market system when a select few of the corporate elites earn stratospheric salaries, far more than the mythical "free" market would allow, the inequality is inherent in the structural nature of competition in the marketplace itself. There is no necessary trade-off between market "efficiency" and inequality.[12] Competitiveness becomes a myth in a market already distorted by oligopolistic competition and by the strategic interaction between governments and corporations. It is these forces, rather than the "invisible hand of the market" that determine the state of competition, according to a 1992 OECD study.[13] And it will also take more than a visible hand or a new version of capitalism to bring about the profound changes in the system of ownership and management of society's productive wealth that would be required to guarantee humanity a survivable future.

Free marketeers would neglect politics and technology, along with history and recent experience. Government management, in one form or the other, has been present, not simply in its most desperate expression during the Great Depression, but after World War II when free capital markets and private ownership of giant corporations were simply goals on the horizon. This was not practiced in France, Japan, or Germany after World War II, when corporations were virtually assigned capital instead of competing for it. Nor can the interlocking financial industrial groups known as the *keiretsu* in Japan be held out as a shining example of laissez-faire capitalism.[14] As Schumpeter once pointed out, economics cannot possibly claim meaning outside historical facts and an approximation to historical experience.

MULTILATERAL MYTHS

To speak of the unprecedented concentration of global decision-making powers in the hands of the North has become a truism. There is little argument, for example, with the notion that the G-7, in callous fashion, seeks to control trade and currency issues that affect the lives of most of the world's population without any representation by the South. In the political sphere the marginalization of the South is even more evident; it is not accidental, but part of a strategic effort to concentrate global decision-making in the hands of the United States and its allies congregated in the UN Security Council. It should be no surprise, therefore, that the current initiatives to restructure the Council viewed as potentially possible are those seeking to enlarge the permanent membership of this body to reflect more closely the composition and interests of the G-7.

The control that the world's most industrialized countries have wielded in and through the IMF and the World Bank has become institutionalized through the G-7 — the de facto governing body of these institutions. In this way a small group of governments use the legitimizing cover of supposedly technical, non-political, representative, and multilateral bodies to create broadly applied policies that respond to the interests of a few, and not to the official objectives of development and economic improvement established in the statutes of those institutions.

The same contradiction between democracy and power emerges in regards to the United Nations Security Council. And the same question arises: Is the distribution of power within the Council and the G-7 an equitable one? Are the G-7 or the Security Council the unchallenged world governing authorities in all economic and political questions? Apparently not, since they must also take into account the actual shifting claims for power among their members, making these institutions microcosms of the continuing competition among national state apparatuses.

In their decision-making proceses some nations are more influential than others, and therefore the same decisions reflect hegemonic standings. There is no doubt that nations of the South are little more than bystanders. But there are bystanders in the North also, including some members of the G-7 and the Security Council, all too agreeable to U.S. dispositions or unable or unwilling to stand up to these in a serious fashion on certain issues.

There are too many "hands" in the G-7, the Bretton Woods institutions, the UN Security Council, or in the corporate industrial-banking spheres to view them simplistically as monolithic. These institutions are less true sources of power than they are simply the agents of power, entrusted to deepen the colonization of the life of the great majorities of the world population. A more useful question might be whether these institutions are capable of resolving North-North contradictions provoked by recurrent economic or political crisis.

The notion of an all-powerful multilateral governing global authority tends to reflect free market premises. It denies that the very chaos produced by the market requires higher degrees of political and economic control by specified states, to uphold the norms and insure stability for the new order. In the first place, of course, that means minimizing, to some degree, the impact on their respective populations of the negative impact of economic globalization. And, of course, it skirts the issue of the continuing, if changing, existence of the nation-state, and in particular the role of United States imperialism, which some find it convenient or fashionable to obscure or relegate as anachronistic.

The post-Cold War period has witnessed no significant changes in the core features of the dominant international power structure. That is, power continues to reside in joined state-corporate structures where each acts upon the other in mutually reinforcing terms. But while that has not changed, what has come under debate is the notion that the State-centered system is giving way to a new system dominated by transnational corporations, in which the State plays a limited role, chiefly as vigilant and facilitator.[15] (There is a supreme irony, of course, in this vision of declining power of nation-state structures in a period characterized by escalating and often violent nationalist — or, more accurately, micro-nationalist — insurgencies.)

But let us be more specific about the concentration of power, and let us move beyond the usual enriching of the North by the South, pointing the finger at the IMF/World Bank, GATT (now the World Trade Organization), G-7, transnational corporations, and other systemic components responsible for what some have called the "recolonization" of the socio-economic and political life of billions of human beings. United Nations "peace-enforcement" operations would fit neatly into this scheme, being called in to secure and legitimate new forms of intervention.

However, none of the multilateral institutions, or capital markets or corporations, stand as independent centers of power. They may be capable of largely commanding the economies of the South and East, but not of the North and much less its global component. It is true that the multilateral institutions have assumed greater power as national economies have themselves become more "globalized" and as national governments have lost much of their power to direct or isolate economic movement on a national level. However, it has not been an even-handed or across-the-board shift. Some governments have lost more than others, principally those in the South, while some in the North, principally the United States, have powerful means of compensating for such losses. We cannot forget that all of these bodies were created to reflect, not challenge, the will and weight of the powerful; they are not, and were not designed to be, democratic. And having done away with the Soviet bloc, big business in the West now seems determined to take a direct hand in the restructuring of the UN in order to make it subservient to the global market order.

The primary task of the international economic institutions is to extend market frameworks, chiefly in the South, in a manner responsive to the needs of transnational corporate investment. In the North it is a different story, because the same bodies — the IMF, the World Bank, and the GATT-WTO — are virtually powerless to rein in brazen mercantilist policies in the U.S., Japan, and Europe, as they engage in arm-twisting and threats to attain commercial advantage, seizing on any pretext to impose barriers on the import of goods from their competitors or even from low-wage countries.

Not only is there an absence of an even-handed commitment to free trade, there is outright opposition to any multilateral initiative to structurally redress the framework of international exchange. The Bretton Woods groups have by and large been oblivious to this necessity, and the free marketeers have resisted the few UN attempts to promote economic justice and redistribution at a global level. A new effort is underway to diminish and dismantle all UN activities tending toward meeting demands for greater accountability of transnational flows of capital and the power of the Bretton Woods institutions. For example, at the 1992 Rio Earth Summit, the UN Conference on Environment and Development, the U.S. and some of its allies defended transnational corporations by deleting measures that called for greater monitoring or regulation of corporate behavior in terms of health and environmental effects. Similarly, the United States also succeeded in shelving efforts to promote a code of conduct for transnational corporations. And already, in one of his first moves as UN secretary-general, Boutros Boutros-Ghali orchestrated the closure of the UN's Center on Transnational Corporations, a leading source of documentation and monitoring.

The Bretton Woods institutions, however, are expanding in power, but only in regard to the amount of influence they wield over the economies of countries in the South and the East. In regard to world financial markets, corporate conglomerates, and the core governments, their influence is actually receding. Nominally, the multilateral financial agencies are part of the United Nations system; in practice they are independent and respond chiefly to G-7 and particularly United States visions of a manageable world economic order responsive primarily to large corporate interests and investment firms. Their job is to reward governments that grant market access and to penalize those that don't.

The IMF, as with the UN Security Council or the World Bank, responds primarily to its chief depositors and principal shareholders. While many in the North view the UN system as too democratic and overly sensitive to the concerns of developing countries, the governing bodies of the Bretton Woods institutions are constructed quite consciously to favor the U.S. and other major economic powers. Those countries, the G-7 and its friends, use their domination to promote their own national economic interests, while ideologically endorsing the drastic neo-liberal recipes imposed on receiving countries as "objective necessities" to "save" their economies and, crucially, to win the IMF stamp of approval and resulting capital disbursement.

Exceptions, such as those accorded to Russia, are decided not by the agencies as a whole, but by the most powerful donors. Both the

IMF and the World Bank have their headquarters in Washington; the U.S. government appoints the World Bank's president as well as the chief of the United Nations Development Program. And, increasingly, social and environmental issues are being redirected away from the UN to the World Bank in an attempt to "privatize" global thinking and action on these problems. All this spells further reductions in the space available for the South's voice in international affairs, and a further concentration of the world's financial, economic, political, and social power in the hands of a few countries.[16]

The IMF and World Bank's neo-liberal approach to economic development was chiefly a product of the U.S. Treasury Department during the Reagan and Bush administrations; more often than not, U.S.-born or U.S. government-appointed economists are the ones who achieve high rank in the Bank.[17] Beginning in the late 1940s, the Bretton Woods institutions, once touted as specialized agencies of the United Nations system and allegedly subject to its democratic control, became agents of the capitalist powers, particularly the United States. The IMF abandoned even its nominal objective of monitoring and regulating international monetary exchange when in the early 1970s the United States unilaterally abandoned the gold standard and the fixed-rate system collapsed.

Since then, the Fund has been assigned exclusively to the task of bailing out governments in financial distress. Yet increasingly obsessed, as were private bankers, that such loans could finance autonomous or statist development policies, the Fund also created for itself a new international role: restructuring the economies of the receiving countries by imposing management conditions on the loans. The greater the problem of insolvency, the greater the IMF insistence on conditionality, and usually, the harsher the terms.

Many believed there would be no contradiction insofar as the IMF, the World Bank, and later GATT responded to a market logic intended to help countries correct temporary imbalances and credit difficulties that ostensibly inhibited private investment; they were all to serve as pump-priming for the world market while protecting local pro-West and pro-market elites against socialist models or the adoption of protectionist measures. The problem, as the bankers defined it, was that if some governments were at once lenders and borrowers, and if the UN could not be politically trusted on account of the presence of a Soviet bloc and nationalist states, then the expansion of free market capitalism was not being achieved.

More than anything else, the multilateral economic institutions were designed to help bring about a safer order for the operations of large transnational corporations, in part by securing the allegiance of foreign governing elites to a liberal anti-communist economic order. Still, as not all governments represented at the UN were militant free market radicals, the multilateral institutions created ostensibly as specialized UN agencies could not be fully trusted as arbiters of which countries would receive international loans and on what terms. Before that power could be conceded, the Bretton Woods institutions had to be made secure for the benefit of corporate capital in general and the United States in particular, for the benefit of the colonizer and not the colonized. If there was little space allowed for discussion of redistribution as a means to expand internal markets in the "developing" countries, there was even less tolerance for full-scale disregard of the market institutions per se.

Invoking the need for the institutions to secure credit ratings on Wall Street for the World Bank and the IMF, the United States directed the renegotiation of the original agreements between the Bank and the IMF with the UN, obtaining exemptions and privileges despite opposition from a number of countries. The functional result was the removal of the Bretton Woods organizations from UN control. Membership in the economic world bodies became subject to financial subscription, with voting weighted according to members' shares (wealth), giving a few countries a veto power over loans; commercial borrowing was allowed, and staff were paid at much higher rates than the international civil servants of the UN.

Neither institution holds much influence over the policies of their largest contributors as they pressure the poorer countries on behalf of purer market principles far removed from the development objectives laid out in the UN Charter. Decisions tend to respond to the political orientation from the United States and its allies, as the Bank and the IMF assume greater authority over the internal workings of borrowing countries by imposing essentially punitive measures. The developing countries — the major field of operation for the IMF — account for less than 10 percent of its liquidity and control.[18]

Yet "developing" countries (excluding Taiwan, which is not a member of the IMF) account for 43 percent of world output, 30 percent of world trade, and 45 percent of foreign exchange reserves. This would nominally entitle the South to some 40 percent of the IMF's quotas, but the reality is that political representation and power continue to ignore the concentrations of wealth in the South. Asia, for example, remains grossly under-represented with only 9 percent of quotas, notwithstanding its holding 17 percent of all world output, trade, and reserves — the original criteria for defining quotas.[19]

By the same token, the World Bank and the IMF have exerted less and less influence over economic policy-making in the wealthier countries; major financial markets and huge movements of capital went on outside its control. The Bretton Woods institutions came to reflect the political realities of private and governmental power acting as the instruments of capital when necessary. The same realities have an economic expression: according to one calculation, in 1990 there was a global surplus of $180 billion, yet the IMF used virtually none of it to alleviate the crippling indebtedness in the South amounting to eight times that amount. Most of the capital went to private capital markets in the North. For its part the World Bank was taking in $1.7 billion in interest and principal payments *from* the South. Between 1984 and 1990, World Bank debt collection resulted in a net transfer of $155 billion from poor countries to rich ones.

In 1993, the World Bank's net disbursement in the Third World and Eastern Europe was $6.5 billion, but those same projects financed by the Bank paid back $6.7 billion, representing a net profit to the Bank of some $200 million. On top of this, a good part of that reimbursement was for goods and services provided by the largest transnational corporations contracted by the Bank, thus making the corporations themselves, many of them state-supported, into the Bank's principal beneficiaries.

Indeed, two-thirds of the Bank's current capital stock comes from private capital markets in the North, making the Bank one of the greatest public-sector lenders in the world, as well as one of the key clients of finance capital represented in investment banks.[20] Until recently, a principal activity of the Bank was to finance massive government development projects considered too large or venturesome by private capital yet necessary to create the basic infrastructures required by corporations, especially in the South. As world capital markets have multiplied in dimension, this lucrative task is now being shifted back to the corporate-banking conglomerates in the form of tens of billions of dollars in contracts for roads, ports, telecommunications, and energy generation.[21]

If the original intention was for the IMF and the World Bank to promote economic stability and growth by re-routing funds around the world, that is to defy the trajectory toward the centralization of capital and power, the results seem much the opposite. Bretton Woods institutional policies, whether accepted freely by borrowing states or not, result in reinforcing and deepening poverty on the one hand and capital accumulation on the other, in true reflection of the interests of the transnational corporations and the governments of the industrialized countries. Their job is to help define and indeed codify into international law rules that will guarantee the free flow and protection of international capital and multinational production.

Keeping the system on course means demanding adherence to a legal underpinning for international trade in services, intellectual property, and foreign investment — in short, to make the world safe for corporate and capitalist expansion, and dangerous for those nations or sectors that refuse to accept "globalization," while making, of course, the necessary discrimination between rich and poor in the application of the law.

Thus the doubling of the gap between rich and poor experienced over the 1980s is also a manifestation of the growing concentration of capital in general, and the implementation of IMF and World Bank structural adjustment programs in particular — programs designed to keep the flow of capital going in both directions while ownership and profits largely remain at the top. This is visible not simply on a North-South geographical basis, but on a global social one as well, as the pockets of the North in the South become richer, and disempowered sectors of the South in the North also grow poorer.

A similar logic of inequitable relations is to be found in regard to GATT and its successor, the World Trade Organization. Again the tendency is toward the self-interested selective strengthening of multilateral agencies, converting GATT into the WTO with greatly expanded corporate control over investments, intellectual property rights, and services. In the late 1940s, the United States and the Western powers conceived of a similar organization, the International Trade Organization, with broad powers — but they were too broad for the comfort of many in the U.S. Congress and in the rest of the international community not ready to sacrifice quite that much sovereignty. GATT was then conceptualized as part of the Bretton Woods order but did not come into being until the 1950s, this time with full autonomy from United Nations oversight.

GATT was also designed to uphold and expand the market order, dealing with commercial questions and providing an instrument, principally for the rich countries, to negotiate reduction in tariff barriers. Ostensibly, they are even-handed agencies dealing with the trade practices of rich and poor countries alike. In reality, instead of finding ways to regulate commercial flows and capital transactions, the GATT-WTO agenda deals more with trade deregulation for goods, services, investments, and intellectual property. According to OECD and World Bank studies, there will be some $213 billion in overall trade gains resulting from GATT liberalization, and of that amount

$142 billion would accrue to the North (including $94 billion to Europe, $19 billion to the U.S., and $26 billion to Japan); $37 billion to China; and $21 billion to "upper income Asia." Africa, however, would suffer a net loss of $2.6 billion, Indonesia $1.9 billion, and the Mediterranean region some $1.6 billion.[22]

Thus even by the Northern institutions' own estimates, "free trade" and "liberalization" is not a "win-win" proposition. Those who draw up the rules are powerful enough to claim exemptions while at once legislating that others remove national barriers on corporate expansion and profit remission. The WTO has even greater coercive capacity against countries of the South that do not adjust their domestic policies to the global-liberal standards. A mechanism is in place to apply trade retaliation based on newly defined "trade-related" issues that the North is interested in and insists are necessary to the workings of the free trade system. This encompasses "trade-related intellectual property rights" and "trade-related investment measures," forcing countries in the South to change their national patent and other intellectual property laws to bring them in line with Northern and particularly U.S. norms, thus further detracting from the possibility of developing independent technological capacities in the South, and insuring a steady outflow of royalties and other technical payments to Northern corporations.

United States officials were most insistent on this point and made clear their intention of using the "trade-related" negotiation process as an instrument for the protection and enhancement of U.S. power against external challenges, but also to further adjust the globe according to its specifications, setting new world norms in regard to environment, labor, and social standards, legitimizing the taking of reprisals against "backlash" nations.[23]

The WTO is neither able nor intended to control transnational corporations, whose internal operations dominate more than 25 percent of world trade and international private banking. Large firms, at least, would not be subject to arbitration mechanisms, particularly if they are United States corporations. A Clinton administration official argued that few countries would be willing to challenge the United States or its powerful allies because the risk of retaliation was too high and costly given the size and importance of these markets in the North to nations in the South.[24]

In addition, intimidation flows from the very size and economic power of the corporations themselves — the 15 largest transnationals have net incomes greater than 120 countries and the 100 largest ones control more wealth than half the member states of the UN. The result is the political and legal contraction of governmental authority, principally in the South, as states now are compelled to establish "non-discriminatory treatment" for their economies, supervised by international authority and regulators.[25]

In this and other ways, the multilateral financial and trade organizations serve as weapons to transform the West's victory over the East into a victory over the South, to globally reward the winning of the Cold War, to further institutionalize the free market model. An ideological zeal accompanies the new needs for capitalist expansion, updating international trade and investment rules to better reflect and serve corporate interests, and the sharper undermining of the right of peoples to determine their own development and defend their other human rights. The U.S. demand for stronger mechanisms internationally, while resisting any application of them at home, is at the heart of much of Washington's domestic opposition to GATT and the WTO.

But internal misgivings over sovereignty notwithstanding, there is little doubt that corporate capital as a whole benefits and the South loses, although winners and losers are to be found in each. For example, labor unions in the United States argued that their workers would lose jobs because of imports coming from countries that pay their workers little, freely pollute the environment, or run unsafe factories.[26] According to one OECD calculation, less than a third of the income to be gained from the GATT accord will accrue to the South, and most of that will go to small privileged sectors in a reduced number of countries.[27] The costs are not only monetary: GATT-related trade and investment liberalization facilitates the movement of some $400 billion annually in drug trafficking, of which some $100 million, according to Interpol, is "laundered" by international private banks.[28] The result is a WTO serving to reinforce power patterns and structural imbalances.

Particularly apparent over the course of the last two decades is the increasing tendency for organizations such as the World Bank and the IMF to function as submissive instruments of their chief financiers, principally the United States, in implementing a vast social engineering project to "structurally adjust" more than 75 countries into North-oriented and North-controlled "properly functioning" market economies. There is little need to pile on documentation of the disastrous effects of the free market blueprint on most countries, when even World Bank officials have admitted publicly that Bank experts have been "a systematic destructive force" in Africa. Deepening economic recession and social tensions, greater internal and international polarization, both economic and political, are seen as a consequence of the ready-made formula of drastic devaluations, deregulations, and budget slashing for social programs, all of which exacerbate the combined impact of reduced market prices for most primary products of the South and growing protectionist measures in the North.

Globalization is reducing the power of communities and individuals, as well as the range and depth of social programs in both rich and poor countries, but it is also further concentrating the power of capital not just to relocate, but, perhaps even more important, to draw on the resources and power of the imperial national governments to do so. Government economic power has been weakened, but principally among the have-nots and the wannabes, both North and South, and in relation to transnational corporations. Power shifts entail corporate benefit as such power is wielded in a way to secure unfettered access to trade and investment markets.

We can expect the U.S. and its economic rivals to continue to rely on "managed trade" to arrange their own intra-North economic relations, leaving only the countries of the South to comply with WTO rulings. Indeed, a 1988 study by the Bank for International Settlements estimated 50 percent of global merchandise trade was in effect "managed" or subject to non-tariff barriers of one sort or another.[29] WTO is for the birds, for the South — it deals with yesterday's trade oblivious to the neo-mercantilist trends of the mid-1990s. In fact, doctrinaire senators in the United States are already criticizing the Clinton administration for its approval of a GATT/WTO agreement that permits continued governmental subsidies for key technologies; but this was precisely the intention of the U.S. and the Europeans who, by far, are the chief resorters to non-tariff barriers.[30]

U.S. politicians continue to insist that reciprocity and "fair trade" must replace "free trade." But the United States, like other major industrial powers, has always violated market principles and discipline when it suited its needs. That is why most of the industrial countries are more protectionist now than they were a decade ago. The U.S. Congress has given the administration great powers to impose sanctions on countries that do not open their markets, and the Clinton administration has not been shy about threatening to employ this authority.

Under the agenda of globalization, corporate elites supported by the governments and multilateral financial institutions of the North thus assume the right to force open the markets and economies of the smaller nations, all in the name of reciprocity. That is to say, they insist that any nation wishing to be part of the dominant worldwide economic system must abandon its sovereign right to chart its own development path.

The militarized consequences of outright economic or political rebellions against that abrogation of sovereignty — as in the case of Iraq, Cuba, or North Korea — are evident. Less apparent is the political and economic coercion applied by the United States and the multilateral institutions: what the *New York Times* terms an "economic diplomacy which requires the United States to get involved in the plumbing and wiring of other nations' internal affairs more deeply than ever before."[31] But larger capitalist countries do not escape this sort of systemic disruption either, first on account of the compulsion that the world capitalist market itself imposes upon societies and governments, affecting economic transactions and social relations; and secondly, the drive of the United States government and corporate elite to hand off onto other nations, rich and poor, the costs of U.S.-defined regulation mechanisms.

In this way, what some assume to be an almost natural process of a globalized market system takes on very distinct and coercive features as part of a much wider push to achieve a U.S.-led global market society. The end of the Cold War and the emergence of a global market signifies a singular opportunity for the United States power elite to attain unchallenged and undivided dominance, able to marshall both the market and the military to inflict carefully calibrated costs upon all who do not embrace the *pax Americana.*

Notes

1. United Nations Development Program, *Human Development Report, 1992* (New York: Oxford University Press, 1992), pp. 34-36.

2. Ruth Leger Sivard, *World Military and Social Expenditures, 1993* (Washington, D.C.: International Peace Research Institute, 1993), p. 20.

3. See Susan Strange's discussion of theory in social science in "Toward a Theory of Transnational Empire," in Ernst-Otto Czempiel and James N. Rosenau (eds.), *Global Changes and Theoretical Challenges: Approaches to World Politics for the 1990s* (New York: Lexington Books, 1989), pp. 163-165.

4. Sivard, *World Military and Social Expenditures, 1993,* p. 5.

5. Ibid., p. 56.

6. "Profits Without Honour, "*Economist,* January 22, 1994.

7. UN General Assembly, Report of the Secretary-general, "Critical Economic Situation in Africa: United Nations Programme of Action for African Economic Recovery and Development, 1986-1990," August 10, 1988, p. 29, cited in "Challenging the Leadership of the Global Economy," in *Global Exchanges,* no. 20 (Fall 1994), p. 3.

8. Davidson Budhoo quoted in Kevin Danaher (ed.), *Fifty Years Is Enough: The Case Against the World Bank and the International Monetary Fund* (Boston: South End Press, 1994), p.7.

9. *Forbes* (July 1994), cited in "Verdict of the People's Permanent Tribunal on the World Bank and the IMF," *Envío* (Managua: Universidad Centroamericana), vol. 13, no. 161 (December 1994), p. 34.

10. *Human Development Report, 1992*, pp. 35-36.

11. Dot Keet, "Regional and International Factors and Forces in the Development Perspectives for Southern Africa," *Southern African Perspectives* (Centre for Southern African Studies, University of Western Cape), no. 29 (November 1993), p. 17.

12. Robert H. Frank, "Talent and the Winner-Take-All Society," *American Prospect*, no. 17 (Spring 1994), pp. 103-109.

13. Noam Chomsky, "The Clinton Vision: Update," *Z Magazine* (January 1994), p. 32.

14. Alice Amsden, "Beyond Shock Therapy," *American Prospect*, no. 13 (Spring 1993), pp. 97-102.

15. Such an argument is made by analysts of different political persuasions. See, for example, Noam Chomsky, *Year 501: The Conquest Continues* (Boston: South End Press, 1993).

16. Martin Khor, "UN Restructuring Against South's Interests," *Third World Resurgence*, no. 23, pp. 15-16.

17. This is the case of Lawrence Summers, previously a World Bank vice-president and chief economist. See Amsden, "Beyond Shock Therapy," p. 96.

18. Erskine Childers and Brian Urquhart, *Renewing the United Nations System* (Uppsala, Sweden: Dag Hammarskjold Foundation, 1994), p. 84.

19. "The Global Economy," *Economist*, October 1, 1994, p. 42.

20. Childers and Urquhart, *Renewing the UN System*, p. 82. "Verdict of the People's Permanent Tribunal," p. 36. Additional data is presented and analyzed by Bruce Rich in Danaher, *Fifty Years Is Enough*.

21. *World Development Report 1994: Infrastructure for Development*, quoted in "Beyond Bretton Woods," *Economist*, October 1, 1994, p. 28.

22. Estimates are from the controversial book *Trade Liberalization: Global Economic Implications*, published by the OECD and the World Bank, calculating a 30 percent cut in tariffs and subsidies as then envisioned in the GATT round. See Martin Khor, "The South at the End of the Uruguay Round," *Third World Resurgence*, no. 45 (January 1994), p. 38.

23. Martin Khor, "The World Trade Organization, Labor Standards and Trade Protectionism," *Third World Resurgence*, no. 45 (January 1994), p. 33.

24. "We are a huge market for the rest of the world and most countries will want to stay on our good side," said one U.S. trade official. "Trade Accord Up for Votes This Week," *New York Times*, November 27, 1994.

25. "Verdict of the People's Permanent Tribunal," pp. 32-33.

26. "What's What in the Trade Pact," *New York Times*, November 27, 1994.

27. Childers and Urquhart, *Renewing the UN System*, p. 85.

28. "Verdict of the People's Permanent Tribunal," p. 33.

29. Harry Magdoff, "What Is the Meaning of Imperialism?" *Monthly Review* (September 1993), p. 5.

30. "Republicans Complain on Trade Pact," *New York Times*, February 1, 1994; "GATT," *Economist*, December 4, 1993.

31. "Diplomacy Is Minding Other Nations' Business," *New York Times*, January 30, 1994.

2

The Global Underclass: Unemployment and Underemployment Link North and South

For real people in the real world, this "new" economic order is not one of global integration and an egalitarian trajectory, but rather the opposite: one of escalating social polarization. As global competition for jobs and profits increases, the basic living conditions of global society decrease. The collapse of the Berlin Wall and the Soviet Union, and the ensuing hollow proclamation of victory and the end of history in the West, had no impact on the harrowing living conditions in which the bottom 20 percent of the world is forced to live. In the meantime, the top 20 percent enjoy an income which is 60 times higher. That includes elites in the South, the cellular phone-wielding sector of our societies that feels much more at home in Miami or London than in their own countries.

The economic and social instabilities in the world have called forth new cadres of spin doctors, whose assignment is to disguise the unfortunate consequences of globalization, making them more acceptable. "NAIRU" is a term invented by some of these economic wordsmiths that stands for "nonaccelerating inflation rate of unemployment." It is also referred to as the "natural" rate of unemployment, or "structural" unemployment. The assumption in all cases is that joblessness, and the poverty that usually accompanies it, is an inevitable social cost a market economy must pay in order to attain a level of "stability," which in turn is defined by the rates of growth (profit) without inflation, which of course is said to derive from wage pressures. Stifling wage pressures entails the existence of what Marx called "the reserve army of the unemployed."[1]

Better to disguise unpleasant realities by simply redefining "full employment" to signify a NAIRU rate of joblessness of 6.5 percent in the United States. What would be the NAIRU rate in a free trade world? How many hundreds of millions would have to be unemployed in order to keep the global economy from "overheating"? How to contain the demand for a more effective and equitable insertion into the marketplace? Better then to keep people out, and those "in" under tight control, rather than to risk inflation or rebellion.

Small wonder that the enthusiasm of corporate minded zero-inflation zealots around the world is not shared by incalculable numbers in the North who fret that their jobs are at risk, or who in the South could go from subsistence to sub-subsistence as the result of a capital-oriented globalization process. Free marketeers feel everyone should aspire to become an avid credit-card-carrying consumer, but obviously not all or even a majority can materialize that dream — as the system requires some degree of marginality in order to stay healthy; and the more global the system, the higher the margin.

The logic may not be new to the South — where the NAIRU rate has always been quite high. The United Nations calculates that some 75 million people are leaving their countries annually as refugees, displaced people, or economic emigrants. Elsewhere, the World Bank states that 1.2 billion people live on less than $1 per day.[2]

Poverty spreads and income disparities grow — not a new development. What is new is the growing number of affected citizens in the North whose concerns over the future are dismissed by their own elite politicians and economists, along with a corporate media, whose own incomes are insulated from global economic restructuring and foreign competition. The non-poor and their spokespersons shrug their shoulders and insist that the free flow and growth of the market inevitably entails disruptions, but that in the "long run" the gains in productivity will trickle down to other segments of society as free trade brings along bigger markets, faster growth, and higher earnings for all. There is therefore no need for welfare in the North, or for development assistance for the South. "Job training" and freer markets are the solution, greater and freer flows of trade and investment worldwide will bring rewards; there can be no hiding from the global marketplace, retreat from free trade, or escape from the "discipline" of the market.

But just how free and how disciplined is the market? Indeed, the more global and concentrated, the less the market is "free" and subject to control. Just who then is benefiting from the expansion of capitalism and the acceptance of corporate logic? Certainly not most workers in the rich countries. A survey by the conservative U.S. weekly *Business Week* of U.S. national income generated by the corporate sector indicated that "workers are getting the short end of the stick." The share of that income going to labor continues to decline, as revealed by the fact that the percentage of corporate income represented by wages, salaries, and benefits is at its lowest since 1969. Real salaries of U.S. workers were lower in 1994 than they were in 1973, while the real unemployment rate in 1993 stood as 13.8 percent, almost double the official unemployment rate. One out of every four people in the U.S. lived in poverty, the highest rate since 1960. Distribution of income was less equitable than at any time since the Second World War: the Congressional Budget Office calculated that between 1949 and 1989, the income of the poorest 20 percent of all families fell 10 percent. Profits on the other hand, as measured by the government, had risen to their highest level in almost 20 years.[3]

Neither the stagnation in labor income shares and real wages, nor the accompanying surges in productivity and profits can be attributed exclusively to global relocation. But this is part and parcel of corporate business strategies in an increasingly "de-regulated," "competitive," and consolidated world economy characterized by job cuts, benefit cutbacks, and foreign relocation. Downsizing, however, seems more oriented to fragmenting the workplace, while for multinationals the trend is to continuously regroup into larger units of centralized capital. The two phenomena are inseparable.

In the United States, the proportion of assets controlled by corporations worth $1 billion or more grew from 49 percent in 1970 to 72 percent in 1992. On the global level, multinational corporations now control 40 percent of world assets and commerce. Labor is being pulled apart, but in another sense it is coming together as part of the same process by which multinational corporations denominate the chain of contracted production running from capital-intensive plant to sweatshops, from high-tech service to part-time workers, linking one corner of the globe to another.[4]

These are new forms of old inequalities, with new formulas bandied about to assist in the "restructuring" of economies, featuring cost-slashing principally at the expense of labor. Markets and investors cheer the resulting surges in profit margins, but this cannot be translated into more equitable redistribution. Why? Because global competition will eventually squeeze profit margins and drive down earnings. Under conditions of world frontier capitalism, not even middle-class white collar workers feel safe, as they too are being downsized out of their jobs, often in the name of competition. One prominent banker has claimed there is no simple solution to the technological-economic upheaval, no way to stem the transfer of wealth from lower-skilled middle-class workers to a new technological aristocracy capable of directly tapping into corporate compensation, and that a smaller and smaller elite will eventually take the place of most workers.[5]

Corporate gurus insist on the technological revolution and the importance of building up new skills and values in order to stem a growing anti-free trade sentiment produced by job insecurity. Officials in charge of labor affairs in the United States and Europe claim that an irreversible shrinking demand for unskilled labor calls for massive retraining and greater government involvement. But their colleagues in charge of finances have usually won the argument that the scaling back of "labor-unit" costs is required in order to remain "competitive." No one, however, seriously envisions retraining the 17 million unemployed or underemployed or the 30 million underpaid in the United States alone.[6] And virtually all officials join in the chorus preaching the virtues of competitiveness and the free market as the determiners of global and national futures, bringing jobs and joy; the only debate being over how much the U.S. government should pry open markets that refuse to play by the global ground rules of liberalization and structural adjustment.

The situation of economic crisis experienced by the global underclass spells increases in poverty and violence, in what looks suspiciously like the old class struggle, as growing numbers of jobless appear as a new reserve army of the unemployed.[7] Unlike past reserve armies, many of the new global poor, in both the North and South, in cities and rural areas, have little chance of re-entering the globalized and increasingly high-tech formal labor market, if indeed they ever formed part of it. The "new" poverty and unemployment is not cyclical or residual, subject to alleviations with upswings in the economy; it is structural and systemic and it has come to stay.

Many economists believe that since 1988 the world economy has undergone its most profound economic decline of the last half century. But no such crisis was being experienced by the corporate elite. U.S. government calculations indicated that the richest 1 percent of families increased their income by 105 percent between 1973 and 1993. And in the case of general managers of transnational corporations, average 1993 salaries of $1.85 million increased 30 percent between 1992 and 1994, according to *Business Week*.[8]

Profits have been growing, but at the expense of workers of the North and South. At the beginning of 1994, the *Economist* forecast that profits as a percentage of GDP in the U.S. and Britain could reach their highest levels since the 1960s, and almost double the rate of the early 1980s. Productivity is purported to be growing but real wages have not kept up — no surprise in the light of the declining power of labor unions over the past decade. Even the reviewers could not escape the conclusion that this was a process of "profits without honor."[9]

MARGINALIZATION AND UNEMPLOYMENT

After 1973, when U.S. growth and especially wages began to stagnate, the tendency among politicians and some economists was to blame the economy's problems on the "uncompetitiveness" of U.S. industry in the international market. But even *Business Week* speculates that "the global economy may be just a scapegoat for domestic problems only slightly affected by changes beyond our borders." Less popular voices warned that U.S. difficulties were overwhelmingly domestic in nature, pointing to data covering the past four decades ostensibly indicating that the shrinking manufacturing base cannot be attributed to increased foreign competition. It is not a flood of cheap goods from abroad, but rather new technology that supposedly explains the divorce between the rise of manufacturing productivity and manufacturing employment, between corporate profits and declining living standards for entire sectors of society from middle to lower.[10]

Each explanation carries some truth yet remains basically apologetic for the role of corporate capital. Recipes calling for retraining or export drives also miss the point. Conventional economic models dealing with regional and international integration are simplistic in their assumptions (thereby facilitating their conclusions), usually invoking the law of comparative advantage and presuming full employment and pristine politically unrestricted markets.

Just as official rates of unemployment are calculated to keep the acknowledged figure suspiciously low, so too with the predictions of integration's effects on the job market. Governments take political cover by proposing retraining schemes or resorting to loud denunciations of foreign "protectionism" and the Japanese "exportation of unemployment." And countries in the South are told that the "Asian" miracle is reproducible in an unrestricted world economy; that the solutions to the problems of a free market economy lie in greater liberalization.

But trade, or lack of it, is not to be blamed or credited as the magic formula or culprit. The problem is that advanced capitalism, with its huge technological breakthroughs, is not capable of providing jobs; it requires fewer and fewer workers to produce more and more goods.

It follows that both "protectionist" and "free trade" policies are largely irrelevant to the roots of a crisis of overproduction — and neither path will create high-tech, high-paying jobs in nations that must "compete" in a global trading order that is structurally unfair.[11]

On the one hand, corporate managers will laud U.S. presidents for forcefully pushing for market access regimes and reforms, for "accepting the role of CEO of America, Inc." and assuming the job of a car salesman haggling over auto parts with Japanese leaders.[12] On the other hand, the same corporations question official rhetoric linking trade to jobs. If business is to succeed, then jobs cannot be placed ahead of profits and investment will take place wherever opportunity is greatest. According to *Fortune* magazine, "Much of American industry, whether or not it gets new markets in Japan, needs to keep shedding jobs to increase competitiveness."[13] Such quantitative shedding — equating workers with unwanted dog hair — is best undertaken by turning abroad.

Northern labor unions and their allies are not likely to accept the new gospel that unemployment is a fact of life and that even under conditions of economic growth there will still be large numbers left out in the cold. This would amount to accepting the same market logic that entails the destruction of lives and the environment along with the possibility of new wars.

In the South, that logic may result in cheaper consumer goods and more jobs in export industries, but it will not be sufficient to offset the displacement of workers from traditional agricultural activities and basic consumer goods industries; at the same time the public sector will be less capable of insulating the majority from the impact of recession and price and market fluctuations abroad. Governments are also constrained from intervening to protect those most severely affected by the glorified profit drive.

"Integration" is therefore seen as the global way out for the South. It flows out of structural reform programs, supposedly spelling substantial increases in foreign investment and a consequent increase in the export of manufactured products to the core industrial markets. Low wage rates and a regulatory atmosphere congenial to big capital are further reinforced. The presumption of policy-makers is that in the long run the boom in export production will more than offset the loss of jobs in those sectors overrun by less expensive imports. But even in the event of full integration into the marketplace, along with the transformation of productive structures, there will also be a loss in the domestic capacity of the society to provide for its own basic needs. As a result, whole sectors of societies face the threat of being left out of full and equitable incorporation into the global marketplace. The market will accept only those who are productive and competitive; the economically irrelevant will be left by the wayside.

At the same time, global or regional integration schemes encourage the less developed countries to maintain low wage levels, spelling continued impoverishment of local workers but also downward pressures on the living standards of workers in the North. Unions oppose agreements that encourage big corporations to roam the world for the lowest possible wages instead of focusing on product innovation and investment in the education and skills of their workforces. Free trade in this context is deemed worthless for workers with nothing to buy, with no jobs, or with limited purchasing power on account of lowered wages.[14]

The modern morality of globalization demands that governments and institutions follow the market, and hence traditional political bodies — including those of representative democracy — cease to be effective instruments for insuring justice and equality. States are deprived of their capacity to foster greater participation in the market economy, of enlarging consumer markets through measures that mobilize the latent productive potential of "traditional" sectors of the economy and society. Defying its own long-term interests, the market-driven version of global integration closes off opportunities, excludes people, accentuates income differentials, and produces socio-political polarization and rebellions, not to mention ecological disaster.

Yet all this forms part of the neo-liberal strategies of new and old elites in the South and East, and remains perfectly congruent and subservient to international capital. Globalized "development" strategists now discover that the evils of statism, corrupt bureaucracy, inefficient public enterprises, oppressive regulation, outmoded industry and agricultural bases, while excessive social welfare and disorderly unions are incompatible with "modernization." The scenario is then set for an "activist" foreign policy oriented to secure uniformity in or "reciprocity" from other nations.

GLOBAL SOCIAL ENGINEERING

At the national level, some believe the State stands between the elite and the rest of the population, between capital and labor. It is rarely positioned equidistant between them — overall state orientation remains with the elite — but the precise role of the State depends on the level of popular democratic accountability and left-over allegiances to vestiges of the welfare state. Labor, however, is defined in broader terms, to encompass not only workers but all sectors of the underclass, including the unemployed and immigrants, who might press, not always peacefully, for responsive governmental policies. As the Keynesian or state welfare options are foreclosed, the large-scale transfer of capital from the public to the private sector through brutal reductions in indirect income of working people (such as health care, clean air, education, etc.) also entails a transfer of power and an assault on democratic rights themselves.

Calculations are made, however, that the system is sufficiently strong and the opposition sufficiently weak, both nationally and globally, so as to not provoke a social crisis that would place the market system as a whole at risk. The result is a slow unrelenting yet unmistakable reduction in basic living conditions for the vast majority, along with steady falls in real wage levels for the working class, as the few concessions won in the past are taken back by the modern market-subservient State.

"Free trade" is the continuation of privatization at the international level. Transnational corporations grow impatient with what they see as the slow pace with which those few remaining "profit-draining" social protections and legal barriers to their unfettered expansion are dismantled. They press for new investment "opportunities" in the world where the barriers are even more feeble or nonexistent, where labor is cheap and unions are weak, and where environmental standards are ignored, and therefore costs of production are low. What Clinton administration senior policy advisers term an "enlargement of the world's free community of market democracies" underscores the standing U.S. commitment to help those corporations with huge market power take control of the economies of other nations, through pressing for the elimination of barriers and restrictions on the generation and repatriation of profits. The stress is on market, not democracy. Exports of goods and production benefit the U.S. economy as a whole, they argue, and the government need not apologize for its commercial aggressiveness.

At the corporate level, this means that protection of the environment and creation of employment remain afterthoughts, if they are considered at all. Yet it is these corporations that are at the heart of the global economy. According to the World Bank, about 40 percent of all global trade takes place among the 350 largest corporations in the world.[15] Foreign direct investment by multinational corporations amounted to two trillion dollars in 1992. The combined assets of the top 300 firms make up about a quarter of the productive assets in the world.[16] The top 100 companies employed 73 million people, of whom some 61 million were in the OECD countries. Of the remaining 12 million employed in the South, half were in China earning relatively low wages.

Governments in the North condone and even reinforce such inequity. Politicians provide a patriotic gloss to corporate "free trade" norms. This reflects a larger consensus among corporate elites in the North in general as well as their bureaucratic partners in government and supranational institutions. But once elevated to the level of policy, the privatized version of democracy and development spells active governmental and inter-governmental involvement in and responsibility for the increase in poverty and environmental destruction. In 1994 some 90 governments were implementing World Bank structural adjustment programs, with loans made on condition that economies undergo free market "restructuring."

Societies pay the cost of allowing decisions affecting the distribution of productive resources to be assumed by the corporate sector. The free market itself cannot guarantee the very growth it purports to generate, much less distribute it equitably, which is why human needs have traditionally been assumed by the State.

Yet states in the South and East are increasingly forbidden to assume the social role that some of their counterparts in the North continue to play. There is a logic in this, since power structures in the North are far more accountable to, and have assigned themselves the task of insuring the preconditions for, the continuous expansion of the marketplace. Therefore, national interference from other governments in the "global system" is not acceptable. Those governments are expected simply to accept the loans from the IMF, which presides over cash flow problems, and the rules enforced by the World Bank's structural adjustment policies to insure the loans. Market liberalization, deregulation, and privatization are the necessary price to be paid not only for the loans, but also to receive private investment. States in the South reneging on their responsibilities to those financial institutions of the North face sharp economic and social dislocation. But those that comply arrive at the accentuation of income inequality, and, over the long haul, the same social unrest.

Unions and an activist State have served as instruments of economic and social equilibrium. But those instruments are falling into disrepute or are under attack, and few of the governing elites anywhere acknowledge their beneficial function. This dilemma is heightened by the rush to free trade. Prominent economists have argued that establishing free trade areas among nations with gross disparities in living standards widens the gap, particularly if the have-not governments have abandoned any pretense of pursuing full employment. [17]

Globalization in this context unfolds in part as the latest chapter in the long-standing struggle between labor and capital in regard to the distribution of wealth and power. Because the forces of labor have been thrown on the defensive worldwide, we are witnessing how capital institutionalizes and enhances its gains. Those gains take the form of a further effort to entrench and institutionalize the anti-social policies of Reagan and Thatcher, winding down governmental regulations and the role of the public sector in general. Free trade and the free market constitute tools, both ideological and political, in the effort to provide the private corporate sector with as much decision-making power as possible, shrinking "barriers," domestic and foreign, governmental and social, on trade and investment, as well as relaxing the constraints represented by organized labor, democracy and national liberation movements, and also environmental standards. In an era of global deregulation, where capital is free to compete freely in search of cheap labor, the corporate establishments say that the "welfare state" is a luxury that is no longer affordable, and the people must realize there is no way out.

Yet the same ideologues and governments tell us that freedom and democracy go hand in hand with the extension of market competition, and that freedom for the corporation is part and parcel, perhaps the most important component, of individual freedom, which is why wealthy individuals and entities should be allowed to make decisions on investments. The Bush administration's trade representative, in defending the "bold new spirit of freedom and free markets" sweeping Latin America, concluded that such extraordinary achievements as unpopular IMF-imposed economic reforms were possible only "when the imagination and industry of the individual are allowed to emerge from the shadow of government control into the bright light of liberty."[18]

Ironically, European bankers and corporate pundits are now hailing U.S. economic management as the model to be followed, arguing that the challenge of "global competitiveness" and the "global market" can only be met through cutbacks in social benefits and the dismantling of so-called labor market "rigidities." That is what they call "securing labor flexibility," a euphemism for union-busting.[19] Much the same thinking was responsible for the weakening of the European Union's Social Charter, which attempted to introduce regional social protection standards. The corporate position was that such high standards would place European producers at a competitive disadvantage vis-à-vis East Asian and U.S. firms. In both cases, the notion of using trade and integration to raise instead of lower social standards, as proposed by critics of the regional agreements, has not, to put it mildly, enjoyed a warm governmental response.

Behind all the government and corporate rhetoric of globalization lies the age-old effort to reduce wage levels, only this time toward the lowest international levels possible. At the same time, the effort goes on to encourage the import of goods produced at those low wages, often manufactured by the same transnational corporations themselves. Capitalist global restructuring, engineered by capital and abetted by governments, has exacerbated the erosion of autonomous national economies, thereby placing national labor movements and their political allies on the defensive.

When corpulent bankers and politicians call for "belt-tightening" they are referring to someone else's stomach. It is not their job that is being "downsized" or "restructured" (although they could use some retraining). Across the industrialized world, social contracts are being broken and rewritten to the detriment of workers. According to the president of the German Chamber of Commerce, "Either German unions will accept substantial reductions in incomes and wages or we [sic] will lose more jobs. We also have the possibility of moving jobs abroad." Indeed, firms such as BMW have done so already, branching out to the North's own South — the state of South Carolina to be exact, where laborers drawn from the black working class can be paid less than half of what a factory laborer earns in Munich. One out of eight workers in the German auto industry has lost his or her job since mid-1991, as unemployment reaches its highest point since the Second World War.

Social welfare has never been a corporate concern, and of late corporate thinking insists it should no longer be a governmental one either. This of course relates to ongoing contentions with organized labor, and the attempt to reverse historical labor gains under the guise of liberalization. Obviously, such a situation is ideal for corporate managers in their bargaining with labor, as the adverse global picture forces new concessions. This image of liberalization's inevitability sets the basis for new labor concessions by weakening the capacity of governments and societies as a whole to generate alternative means of providing social protection. Trade and investment are then acknowledged as profit-making ends in themselves, not as possible instruments of development. Social problems in undermined states are dumped on the laps of corporations and the market, which is to say they are ignored unless and until they threaten to unravel the entire system through social unrest or upheaval.

A period of strife in Western Europe is in store because, in the words of one German analyst, "Americanization is not to be expected. The unions here are much stronger than in the United States and they will resist with all their resources and political power."[20] Yet social contracts along with social democratic welfare states are even breaking down in Scandinavia and unemployment is growing not only in Germany but throughout the North, acquiring a "structural character" — 18 million alone in the European Union, with proportions among women, non-whites, and youth sometimes twice the national average.

Neo-liberal integration schemes between powerful economies of the North and their dependent Southern "partners" are largely designed to lock in structural adjustment policies. In the process they also institutionalize two-tiered economies and societies between the states and within them. NAFTA, for example, will further accelerate the economic decline of the U.S. working class in general and the black community in particular, situated as they are in those industries most vulnerable to the international flight of capital.

NAFTA and its clones are not principally about trade; they are about defending the ability of capital to move across borders without being politically hindered by governmental democratic accountability. They are about the ability of capital to reverse every one of the gains attained by social struggles over the course of the century. In each country they are about the imposition of a new type of sovereignty, where corporate rights prevail over democratic ones: a sovereignty defined by corporations that assume the power to legislate and even enforce the new rules. What they are not about is defending the rights of labor to challenge capital unimpeded across those same borders.

Corporate-directed and government-implemented global structural engineering is crafted in such a way as to prevent the ordinary citizen from learning about, much less participating in, the negotiations on trade and financial agreements. In the global economy, what hurts workers in one country usually hurts them everywhere. And there is considerable empirical evidence that globalization, in the form of direct foreign investment as a source of profit for U.S. corporations, has significantly increased inequality in the United States over the past two decades. But the public is told the opposite: that what is good for the corporations and capital is good for the country and society, that jobs depend on the level of national exports, and that requires slashing costs at home, dismantling the "unfair" obstacles to the penetration of overseas markets.

THE INVASION OF THE JOB SNATCHERS

At the heart of much of the obsession with the reordering of the global economy lies the widely accepted view among governmental and corporate elites in the North that the big tantalizing "developing" economies of the South will account for at least half of the world's output by early in the next century. This endless boom would represent insatiable demands for goods, capital, and services of every type. According to the United States Commerce Department, the "big emerging markets" are expected to increase imports by $972 billion between 1990 and 2010, while the industrialized countries will increase their imports by $658 billion.[21] Zealous free marketeers go on to predict the end of national and technological boundaries that have kept rich and poor apart, a surge in standards of living everywhere, including the appearance of three billion modernized, middle-class, democracy-demanding consumers the world over with Mastercards and Visas at hand.

But in fact there is no direct tie between levels of corporate expansion and meaningful employment. Globalization is threatened by "extremists" in the South who seek more independent national paths of development, or their maverick counterparts in the North — such as Japan — which restrict imports and therefore supposedly provoke job losses elsewhere. In the worst cases (from elite Northern vantage points), a school of politics and thought comes into being in the South demanding equal market access abroad for its capital and goods.

When nations in the South depend not on technology but rather on cheap labor as their principal source of income, and when their governments seek to exploit that "comparative advantage," some in the North will cry "social dumping": competing unfairly by denying their workers basic rights and decent conditions. The "unfair" advantage of cheap labor, poor working conditions, and lax environmental controls, it is claimed, amounts to the "stealing" of jobs by the South from the North — the "giant sucking sound" related by Ross Perot.[22]

Economists of different persuasions accept the fact that the decline in the jobs and real wages of low-skilled manufacturing workers in the North is also an inevitable facet of the global "adjustment" process, as capital and production seek out new markets, thereby reducing demand for unskilled workers in the North and affecting their wages. This is the essence of how NAIRU in the North becomes institutionalized through globalization. It is also true that skilled workers in fast-growing economies in the South are operating complex technologies once seemingly reserved for the North. And the same production worker paid some $25 an hour in Germany or $16 an hour in the U.S. could be hired for only $5 an hour in South Korea, $2.40 in Mexico, $1.40 in Poland, and 50 cents in China, Russia, or Indonesia to perform the same tasks.

One common argument is that labor productivity and not labor costs is the essence of competition, and that as long as rich countries have higher education standards and superior infrastructure then the most important high-wage jobs and, in particular, profits are safe. This underestimates, however, the growth in productivity in certain areas of the Third World; increasing output per worker, when combined with persistent North-South wage differentials, spells a growing capacity to attain levels of productivity that could approach those in the North at a fraction of the wage cost. Cases abound, for instance, of workers in English-speaking countries in the South processing data and creating computer programs for Western corporations, affecting software firms in the U.S.[23]

Although strategic skills are tightly guarded in the North, politically and economically disempowered workers in the South can be made to multiply their productivity without their employers being forced to equally multiply their wages. The result is greater returns on investment in the South and net job losses in the North. Perhaps the new ease with which capital and technology can be transferred across borders has already broken the ties between high productivity, high technology, and high wages. Cheap labor can now be harnessed to the latest technology and skills enhancements in certain sectors of the South in order to yield extraordinary profits for multinational corporations based in the North.

As overseas investment becomes more profitable than home investment, capital flow increasingly migrates from the First World toward the South and East, coming back in the form of profits and goods, but at the expense of employment and wages in the North. Under these new rules of the game, for example, U.S. firms with foreign operations cut their domestic manufacturing employment by 14 percent between 1977 and 1989, even though in the domestic economy as a whole, manufacturing jobs fell by only 1 percent.

During the same period employment by U.S. multinationals in the South rose by 6 percent, whereas jobs in European subsidiaries fell by 23 percent. The number of employees in the South working for multinationals as a percentage of their total workforce is also rising. Although the poor countries accounted for nearly two-thirds of the total increase in multinationals' employment between 1985 and 1994, it must be kept in mind that it is still a small percentage of total corporate employment. As noted above, according to the 1994 World Investment Report of the United Nations Conference on Trade and Development (UNCTAD), multinationals employ only 12 million workers in "developing" countries compared with 61 million in "developed" ones.[24]

Domestic wage differentials within both rich and poor countries are widening, even though the gap in average national incomes between rich and poor countries as a whole may sometimes appear to be diminishing. Increasingly, inequitable income distribution, therefore, does not lend support to predictions of huge new middle classes of frenzied consumers in the South, sustained by high-tech jobs and incomes transferred from the North. Conservative analysts tend to claim that globalization has reduced the income gap between developed and developing countries, but even the *Economist* is forced to admit that international market liberalization "will also widen income inequality within rich economies, as the pay of unskilled workers falls relative to that of skilled workers. Reduced job opportunities and widening income inequality could easily ignite simmering social and racial tensions."[25]

Official political circles in the U.S. and Europe find it easier to blame "job losses" on immigration and manufacturing competition from the South. Nothing is more convenient for corporate capital than for its victims in the North to blame its victims in the South for their common predicament occasioned by a "global boom" that just happens to leave people out. Unscrupulous politicians throughout the North go so far as to state that national security is being undermined not only by job-snatching immigrants but also by the rapid economic advances made in certain countries of the South. In a win-win rhetorical flourish for corporate interests, it now turns out that enrichment *and* impoverishment in the South spell equal threats to the North! The accusation is that the fall in the North's percentage of world output, particularly that of the United States, is at least partly based on global income redistribution, as poor countries "catch up" with the North.

According to this version, impoverishment in the rich countries is the product of trade with new industrial "upstarts" from the South, to the point where the Third World is beginning to threaten the First World's prosperity. Prejudices become rooted and can give way to perceptions and policies denouncing unfair and "excessive integration" in the world economy. Corporations are not above propagating alarmist interpretations, as part of their attempt to induce Northern governments to provide further subsidies for technological development on the one hand and rolling back labor union demands on the other — all in the name of maintaining a "competitive" economic and national security edge: to save jobs and to stem a possible shift of political-economic power from West to East, this time, given alarmist expectations of China's growing economic clout, across the Pacific Ocean.

But an increase in "average incomes" does not necessarily imply improvement in the livelihoods of poor people in either rich or poor countries. The truth is that globalization entails winners and losers inside every country, as economic elites the world over demand and win greater and greater social cutbacks from their government-partners, to create ever more profit-friendly climates.

Businesses with workforces in the North, unable to compete with their transnational counterparts, would be forced to shut down, throwing workers into unemployment. But workers in the North, especially those in manufacturing, are not easily moved into new industries and services, and unemployment mounts. With pressure on governments to protect industries' profitability, blame often shifts to the "unfair" trade or production practices of other countries. While attacking enemies abroad, U.S. corporate structure also advances at home, demanding an end to "labor market rigidities" (wages and benefits), seen as barriers to global structural adjustment. According to the *Economist,* making labor markets less rigid means "scrapping minimum wages that prevent relative pay from adjusting; pruning welfare benefits that discourage the jobless from seeking work; and relaxing restrictive hiring and firing rules that hamper recruitment."[26]

In other words, while governments in the rich countries proceed with the dismantling of labor gains at home, they also demand low labor standards abroad. To pose the question of whether the "Third World" should be forced to meet minimum labor and environmental standards is to miss the point. It also presupposes a usually nonexistent governmental inclination to impose restrictions on new investment ventures. The real issue is whether any meaningful labor and environmental standards will be left in the wake of the tornado of globalization — in developing countries of the South or in the U.S. itself. So far, corporate interests have succeeded in convincing many jittery Northern workers that the "real" threat to "their" jobs comes only from workers in the South who foolishly agree to work for virtually no money with no protection.

The result is that labor standards and environmental issues play an increasing role in international trade disputes — a positive result although for the wrong reasons. Pressured by domestic (non-corporate) constituencies appalled by working conditions in Third World factories (accident death rates in manufacturing industries are nearly ten times as high in Pakistan as in the United States, according to the International Labor Organization), the G-7 governments virtually held up the signing of the Uruguay GATT round in April 1994 as part of a drive to place labor standards formally on the agenda of the new World Trade Organization. This was fiercely resisted by governments from the South as well as by those corporate interests that benefit from lax standards.

With good reason, governments of the South contended that the rich countries were concerned less with the lot of destitute workers than with the need to justify protectionist practices — in economic terms, an attempt by the rich countries to deny the South the "benefit" of one of its few comparative advantages in cheap labor. According to one corporate-oriented analysis, to demand that all countries apply similar labor and environmental standards is tantamount to asking for all comparative advantages to be eliminated before trade begins: "It is like Finland arguing that Ecuador has an unfair advantage in growing bananas because it has more sun."[27]

Clearly, the push by countries in the North, led by the United States, for the WTO to establish a link between trade and international labor standards has little to do with solidarity with Third World workers, but rather involves a media-friendly rhetorical mechanism to justify protection against competitive imports from the South.

There could be no denying that much of the Northern trade union argument for leveling working conditions is in large part a response to fear of competition. But at the same time, concerns about the exploitation of child labor, slavery, and minimal trade union rights have found and deserve broader acceptance. Nevertheless, to many in the South, the linkage of trade to labor and environmental standards looks like further evidence of the one-sided approach to liberalization — inventing new rules and new concerns historically absent in North-South relations. The goal, some believe, is simply to find new pretexts for mandating sanctions, including the imposition of "Northern" conceptions of human rights over local values in order to continue to rule over the international political economy. The objective is to increase Northern authority over nations in the South, particularly those that over the next ten years may account for two-thirds of the growth in world production and trade.

There is also the need to avoid explaining the real meaning of "structural unemployment" in the North. Structural problems would call for structural remedies in the North — but that is not on the Bretton Woods agenda. Instead it is the South that is required to undertake painful World Bank and IMF structural adjustment policies. The South appears therefore as both cause and remedy to the core Northern problems resulting from global capitalism.

The North cannot escape the effects of this unprecedented global social disequilibrium, reinforced by the disproportionate growth of the population among the poor and the surge in migration. There is growing awareness, at least in much of Western Europe, of the fact that current high levels of unemployment are not a passing phenomenon, a phase in the commercial cycle, but rather a dramatic indication of a global readjustment of the capitalist system at the expense of laborers and labor rights. It is still easier, however, to blame other victims, particular non-white immigrants. Laborers in the South and East are also reeling under the effects of shock therapy. As they flee Northward, they encounter the racism and xenophobia that could threaten the internal balances of the North, providing an opening for the extreme right. Global structural adjustment is indeed upsetting the treasured stability of many rich countries.

The "competitiveness" myth becomes a new justification for ignoring the plight of the poor and of labor in general, as corporate capital demands a free hand in markets as free as possible from welfare or redistributional schemes. Societies are asked to "adjust" and accept "discipline," that is to say accept market-oriented governmental policies, while resigning themselves to the logical consequences of lack of competitiveness — to unemployment and poverty, or even elimination of those functionally disabled by the marketplace and those social sectors, North and South, whose presence only detracts from overall profitability.

In such a system of global apartheid, growing numbers of human beings, especially women, in both the North and the South, have gone from being exploited by, to being excluded altogether from the glories of a global market economy. The North will be arbitrary, often media-driven, in responding to the manifestations of the crisis. Televised scenes of starving children in Somalia are directed at unemployed workers who are supposed to applaud loudly when their armies march in to force-feed all those starving people. But the same year that Somalia underwent humanitarian intervention, World Bank lending to CNN-invisible sub-Saharan Africa fell by $1.2 billion, or 30 percent, while contributions to Eastern Europe, a media favorite in the West, rose from $1.7 to $3.8 billion.

Of course, new definitions of global economics purposely fail to mention that one-third of humanity no longer fits into that imaginary globe. Under the new economic rules, only those fit to "compete" in the international market are able to survive. Those who are not competitive — entire nations, regions, or more often, non-productive and therefore expendable sectors of society — are cast aside regardless of their numbers. For them, perhaps a majority in the world, there is no such thing as a global economy, nor a global market, nor a global village: they have been left out of the development equation altogether to the point of being deprived even of an earlier era's means of subsistence living; forced, as Mexican peasants are, to leave their eroded plots and migrate to the cities as a result of the liberalization of agricultural prices (while U.S. agri-business leaves fertile land fallow to profit from Washington's own subsidy programs).

A global slum of the poor surrounds global suburbs of the rich, with walls that run across countries separating those who consume goods and capital from those who consume only images. Some small sectors in some countries of the South will stand to benefit, at least until the copious capital flow dries up, and pandemonium follows the shut-off.

Some countries, such as Mexico, may feature the fastest growing number of multi-millionaires, and in East Asia there are ministers and prime ministers who earn salaries four times as high as their counterparts in the West, but the social record belies the blithe presumption that the free market, equitably shared economic growth, social stability, and democracy are all inextricably linked. Globalization translates into a global downward spiral of wages along with working and living conditions, environmental devastation, rural-urban polarization, reduced food security, depopulation of rural communities, and enhanced appeal to narrow ethnically-defined nationalism, fundamentalism, or fascism. The vision of happy "developing" nations on the verge of joining the First World thanks to the global marketplace clashes with the various expressions of social and economic displacement and instability. The sobering fact of massive impoverishment is the true reflection of the hideously unequal character of economic growth in a system in which people are subordinated to the corporate-market agenda. The result is the greatest social division between rich and poor in history.

Economic growth rates might soar, and giant strides are made in science and technologies, but hunger and violence are on the rise. In the framework of neo-liberal market fundamentalism, the advances are more in the interests of corporations than of peoples or of peace. Poverty becomes entrenched, and immediately tends to be forgotten, because from the dizzying vantage points of the rich, it seems to have no bearing on the general health of the free trade corporate global economy. Funds to rectify the drastic effects of a socially dysfunctional economy are scarce, while attempts to introduce structural political or economic corrections are branded as subversive and incomprehensible to the technocrats unaffected by and oblivious to the stark reality of growing poverty in an expanding national or international economy.

Social policy issues re-emerge as the effects of desperate social crisis take hold. Health, for example, simply begins to disappear as a public responsibility: in India, cutbacks in support for elementary sanitation opened the way for the reappearance of a plague that was the scourge of other centuries, provoking a stampede of over half a million people and billions of dollars in lost production, ridiculing the claim of local elites to the effect that their country had joined the team of the modern "tiger" economies. Not even nations as rich as the United States escape such pitfalls. Easily prevented childhood diseases are on the rise as public health budgets diminish: fewer than 1,500 children contracted measles in 1983, but in 1990 some 27,000 cases were reported.[28] The World Bank's 1993 *World Development Report* estimates that child mortality in low-income countries could be reduced by as much as 70 percent and life-expectancy raised to near Northern standards for a cost of $22 billion. The Clintonite Democratic Leadership Council of the Democratic Party in the U.S. calculates that various U.S. government subsidies to corporations — corporate welfare — cost between $60 and $75 billion per year.[29]

Notes

1. "Alan Knows Best," *Newsweek*, November 21, 1994.
2. Cited in "Verdict of the People's Permanent Tribunal on the World Bank and the IMF," *Envío* (Managua: Universidad Centroamericana), vol. 13, no. 161 (December 1994), pp. 32, 34.
3. "Plumper Profits, Skimpier Paychecks," *Business Week*, January 30, 1995, p. 34. Paul Krugman, "The Rich, the Right, and the Facts," *American Prospect* (Fall 1992).
4. Kim Moody, "Pulled Apart, Pushed Together," *Crossroads* (October 1994), p. 7.
5. "The Real Revolution," *New York Times*, January 6, 1995.
6. "Ministros de Economía de la UE quieren reducir las ventajas laborales," *El País*, December 12, 1994; "Europe: Nose to the Grindstone," *Business Week*, December 5, 1994; John McDermott, "And the Poor get Poorer," *The Nation*, November 14, 1994, p. 578.
7. Some would insist on blaming technology, but it was Marx who warned that "as large-scale industry advances, the creation of real wealth depends less on the labor time and the quantity of labor expended than on the power of the instrumentalities set in motion during the labor time. These instrumentalities, and their powerful effectiveness, are in no proportion to the immediate labor time which their production requires; their effectiveness rather depends on the attained level of science and technological progress; in other words, on the application of this science to production .... Human labor then no longer appears as enclosed in the process of production — man relates himself to the process of production as supervisor and regulator ....

He stands outside of the process of production instead of being the principal agent in the process of production." Quoted from the *Grundrisse* in Shegeto Tsuru, *Japan's Capitalism: Creative Defeat and Beyond* (Cambridge, U.K.: Cambridge University Press, 1993), pp. 220-221.

8. "Verdict of the People's Permanent Tribunal," p. 34.

9. "Profits Without Honour," *Economist*, January 22, 1994.

10. *Business Week*, November 15, 1993.

11. Philip Green, "Talk Opportunity, Not Trade," *The Nation*, January 3-10, 1994.

12. Praising President Bush for his managed trade approach to the Japanese, James D. Robin, chief executive officer of American Express, said, "This is the first time the U.S. has come out united — the Commerce Department, the Treasury, the President, the business community — to declare that trade is a national priority on a par with our security interests. For better or worse, we have crossed that line in the sand." "What Now for the U.S. and Japan," *Fortune*, vol. 125, no. 3 (February 10, 1994), p. 55.

13. Ibid., p. 55.

14. Interview with Richard Rothstein of the Amalagamated Clothing and Textile Workers Union in *New Perspectives*, vol. 8, no. 1 (Winter 1991), pp. 32-35.

15. *NACLA Report on the Americas*, vol. 27, no. 6 (May/June 1994), p. 5.

16. Richard J. Barnet and John Cavanagh, *Global Dreams, Imperial Corporations and the New World Order* (New York: Simon and Schuster, 1994), p. 15.

17. Robert Kuttner terms it "the victory of assumption over efficiency." "Market, State, and Dystrophia," *American Prospect*, no. 15 (Fall 1993), pp. 7-9.

18. Quoted in "Rethinking the Economics of Free Trade," *Resource Center Bulletin*, no. 27 (Spring 1992), p. 5.

19. Conclusions of the World Economic Forum held in Davos, Switzerland. *El País*, February 7, 1993.

20. "Rewriting the Contract for Germany's Vaunted Workers," *New York Times*, February 13, 1994.

21. *New York Times*, January 3, 1995.

22. *Economist*, April 9, 1994.

23. "The Global Economy," *Economist*, October 1, 1994.

24. See the study of labor productivity in the Mexican steel industry made by McKinsey Global Institute and the study by Kalus Schwab, president of the World Economic Forum, as well as the report on UNCTAD in "The Global Economy," *Economist*, October 1, 1994, pp. 16, 27.

25. Ibid., p. 44.

26. Ibid., p. 44.

27. Ibid., p. 39.

28. Praful Bidwai, "Plague Warning," *The Nation*, October 31, 1994; Laurie Garrett, *The Coming Plague: Newly Emerging Diseases in a World out of Balance* (New York: Farrar, Straus, Giroux, 1994).

29. "Go After Corporate Welfare," *New York Times*, January 17, 1995; *Economist*, January 21, 1995.

3

States and Markets

Where does the responsibility lie for the creation of wealth amidst poverty? Is it markets (economic forces) or states (political forces) that constitute the determining forces? Historically, one has served as an indispensable complement to the other as states assumed the task of sustaining and expanding the interests of dominant national economic elites. In the era of so-called globalization, the question posed is whether economic forces have overcome their dependency on political structures, assuming many of the functions previously assigned to governments; a process accelerated as territorially-centered nation-bound governments appear to lag behind while market forces assume a global reach.

Here we should have no illusion about a magical marketplace in which the sum of thousands or millions of individual business and consumer decisions determine the thrust and direction of economic growth. Much to the contrary, the trend toward market "globalization," as that of market nationalization before it, entails a sharp concentration of economic resources. Theories of economic and political liberalism notwithstanding, the centralization and concentration of capital shaped the character and content of the modern capitalist nation-state. Economic (and often territorial) expansion was in many senses a highly directed and politically-charged process. From the sixteenth century onwards, the unequal distribution of resources, upheld politically at the level of European nation-states, acquired new territorial dimensions in which the old social division between core and periphery acquired new geographical and ethnic characteristics. Economic groupings made use of their political connections to define and maintain monopolistic privileges, thereby further accumulating wealth and influencing polities.

Some theorists would have us believe that the contemporary era is fundamentally different: first, because there are no equally matched global powers engaging in a multi-faceted imperialistic competition with one another; secondly, because contemporary corporate power is so great as to impose global rules of economic engagement and trans-elite profit distribution; and third, because states themselves are rushing to remove the shackles on the "free" movements of capital and commerce.

There is some truth to such ideas. The "globalization" of the world economy is increasingly the product of internal corporate transactions. Trade becomes "freer" because it flows with greater smoothness across national borders, but it is less "free" in that peoples the world over have fewer opportunities to influence that trade. Twenty-five percent of the world's productive stock is concentrated in 300 corporations. Between 1982 and 1992, those companies increased their control of world production from 24.2 percent to 26.8 percent. This means that the 15 largest transnationals have net incomes greater than 120 countries, and the 100 largest ones control more wealth than half the countries in the world. Three hundred and fifty billionaires have a combined net worth of $760 billion, the equivalent of the bottom 45 percent of the world population.

By and large intra-firm trade — up to a third of world trade linked to some 200 corporations — is not subject to free market rules and is frequently able to circumvent state regulations. Nor does government concern itself much with the absurdly wide gap between corporate salaries and those of workers on the lower end. Nothing demonstrates better the growing degree of economic centralization and concentration of wealth, while the level of poverty and the economic marginalization of peoples and even nations are intensified as part of the same "globalization" process.[1] Mega-companies and corporate bankers roam the world in search of customers, savings, and investment outlets.

Today less than 7 percent of world trade is free trade. The rest is directly or indirectly administered by states, be it through the negotiation of access or by way of protection. According to the UN Development Program, of the 24 wealthiest countries, 20 had more protectionist regulations in 1992 then they did ten years earlier.[2] Free trade is less about freeing trade, and more about adjusting national frameworks to permit the free movement of capital across borders. As for capital markets, these are not non-political bodies reflecting the invisible convergence of thousands of buyers and sellers, but are indeed subject to the manipulation of a limited number of financial operators and politically-influenced central banking authorities.[3]

Specialists of different political persuasions tend to admit there is no arms-length distancing between business and government at the highest national levels. Central banking and political authorities are very much involved in operations seeking to prevent or remedy defaults or collapses. And in terms of commerce, no bones are made about government involvement in the promotion of exports coupled with furious campaigns against other nations not practicing "fair" trade. What becomes increasingly apparent in a post-Cold War setting is the drive by the United States to assume the role of world economic governing authority, and to impose its rules for economic international intercourse. Whether markets or other states can effectively be cajoled into voluntarily accepting Washington's version of the neo-liberal order is a question that is explored below, but the existence of an urge to impose self-serving world guidelines is undisputed.

Global corporations, the largest of which are U.S.-based, regularly tap governmental power and are involved in the drawing up of a government-corporate agenda, often supplying ideas and personnel to the bureaucracy in a revolving-door fashion. The common task is to maximize the extraction of wealth on a world scale in order to further concentrate power and resources in fewer hands. Those entities are corporate, but they are also national, and herein lies one source of conflict, since not all governments have an equal amount of power to shape or address global corporate agendas. Only a few governments have such global outreach capacity, which includes military clout, allowing bureaucratic interests to assume a larger role in the definition of that agenda to address non-corporate interests or to push the corporate agenda by non-market means. This is not inevitable, because governments still retain the potential will and capacity to protect the poor from the tendency of globalized corporate capitalism to lower social, wage, and environmental standards.

Evidently, save in the few states where social concerns are given greater priority than corporate ones, the improvement of living conditions for majorities is not the fundamental concern of national politics, save perhaps on occasion where the same conditions threaten to undermine both profits and general stability, leading governments to intervene to shore up long-term corporate privileges, sometimes over the opposition of short-sighted or small business groupings.

Several questions, however, do emerge in modern state-corporate relations. The first is whether the "great" transnational firms can in effect dispense with political state apparatuses completely, taking over the management of an economy that is increasingly equally transnational. A second is whether capitalist governments can effectively resist the tendency for they themselves to become the victims of corporate privatization, or indeed whether governments in the rich countries can effectively insure primordial corporate loyalty to the nation-state. A final question, the subject of a different discussion altogether, is whether non-capitalist states or groups thereof can still have any hope to reverse, or at least change, the direction of corporate globalization, so as to force it to take account of pressing social and ecological demands, also on a transnational basis.

Basic governmental intervention in economic matters has not disappeared from the face of the earth. But the question is whether under transnationalized forms of production and financing, governments can still effectively resort to the age-old instruments of taxation or regulation in order to insure some degree of "loyalty" to broader national concerns, claiming a proportion of profits for purposes of redistribution or the further enrichment of the local elite, including the bureaucracy itself.

To be sure, the thrust of the modern corporate agenda is precisely to banish all profit-detracting statist tendencies and to support profit-enhancing ones. Politically, therefore, the process is selective and far from pure; there are built-in safety measures because a pure adherence to market and deregulatory principles the world over would severely undermine profit-making capacities and risk chaos. Governments must also balance different corporate interests against each other and sometimes the interests of contending social groupings, including organized labor against capital. This is not to say that the principal corporate-oriented governments intend to subordinate transnational companies to global democratic needs. Some governments in the South once thought that corporations could be reined in by concerted multilateral action: evidence to the contrary was the demise of the United Nations Commission on Transnational Corporations along with its plans to impose a Code of Conduct to curb corporate abuses.

Once again, the task of regulation falls principally on the corporate world itself and the governing elites in the rich countries themselves. Their job is to uphold and push the international codification of a more profitable and secure global setting for private corporate transactions. The objection is only to the regulations corporations do not influence or control. Yet precisely because the regulations are also defined by the nationally-based powerful and the few, subject also to competing domestic pressures, the task of articulating a global regulatory framework reflects the sometimes conflicting biases of the few, although usually against the many and the less powerful. In essence, a logic of mercantilistic imperialism prevails, and logically would do so until a single world government run by a handful of corporations controlling the world economy appears on the scene.

In short, if one can speak of governmental regulation, including its foreign policy versions, these are intended to shore up and refine, and not to challenge, the basic iniquitous world capitalist production and exchange system. By the same token, the dividing line between free trade and regulated trade is more rhetorical than real, in part on account of the ability of huge corporations to impose market conditions and also because of the dubious adherence of states themselves to the principles of liberal economics. In practice, Western industrial economies have each sought to enforce free trade on the non-West in order to open markets to their products and capital (free trade), while concurrently resorting to "regulation" or what today is known as national industrial or competitive policy (protection) in order to safeguard Western-centered profit-making.

CORPORATIONS AND NATIONALITIES

Corporations have world strategies and interests, but it would be a mistake to conclude that their nationality is not important either to themselves or their home government. Corporate nationality exists and is important; were it not the case, wealthy nations such as the United States would have no trouble adjusting to a scenario where non-U.S. corporations controlled key sectors of the media, transport, or sensitive military technologies. Under "unfettered" free market dynamics, corporations in their endless pursuit of profit would nominally be free to relocate to other countries with lower wages, less stringent social and environmental standards, and legislation and political regimes that uphold the sanctity of foreign investment. Yet headquarters and authority are located in the North, not the South.

In the case of the modern U.S. corporation, the argument is made that as companies become more global in their operations, the links between them and their original home base economy rapidly disappear. The political implication is that official policy-makers would be wise not to confuse national economic interests with the economic interests of "national" corporations.

Conventional wisdom holds that corporate "competitiveness" abroad helps insure jobs and rising living standards at home. Liberals add that the national economy must also be competitive and attractive to investors, including foreign corporations. In one analysis, the foreign corporation that is willing to invest in the United States is more important to the economic future of the country than the U.S. corporation that simply takes its operations abroad.[4]

Of course, state strategies must also reflect and respond to patterns of corporate concentration and competition for new markets. To different extents and in different ways each of the major industrial states monitors and influences international investments that have a bearing on the structure of the national economy. While laissez-faire may continue to be an article of faith in the United States, a less purist and more accepted elite view is that the economic fate of nations is still tied to the national and especially international success of domestically-based corporations.

Those corporations in turn, however global in their outreach, do not operate in a world free of politically-drawn economic differentiations. The unconstrained free economic space that may nominally exist within a nation-state does not exist internationally, at least not yet. Sovereign political considerations continue to act upon as well as reflect the "global expansion" of the modern corporation and finance capital. Even for states as powerful as the United States, engaging the corporate world is not a question of will, or simply a reflection of internal power line-ups, but also reflects the need to safeguard non-corporate, electorally strategic sectors of the economy and population also at the mercy of decisions of national and foreign corporations and financial conglomerates and markets.[5]

For its own protection perhaps, the international scenario is characterized less by multilateral market access regimes than by protectionist and regulatory-minded governments, sometimes at odds with particular sets of corporate interests. And where several governments play the same game, then problems arise, particularly if economic science and popular belief combine to feed the convenient notion that "jobs" depend on corporate global expansion. There is no disassociating the health of General Motors from the "health" of the "national economy."

There is some truth to the GM assertion, yet ironically it was initially claimed to support governmental inclinations to favor domestic corporate investment over foreign investment, even though neo-liberal theories would insist on eradicating any such distinction. Evidence assembled in 1991 by Laura D'Andrea Tyson, the Clinton administration's chief of the Council of Economic Advisers, found that after decades of massive direct foreign investment by U.S. corporations, "the competitiveness of the U.S. economy remains tightly linked to the competitiveness of U.S. companies." In the case of the chief U.S. multinational companies, domestic operations accounted for 78 percent of total assets, 70 percent of total sales, and 74 percent of all their employees. Each of these figures was growing instead of diminishing as foreign investment increased. Of course, the high-wage, high-productivity jobs also remained at home while the amount of critical research and development activities undertaken abroad was quite small, and in the case of Japanese firms virtually negligible.[6]

With respect to management, there is also very little that is multinational about the composition of boards of directors. Rhetoric about global partnerships aside, another study found that most large U.S. corporations do not have foreigners on their boards of directors. One survey found that the proportion of the top 1,000 U.S. firms with a non-American on the board had declined from 17 percent in 1982 to 12 percent in 1990.[7]

Companies in this fundamental respect are far from being "multinational," even among major U.S. corporations who are least closed in this regard. For Japanese-based multinationals, one 1990 estimate was that the proportion of assets held at the parent operation was well over 90 percent.[8] Still, the weight and role of multinationals will vary from country to country: in Germany and most of Europe foreign-based multinationals play a large part in the economy and behave much like the nationals. This, however, is not the case in Japan, one of the largest single markets in the world. Evidently the lack of reciprocity in the treatment of multinationals there does not support either the notion or the reality of corporate globalization, and of the market access capitalism that is supposed to characterize the new world order.

The principle would appear to be that each corporate state protects its own in the contest for the apportionment of the global market. But here again the United States has another major advantage, inasmuch as few major non-U.S. corporations or global-minded financial firms can afford to dispense with the massive U.S. market itself, as a source of sales, technology, information, and capital. This means that non-U.S. corporations, in their quest to globalize, must also increasingly gravitate toward the New York-Washington power center. No foreign corporation of course can afford to be without domestic political leverage in the country in which it operates, but in the case of the largest non-U.S. corporations operating in the U.S. market, this also entails some degree of de-nationalization in order to better respond to and reflect U.S. standards. The result is an internationalization process that further reinforces and recognizes United States global authority.

Access to the U.S. market has its benefits, but there is also a price to be paid. Japanese and European corporations are anxious to avoid offending political authorities in Washington, and will respond readily to national regulations and requirements, including commercial ones.

They must also closely gauge fiscal and commercial policy-making, which is bound to influence any major corporation's profit-making capacities in the U.S. and world market.

This is done not only for the sake of preserving market shares in the U.S. or obtaining access to its rich financial markets, but also as a means to better position the corporation on a global level. Finance capital, independently of its nationality, finds it indispensable to pay close attention to what happens in Washington, on account of Washington's impact on global market structures, including financial markets the world over — that is, on account of the structural power of the United States. Corporations must physically and politically locate themselves as closely as possible to the seat of imperial power, contribute to as well as to share in and profit from the imperial projection over the world.

In this way it is not so much an abstract "market," but rather U.S. domestic economic policies that determine political influence over what is produced and sold, where, by whom, and on what terms. Regulatory decisions over market operations were once the prerogative of each sovereign state. But while deregulation is now rampant in most countries, global re-regulation is imposed from the North as corporate political interests in the rich countries have now concentrated market tutoring on a global scale; and among those nations, the United States is by far the most significant.

It follows, as Susan Strange has argued, that the structural power of the U.S. is not measured in terms of the goods and services produced within its borders, nor by the volume of its trade, or even by the value of goods and services produced by North American multinational corporations. Its power, if it can be estimated at all, would be equal to the total value of goods and services produced by any transnational corporation responsive to U.S. political decisions.[9] It has been the United States government that has set the terms followed by most transnationals in their dealings with "communist" countries, past and present, pressuring "allied" governments to restrict sales in items deemed sensitive and threatening offending corporations to make things difficult for them in United States operations. In this way the United States can manipulate trade, markets, governments, and corporations.

Yet most governments would agree with the proposition that foreign expansion of U.S. direct and indirect corporate investment is central to global economic growth, including that of the "national" economies. Japan may be an exception, inasmuch as foreign corporate investment there is less important to national economic health than the activities of domestic firms. This is not the case with the United States economy, which continues to depend on foreign capital investment; but unlike other dependent countries, such "weakness" is largely offset by the size (and attraction) of the U.S. market and the undisputed clout of the U.S. military. Aggressive U.S. policy lures foreign investors, for example in the electronics and automobile industries, into building full-scale production plants in the United States. Once again, it has been governments, state and federal, that have actively negotiated with multinational corporations in order to build plants within their boundaries. It is not free trade, but rather its opposite, the interfering hand of the State, offering or threatening import protection that helps set the terms for the development of trade and investment flows. The direction of profit flows tends to follow and reflect the lines of power.

Corporations adapt to levels of government power and vice versa. Corporate strategies adapt to, or take advantage of, those levels of power. Political decisions seem to have more of an impact on investment decisions than vice versa; particularly as governments take economic diplomacy and industrial policy to heart. Corporate reading of governmental trends, set by their own home governments as well as others, may have led Japanese automobile makers to locate production in the United States and in Europe in order to guarantee access to these markets in the event of import problems.

Advances in communications and production technologies tend to make such global displacements that much simpler without affecting central control, but it is government policies that still play an important role in shaping investment decisions. Corporate rivalries become governmental ones, competing for home and local official favor in order to secure the best bases for high-technology production, investment placement, or consumer sales. There is nothing inevitable or non-political about the globalization of capital and industry.

WHO REGULATES THE REGULATORS?

Regulation is not a politically neutral procedure. No multilateral body has sufficient authority to impose rules of investment to apply to *all* countries (and not simply to the South and East). Nor is it clear that an internationally negotiated framework for foreign investment, even where approved, would escape the competitive pressures, particularly at the level of the North, for each nation to secure the best terms for its own.

Governments in the South, of course, are swiftly penalized if they try to enact protection or regulation at the expense of foreign corporations. But for the principal industrial countries in the North, coercion is a more complicated task, and not one of the economic giants is willing to sacrifice its sovereign resort to trade and economic policies that uphold corporate investment, as long as its competitors are not moving first in that direction.

U.S. fingers tend to point to Japan and to the multiple examples of how government-assisted Japanese corporations, particularly in the high-tech field, have come to exercise enormous market power, clearly focusing their strategy toward the penetration of key markets and the dominance of vital technologies at the expense of European and U.S. competitors. The latter are compelled, therefore, to petition governments not only for protection but indeed for greater access to the internal Japanese market, which generates profit margins that permit cut-rate pricing abroad. If the policies of one government slant the playing field, then it is up to its rivals to use their power to correct the imbalance. Otherwise, warned the U.S. head of the Council of Economic Advisers, "If we disarm unilaterally, we leave decisions about the future composition of our economy and its trade, not to the free market, but to the policy decisions of other governments."[10]

Inasmuch as corporate and national well-being are broadly (though erroneously) perceived to be one and the same by governments, the political and economic motivations for globalization also tend to mesh. After all, export shipments between branches of the same firm increasingly account for higher percentages of the total trade of the major exporters — some 40 percent in the case of the U.S.

Classic arguments about free trade vs. protection have little relevance, and are even seen as dangerous to the pursuit of higher corporate and governmental interest in a changing global scenario. With the Soviet Union out of the way, even the definition of strategic interests acquires an economic content, thereby justifying political-governmental involvement. The Pentagon continues to argue, as do certain European defense industries, that foreign ownership or control of industries or products deemed critical to national security is not a good idea.

Globalization is inadmissible in the narrow and traditional U.S. national conception: according to the Pentagon, national defense requires a national economic strategy for local ownership or local production to enhance national control over suppliers in the case of an emergency. This begins with national security provisions in foreign investment laws, and the taking of active steps to enhance domestic competence in defense goods and technologies, including commercial ones with military applications (or vice versa). This is discussed later on.

U.S. "strength" in high-technology industries still depends chiefly on U.S. firms, both on their own and by way of their capacity to secure partnerships and access to external research.[11] But partnership is no substitute for outright ownership and common nationality. Thus on multiple occasions the U.S. government has prompted U.S. companies to withdraw from politically sensitive foreign projects.[12]

The mounting costs and competitive dimension of modern technology, associated with global expansion, has always presented corporations with the need for greater degrees of centralization and concentration as well as access to the public purse and government power. That means either out-perform rivals or create partnerships with them on the best possible terms. Such a pattern of behavior is not new, but it is sharply evident in the modern world where the advantage of one corporation or industrial nation over another is a function of politics as well as product and process technology (the capacity to continuously observe and absorb new skills and methods in industry and in the population more quickly than competitors). This is particularly true in biotechnology, optoelectronics, micromanufacturing, and semiconductors. Yet national boundaries also have an impact here, because the diffusion of technologies is a carefully controlled process, at the level of corporations, researchers, and government — this is particularly the case in Japan, somewhat less so in the United States and Europe.[13]

Foreign expansion, particularly in the "emerging economies" of the South, becomes more important. But market structures or market access regimes demanded by corporations do not emerge automatically as the product of economic engagement and "integration"; if they do, it takes too long. This is why such processes can be politically influenced to fit the requirements of one set of competitors over another. Governmental policies and market structure continue to respond to each other. And it may well be that governmental muscle helps insure that the globalization of corporations and of the market is structured in such a way that one nationality benefits more than others.

Asymmetry in economic as well as political power has undisguised manifestations. This is evident in North-South dealings, but also in relations between the "West" and Japan. In each case, the United States government feels obliged to press for structural changes so as to eliminate the disadvantages its own industrial or financial corporations face in the context of institutions, practices, or policies out of sync with the U.S. version of the "free market" order.

In Japan, a formidable state-directed machinery of political and economic coercion is deployed to insure secure conditions for market expansion. Intervention becomes the norm for the sake of "open market competition." U.S. and European governments claim they must apply political pressure in the face of Japanese unwillingness to further open its market or to curtail its exports. Western political muscle must counteract economic obstinacy. According to one U.S. expert, "An automatic yes to Japanese companies buying U.S. companies is an automatic acquiescence to this asymmetry that belies the assumptions of global corporations operating in politically unconstrained markets."[14]

Governments on the periphery are becoming enfeebled, but the nation-state is alive and well at the core — again, this is nothing new because that is what colonialism, old and new, is all about. In the North, the power of the State is increasing as an instrument for the international expansion of capital, a phenomenon that is complementary to the erosion of the national economy but which sustains the global activities of capital and State.

Whether they choose to admit it or not, corporations *do* have nationalities and do pull political strings to secure advantages. But their real loyalty is to profits, which in turn entail free trade abroad and fair trade at home, including of course a steady diet of direct and indirect governmental subsidies, as well as collusion with bureaucracies and/or military establishments. The latter are especially relevant in the development of key technologies, which for strategic reasons neither the U.S. nor its rivals are willing to submit to the free market.

As corporate global expansion needs mount, so too does the political (and ideological) duty of securing "market access" regimes — abroad but also at home. The "harmonization" or "integration" of national legislative and economic practices cannot be left to the market itself, particularly in periods of recession when domestic social pressures build up to move in the opposite, "protectionist" direction. In a world of "imperfect" competition, where the multinational corporations uphold their own national and structural protection yet insist on the dismantling of each other's, friction is the result. The tensions are exacerbated by both corporate and governmental attempts to scale back regulatory policies that discriminate between domestic and foreign companies. Yet as governments seek to mitigate the social effects of recessions, there is also a tendency to pressure national corporations not to "export" jobs or research and development activities.

In the North, big corporations require big government intervention at both the sending and the receiving end in order to eliminate barriers and contain adverse socio-political pressures. This is different from intervention in the South and East, where pressure mounts to scale back impediments that hinder investment, and instead secure regimes that pursue rapid privatization while offering lower production costs, minimal wage and environmental standards, and therefore optimal guarantees for profit-making.[15]

TRANSNATIONAL ECONOMICS VS. TRANSNATIONAL POLITICS

However uneven the process, economic globalization is placing constraints upon the autonomy of states. Some states, however, lose more power than others: the process does not affect power relationships equally, but rather accentuates existing imbalances. It can be further argued that if indeed the concentration of capital and integration of markets reduce the scope of authority of any one state, they also create vacuums in authority that only the strongest are able to fill. This does not necessarily translate into political control over the economic system, but rather into greater influence within it, particularly where military and ideological factors also intersect with economics.

Of course, even the wealthiest national governments and individual corporations, along with national economies, are beholden in some degree to trans-territorial capital markets, technological innovation, currency movements, or fiscal policies set by other rich countries. The authority of the international state system has not so much been diminished as transformed and concentrated in greater hegemonic fashion, and it does not remain impassive in the face of broader economic and technological forces. The concentration of economic power requires the exercise of global political rule-making, a process much less open and more contradictory in world politics than in world economics.

A U.S.-centered global political system has not yet materialized, but a reading of present tendencies strongly points in that direction. This does not mean that other power centers do not have an independent capacity to influence financial and currency markets, and even to exercise diplomatic muscle to secure liberalized access to external markets. Certainly in the case of the vast majority of states, their own government power influences domestic economics. But the pooling of governmental authorities would not necessarily entail the coherence and the swiftness of action demanded increasingly by economic forces. At stake is not only national but also systemic well-being. There is an imperative to contribute politically to the stabilization of the world capitalist economy: ultimately global economic stability also demands global political enforcers.

A complicating factor is the emergence of relatively autonomous regional economic spheres that purport to transcend the individual state, in order to form new multi-state political authorities capable of competing with the United States in setting the terms of global economic management or at least of having a greater say within their own region. We will return later on to examine the political and economic implications of regional systems. Suffice it for now to record the existence of competing capitalist political forces, national, regional, and international, bent on influencing the shape of the world order, but from different perspectives and with different priorities, thereby further complicating and delaying the emergence of required universal rules for world development and order. As Robert Cox points out, there is an increasingly marked duality and tension between the principles of interdependence and territorial based power, even before all non-economic forces have been factored in.[16]

Setting aside for the moment the argument over whether the U.S. is losing the productivity contest to Japan or Europe, there is little debate that U.S. power remains global capitalism's principal enforcer, the principal regulator of the allegedly self-regulating market. There is no evidence that a new supranational higher authority has come into existence enjoying equal levels of world influence and outreach. None of the principal multilateral institutions, the IMF, World Bank, GATT/WTO, plays this role effectively, nor do the G-7 or the UN Security Council as such.

If it was true that structures of governance tend to coalesce around economic power, it would follow that the multilateral institutions, including corporations, have, in this increasingly "post-state" world, become the managing board of the world political economy. This, however, is clearly not the case, if for no other reason than these bodies are politically and militarily incomplete as governing institutions.

Inter-governmental institutions have not substituted for the State. They may dictate economic and social policies in more countries than ever before, and they may even provide a military vehicle to enforce international conformity, but they hold no such power over the principal rich countries. Indeed, those bodies are the reflection and instrument of international domination. They may dominate the small nation-state by protecting corporate interests and imposing their will on the South, but the Bretton Woods institutions are not more powerful than the most powerful of the "equals."

Indeed, there is no incompatibility between the accelerated globalization witnessed over the course of the last two decades on one hand, and, on the other, the four-century-old tendency of capitalist national states to impose transnational political systems, less euphemistically known as colonial empires, on the South. News of the demise of the State is premature. Although the tendency may be in that direction, national markets have not disappeared or dissolved in the global market. Some may be dissolving faster than others, but this does not change the fact that key national markets, particularly that of the United States, and perhaps those of the European Union, remain the principal locomotive of the "global" economy. And despite or on account of their strength, their governments continue to play a role in enhancing the terms of "competitiveness" for national industry and services, as well as providing indispensable mechanisms for securing advantages over other nation-states.

Large states, directly and/or through multilateral bodies, attempt to attain a consensual regulation of the world market for the universal benefit of capital's mobility. Multilateral bodies lack armies, effective enforcement power, and even the necessary economic resources to deal with political or fiscal emergencies. There are attempts to strengthen some of these authorities, but one harbors the suspicion that the access to power is limited to the principal rich countries, while that power is being used ever more amply against weaker countries. The appearance of regional or multilateral bodies affects the poor more than the rich; indeed they may even enhance the power of the already powerful, giving organizational shape in many respects to the already uneven distribution of decision-making authority. Even where the international bodies pretend to uphold the principle of universal enforcement, the powerful countries simply opt not to comply — a luxury certainly not available to most countries.

Inter-governmental bodies are by and large called forth to administer what has been agreed upon by the powerful states. And in the absence of such agreement, there is no indication that the principal rich sovereign states will submit to external dictates. One rich country's definition of global rules may not be to the liking of another, not to mention the concerns of the poorer countries. Yet because the integration of markets will not wait and because dependency on access to those markets tends to increase, the result is increased North-North and North-South tensions. Unholy alliances sometimes result in the process, as countries of the South can take sides with the European Union against the U.S., or with Washington in particular global economic schemes.

In reality, the complexity stems from the nature of state-centered global hegemony, in an era in which the State must respond both to world market forces on the one hand, while administering society's demand for government social responsibility to provide minimal welfare on the other.

Clearly, whether another state enhances domestic welfare is not the chief concern of the United States. But there is a direct relationship between the degree of wealth and military power on the one hand, and national economic autonomy on the other. States in the South and East, as well as the smaller industrial nations, are not masters of their own economic domain. They become increasingly limited in their capacity to respond to their citizenry, as it becomes clearer that unbridled liberalization and integration into a world economy dominated by transnational capital does not and cannot enhance the general welfare of populations.

The larger core states cannot escape this logic or its consequences, as governments no longer exercise the control they once had over their own national economies. But unlike their counterparts elsewhere, they do have the political leverage necessary to manipulate the workings of a global economy on behalf of national corporate interests either protecting or securing privileged access to external markets. This reality belies the common claim that both North and South have become powerless in the face of economic globalization.[17] While people throughout the North have paid a heavy price in unemployment and social cutbacks, the governments themselves are doing fine. Disempowering the state apparatus itself is reserved largely for the South.

The notion of the decreasing power of the State, defended sometimes in well-meaning quarters, has significant and dangerous implications. Taken one step further, it has a disempowering consequence. If states can have no power, then the appeal or struggle for political control or influence over political institutions has no meaning. National liberation movements become a contradiction in terms. Worse still, the formal state structures that emerge in the South are seen as functional only as part of the globalization thrust. The old politically identifiable colonial master is said to have "given way to a new multifaceted global master, whose hegemony no longer lies within the realm of the state, but within that of the market."[18] Sharing much the same premise, free market fundamentalists would go on to argue, much to the delight of the global power centers, that there is no master at all. And as for the social consequences of globalization, these "soft issues" as well as police functions would be left to the management of what remains of the market-oriented, privatized State.

The system does not substitute for or even transcend the State, but rather transforms it as an adjunct and instrument for the further concentration of wealth and power. In the light of the chaos of market tendencies, some external adjustment is always necessary. As governmental and academic strategists insist on reminding us, international political and economic stability is vital to the economic and political well-being of the core nations, and their bureaucratic elites (and to a lesser extent business ones) are fundamentally beholden to the home base. Multinational democracy has not been the salient feature of historical attempts to build transnational political structures, and where they have been built at all, as in the case of the League of Nations and the United Nations, powerlessness has been the fundamental characteristic. The exception of the Security Council emerges where again democracy is not the norm.

Even on economic grounds, the fact remains that while the "institutional trinity" (World Bank, IMF, and GATT/World Trade Organization) may well dominate the economic relations of countries in the East and South, nevertheless the principal industrial nations can and do ignore these institutions when defining their own priorities, making their own separate deals or their own sanctions. Given their lack of success in effectively stabilizing the international economy, there would be little basis for the claim that the trinity actually manages or controls the world economy. Most prominent producing and consuming nations are politically outside its sphere of control. The transnational institutions effectively serve the interests of transnational corporations, as do most states in the South upon enacting structural adjustment programs mandated by the Bretton Woods institutions. The state-corporate relationship, however, is more complex at the level of the North, where international institutions confront real difficulties in achieving the type of coordination and submission practiced in North-South relations.

The globalization of capitalism notwithstanding, the world is still riddled with political realities that can either block or assist capital's quest for higher profits and accumulation. The search for profits and markets still shapes (and is shaped by) the organization of states and societies. Market "freedom" has always been relative, as capital will employ non-economic agents in attempts to monopolize or tame the market. Competitiveness in this sense is also relative, as a series of forces — social, business, and national — may well fall victim to a process of capitalist change in general, or the shaping of that change by the selected few.

The nature of state intervention has changed, but not the role of the State itself. In the South and increasingly in the East, such state intervention is clearly molded to fit the demands of private capital as interpreted by the multilateral financial institutions, with local elites hoping for a payoff. But in the North, fewer states feel they exercise sufficient power to bend the globalization process in particular self-serving directions.

Today, the U.S. and a selected handful of its allies directly or through multilateral mechanisms dominate and define the operating framework of the world economy. Nonetheless, a power shift is at hand, and not simply of a diffuse economic character: state-based politics accompanies market globalization, and indeed helps insure "discipline." The power shift takes place internationally as well as domestically, placing greater governmental authority precisely in the hands of that corporate sector in each country most linked to global market expansion.

National and international state functions continue to interlock, shaped by broader market concerns. But where "national" economic policies are perceived to be inconsistent with liberal global guidelines, this too is a reflection of the political and power shifts. There is no loyalty to principles, and interdependence means some are more dependent than others, but the resort to state policy in the North becomes a lever that allows particular corporations and banking firms to attain a competitive edge at home and abroad. State policy in this regard continues to be the ready instrument of key corporations to minimize the hazards of going global: securing particular political or fiscal support, obtaining preferential treatments or semi-exclusive access to new markets.

In all the principal capital-exporting countries, going global is a selective, political, and conflict-prone process. Yet it does not affect all states in similar fashion, since the growing disparity in economic distribution has a parallel political effect in which power is further concentrated in the hands of the already powerful. National disintegration coexists with, and perhaps is both cause and reflection of, the further concentration of corporate global power. Simply because the actors are increasingly complex is no reason to throw out the territorially-defined and administratively centralized nation-state. Big power foreign policy may now deal fundamentally with global economic and political issues, but the perspective and the defense of interests remains basically national, not global. What we are witnessing is a process of the reconfiguration of sovereignty, and more specifically, the transfer of the attributes of state sovereignty from South and East to North, and within the North to the United States.

Imposition by force is kept to a minimum, often becoming unnecessary since local capitalists and bureaucracies also see their interests upheld by greater integration, having in most cases already interlocked their capital, organization, and mentalities to those of the global

corporate center. However, intervention, or the threat thereof, remains the linchpin of the entire system. Much the same is true in the
North, where democratic accountability also falls by the wayside as
part of the restructuring process, also designed to become irreversible
in the light of nationalist or labor challenges.

Invoking globalization and competitive needs, global restructuring
entails the re-molding of social relations and societies as a whole. This
emerging world order requires internal and external renovation, at
the level of the State and civil society, at the level of politics and culture. Its objective is to make states and peoples more accountable to
corporate capital and corporate elites. And just how successful the
penetration is is largely determined by the dynamic of contending social forces, principally within the nation-state itself.

True, a tension between globalization and state sovereignty exists
also in the North, inasmuch as the more powerful countries can and
will resist blanket applications of neo-liberalism. The U.S. drive to
constitutionalize neo-liberalism on a world scale is accompanied by
escape clauses, applicable only to itself and allies in need.[19] It is also
true that rich countries retain more sovereignty that poorer ones in
general, and are thus better equipped to combat the social effects of
hyperliberalism and make themselves less vulnerable to external destabilization. But the best way to guard against social effects — or at
least better manage their political manifestations — is to mobilize
state power to influence the process of globalization itself. Increasingly, only the United States seems capable of undertaking such a
task, and even it has uncertain prospects of success. And while the
United States corporate elite may not always manage to control market upheavals, it does exercise a powerful sway over other states and
corporations. One cannot either under- or overestimate the importance of U.S. governmental regulatory influence over markets, capital,
and corporations that operate in its territorial domain.

Given the interlocking of economies, the search for stability is at
once domestic and global. Apologists absolve the new intervention,
denying not only its political intent and responsibility, but indeed its
very existence. Those responsible for disintegration, they claim, are
not the rich, but rather amorphous bodies such as "international interdependence," "economic globalization," or simply "the market"
mysteriously guiding development for one and all. The new self-right-
eous assumption is that market-based global economic integration —
the universalization of capitalism — will lead to stable, cooperative
international relations and a higher living standard for all — at least
all who matter.

But does the "invisible hand" of the market magically allocate resources around the world according to the law of comparative advantage? Or does the State continue to constitute an instrument of power, to place influence in the hands of entities loyal to the global capitalist logic, while disempowering potential opposition? Could it not be that the growing dependence of national corporate elites on global markets, rather than altering the traditional function of the State, instead enhances its political aggressiveness, engaging in an endless quest to achieve "competitive" international advantage, including new markets, in exclusive fashion and by non-economic means if necessary?

Further questions arise here. Is the drive for hegemony, along with political and even military rivalries, simply a feature of a past world system? Have the relations among military power, economic strength, and political and cultural influence suffered radical alterations to the point of segmenting what used to be also considered the aggregate expressions of power? On the other hand, has the march toward "integration" been accompanied by increasing political and social world harmony? Did the end of the Cold War open a new historical period of North-North collegiality based on consensual global rule? Does the spread of market capitalism have anything to do with sharp increases in social inequality, the shattering of national unities, socioeconomic breakdowns, wars, and other human catastrophes? Is the pendulum truly swinging toward universalism and away from nation-statism? Since when have the major powers focused more on universal interests than on national ones?

Is the new order then the product of spontaneous globalization, of new structures of actors and actions? Are modern "market" forces, economic or ideological, creating new forms of power and domination? And if so, is that power a new form of "liberation" or a new mechanism of control and repression, substitutive of traditional military instruments? Is it mere coincidence that the privileged support, and the marginalized oppose, a system that further privileges some while further marginalizing the many?

Or is it in fact the more visible hand of transnational corporations, the imperial states, and their multilateral political and economic agencies that use force to accomplish that same end? An in-between interpretation would land the responsibility at the steps of the multinational corporations and finance capital, along with the World Bank, International Monetary Fund, and GATT/WTO. But, as explained, the historical and present authority of these bodies is more a reflection of nation-state line-ups in the North than of the magic concentration of global economic authority.

GLOBAL HEGEMONY

World orders, past and present, are grounded in social relations. Between the social and the global lie national structures whose own workings are influenced by local and trans-border forces. The saying that all politics is local remains true, but only to a limited extent. At the level of elite politics and social sectors, the structures of domination may well reflect the larger hegemonic forces to which they are by and large loyal. Non-elite forces, however, also impact on national structures, particularly in times of turbulence, when for the sake of stability, national elites are forced to make domestic social concessions. This makes national politics an important unit of global dynamics, often at odds with the demands of economic and technological change.

Thus the process known as globalization does not preclude or overtake national politics. Commercial or financial markets have never been non-political, because they are both the subject and the source of political pressures, particularly as the number of powerful players — corporations and states — steadily diminishes. State-market interaction is more complex, as governments still have responsibility for trying to shape the larger political and economic space required for capital's expansion and mobility. Such a task was rather simple during the period in which national economic spaces were less integrated with global market forces and transnational capital. But governments also play a role in the same regulating and space-securing task that must also be increasingly assumed at the world level. Clearly, not all states are equal participants in the task.

But history indicates that the concentration of power is subject to a number of pitfalls, particularly where it entails the building of transnational hegemonic systems. The picture is now further complicated by the accelerated internationalization of production and finance: political formations have not kept up with economics. Stronger groupings of corporate capital demand greater mobility for greater profits, and therefore demand an end to whatever barriers in whatever potential market stand in the way. But because there are rival profit-seeking concentrations of capital, within or among the principal core capitalist nations, there may also be conflicting demands over which barriers should be removed and when, and which should remain in order to retain certain profit-enhancing privileges. At the same time, the principal capitalist governments will also be subject to local demands for protection of social rights or of business unable to compete under "free market" conditions.

Globalization therefore entails a demand for both the reinforcement and restriction of state sovereignties or state action. And this is where power enters into the picture in determining who gives and who takes. National and global pressures converge on governments. Corporate capital would appear to be winning the battle, insofar as states, large and small, have become increasingly "internationalized" at the expense of democratic accountability. States are increasingly forced, at regional or global levels, to act as purer agents of capital in order to secure the domestic and global infrastructure demanded for the generation of profit — what has been termed the constitutional entrenchment of capital's privileges.

But ideology and corporations alone cannot insure the market discipline demanded by capital, especially if it entails crossing borders. This is the job of the imperial State, which undergoes a process of parallel power concentration as capital's indispensable partner, projecting non-economic power to secure market-access regimes and market discipline and sustain market order. The aim is to arrive at more effective formulas for global social and economic management, steadily diminishing all distinctions between local and foreign capital, local and global interests, collapsing local power formations into larger regional and global ones, steadily dropping domestically-driven pretenses of social and environmental responsibility. Although states have for some time been critical partners of capital in the process of expansion, what appears to be new is that the very dimension and integration of world markets and capital concentration are pushing the contours of the existing nation-state system.

Capital and technology now require that the State assume new functions at an international level, while other functions (including social powers) be dropped altogether. Regionalization and globalization, in this context, are breakouts of a traditional international state system in order to better respond to the agenda set by corporate capital. Capitulation to a global system is not consensual nor is it totally ideological, although it may appear to be so to the local technocratic elites. Others, however, are persuaded to believe that global structural adjustment is a matter of common sense and natural evolution in the search for higher productivity and superior rationality.

Globalization can perhaps dispense with some states, but not with all state functions, particularly the functions of control and coercion. While the authority to police and to legislate according to corporate needs will continue to be elementary state functions in much of the South, the trend is not to remove the State but to privatize its functions on behalf of capital, to deregulate and re-regulate in the interests of capital mobility and profit enhancement, while steadily pushing uneven national deregulation to give way to corporate-controlled global re-regulation inimical to the interests of labor.[20]

As is argued below, it is precisely because cycles of economic instability cannot be domestically contained or treated, and because the search for profits supersedes national barriers or community control, that capital demands that state authority be a) more accountable to corporate needs, i.e. privatized; and b) for authority to be transferred from national to more powerful and protective supranational authorities, better capable of assuring broader better conditions for profit-making, and for the more effective merger of political and corporate power. The European Union or NAFTA models represent advanced steps in this process of capitalist "rationalization," which, invoking the God of competitiveness, demand that not only governments but whole societies reorganize themselves on a market basis.

Under the ideal corporate scheme of affairs, the State, instead of acting as a buffer protecting the domestic economies from external forces, would take on the form of mediator increasingly biased toward global corporate priorities. This would reflect a shifting of gravity from national economies to the world economy and global management, representing not a loss but a shift of power.[21] A question to be explored later is whether the internationalization of production and finance translates into a diminishing of every nation's economic influence, including that of the United States.

This "internationalization" of the State is not an uncontested phenomenon. Important social forces continue to assert themselves principally on the national terrain. At the same time, rival regionalization processes, along with bitter market competition, translate into lack of consensus over the pecking order in the world hierarchical structure. This means difficulties in arriving at a global consensus, much less translating the same into a coherent set of rules for the rest of the world to follow.[22]

Our analytical framework must take account of the uneven relations of power among states, and therefore the varied outcomes of their respective interactions with global forces. It would be as much a mistake to generalize state theorizing on the basis of debt-ridden nations in the South beholden to the IMF, or of Japan in its own relationship with global markets, or that of the so-called new industrial countries of East Asia. Even if we admit the presence of de-statization and other globalization trends, the rate of their progress and the scope of action, or even their seeming irreversibility, should not be exaggerated; nor can their specific directions be anticipated by invoking grand changes in technology and communication whose impact on political systems is more often assumed than explained.

Historically, the capitalist economies have been unable to generate self-corrective economic mechanisms. As long as this is the case, market economics will not transcend politics. In fact, global capitalist economics generates and requires even higher regulation, in the face of the multiplication of state breakdowns and internal governing incoherences that seem to characterize national political authority in so many regions of the world. The creation of a stable international regime required by capital is a political task historically undertaken by the hegemonic power; there is no reason to think that hegemony and globalization are now for the first time in history mutually exclusive propositions.

Thus, the process is global but also imperial, having a definite territorial base and state apparatus at its source, without being state-centered or territorially bound. Hegemony is defined here neither in terms of the absolute dominance of a powerful state within the system of international relations, nor as a dominant structure of values that permeates a state system. It is rather a combination of both: hegemony as the product of the tendency to concentrate economic power, which is then linked to the dominant corporate strata of a particular state. It may or may not entail the acquiescence of the dominant corporate-governmental strata of other states.

The hegemonic force must be equipped to deal with inter-corporate and inter-state conflicts, which by and large would not be anti-systemic in nature and would not require the use of force. But more importantly, it must deal with those anti-systemic nationalist challenges operating at the ideological or state levels, and where the use of force is the preferred option.[23]

Modern U.S. global hegemony is as much a cause as a consequence of the universalization of capitalism. Historical circumstances have equipped the ruling North American elite with the most formidable military, ideological, and economic weaponry ever assembled. Never has one power center had so much influence over so much territory and over so many dimensions of life as has the United States, its government and its institutions, in the 1990s. Power is projected and upheld not only by the imposition of crude pressure over other states, but also by socio-ideological acceptance of profit as the guiding principle of human existence: coopting other social groups and states, fusing identities at the level of global elites. All represent an attempt to perpetuate the system, but they have so far proved unable to achieve systemic stability, notwithstanding Washington's privileged status in the uni-polar world. But the call to imperial duty ("leadership") is unmistakable.

The realm of hegemony, therefore, extends much further than inter-state relationships or to economics itself, centering rather on the relationship of politics and ethics to production. The more that market subservience and recognition of U.S. "leadership" are entrenched at the level of civil societies, the smaller the need for tight control. Hegemony, as opposed to outright control, entails a certain flexibility for political and economic action, though always within the confines of the system's framework and basic power structures. Those structures can be separated on occasion from government policies, but not from basic institutions and their social basis.

State power proved critical to the expansion of capital, albeit often at the expense of secondary states and other concentrations of capital. Corporate capital will not countenance a world of effectively sovereign states or of autonomous supranational organizations, unless those states and institutions are effectively subordinated to capitalist logic. It is in this sense, and in this sense only, that multinational corporations and financial centers acquire a vested interest in overhauling the present inter-state system, forcing all states to gravitate toward the core of big capital as corporate-centered governing elites, international organizational networks, and multinational financial institutions insure loyalty, or at least systemic punishment of those wishing to opt out.

A number of core powers or institutions exist — the G-7 and the Bretton Woods institutions — and sometimes conflict may arise among them, but the tendency is toward integration of purpose and of command. As the accumulation process advances, so too does the propensity to centralize and reinforce certain types of authorities and controls. Multilateral instruments already express the need for greater international economic authority, but at the apex of their pyramid will stand the internationalized state, attempting to shape the rules of world and local economic governance.

What some will view as the rigorous logic of competitive economics at work may best be regarded as the product of a market process working within a political framework. In this scheme, absent democratic control, states also become transmission belts from the global into the national, molders of society according to the demands of transnational capital. But states become internationalized in the same way they are "integrated" into the global political economy: either in subordinate or dominant fashion, with the top ranks of economic power (G-7) assuming differing degrees of autonomy, in relation to each other and to the system as a whole.

Another question altogether is whether a transnational managerial elite is sufficiently strong and coherent to restrict international competition, or to lead the way domestically toward the creation of parallel transnationalized social formations; that is, to incorporate all societies into a single social structure in which pro-U.S. elites are willing to assume their privileged yet subordinate position in a global social pyramid. This presupposes that power has shifted irreversibly from labor to capital in the process of political and economic restructuring; that democracy and sovereignty must be sacrificed or have become irrelevant in a unipolar world.[24]

What will be argued is that the reshaping of U.S. global hegemony — the attempt to encompass all states and societies around its orbit — is challenged, not so much by rival states, as by socio-ideological dissidents as well as the volatility and globalization of financial markets themselves. Attempts are made therefore to reshape the national and international system, to make it subject to legal enforcement and central control, all in the name of sustaining market discipline, political conformity, and allegiance to the U.S.-dominated order. But how many nation-states are eager to transfer sovereignty, along with the human, military, and financial resources, that is power, to the higher authority?

It may well be that global economic interdependence is undermining the capacity of states to sustain independent policies, but it is also true that political and even social barriers hinder the coming of a stateless global economy. At essence is the need to reinject social forces — people — into the analytical and normative framework, to insist that even if long-standing patterns of world politics are undergoing change, and even if the interplay of international politics and the world economy is a fundamental determinant of the direction and nature of the change, that people in social and cultural processes are also sharply engaged in the shaping of the new order.

Herein lies the pivotal subject and target of international history and the global political economy. And the sustained state of turmoil and polarization in world affairs constitutes an unmistakable sign of reaction to the encroachment and iniquitous nature of global capitalist expansion. The crisis in global authority and stability is first and foremost a social one, reflective of growing tendencies to resist, consciously or not, national-global capitalist universalization.

Still, any inkling of national "protectionist" policies in the South is immediately branded by the North as an obsolescent statist development and heretical from the standpoint of a free market theology. This is hardly a new development and not much of an improvement on the days when Spain and Portugal opened the first European capitalist franchises in Africa, Asia, and the Western Hemisphere. The "core" countries dictated what was to be produced and how and at what price in their respective "peripheries," to the greater wealth and glory of the "center," and according to the ideologies of the system as a whole. Then as now, there were natives supposedly eager to receive the white man's trinkets and religion. Economists today call this interdependence, but as always some are more dependent than others and the systems are designed to keep it that way.

What we are witnessing, therefore, is a dramatic acceleration of capitalism's historical tendency to divorce the wealth-creation process from social and/or national controls, particularly in the poorer countries from which the wealth is being extracted. This was and is accomplished by the use of force, yet also by political and ideological means, invoking the concept of "universal benefit" and the "self-regulating market." This invites, as Karl Polanyi once observed, a protective response from society through the political system, in order to reassert the primacy of the social. That is, mobilization and popular resistance in order to break increasing governmental and structural accountability to the rich. Whether society can take back meaningful spheres of political authority is a central question of our times.

Notes

1. "Verdict of the People's Permanent Tribunal on the World Bank and the IMF," *Envío* (Managua: Universidad Centroamericana), vol. 13, no. 161 (December 1994), p. 32; Richard Barnet, "Lords of the Global Economy," *The Nation*, December 19, 1994, p. 754.

2. United Nations Development Program, *Human Development Report, 1992* (New York: Oxford University Press, 1992), p. 34.

3. Robert Cox, *Production, Power and World Order* (New York: Columbia University Press, 1987), p. 301; Richard J. Barnet and John Cavanagh, *Global Dreams, Imperial Corporations and the New World Order* (New York: Simon & Schuster, 1994), pp. 385-418.

4. See, for example, the arguments made by the U.S. Secretary of Labor, Robert Reich, *The Work of Nations: Preparing Ourselves for 21st-Century Capitalism* (New York: Knopf, 1991).

5. See the Congressional testimony of Stephen Cohen, "Corporate Nationality Can Matter a Lot," *Berkeley Roundtable on the International Economy, Working Paper* no. 27 (1987), pp. 1-3.

6. Laura D'Andrea Tyson, "They Are Not Us: Why American Ownership Still Matters," *American Prospect*, no. 4 (Winter 1991), p. 40.

7. Report by Korn Ferry in the *Economist*, cited in ibid., p. 40.

8. Cohen, "Corporate Nationality Can Matter a Lot," p. 3.

9. Susan Strange, "Toward a Theory of Transnational Empire," in Ernst-Otto Czempiel and James N. Rosenau, *Global Changes and Theoretical Challenges: Approaches to World Politics for the 1990s* (New York: Lexington Books, 1989), p. 167.

10. Tyson, "They Are Not Us," p. 43.

11. Ibid., p. 47.

12. Other examples are provided in Cohen, "Corporate Nationality," p. 4.

13. Ibid., p. 8.

14. Ibid., p. 5.

15. "A market access regime acknowledges that active government assistance to firms in many forms is a fact of life," Peter F. Cowey and Jonathan D. Aronson, "New Trade Order," *Foreign Affairs*, vol. 72, no. 1 (1992/1993), p. 184.

16. Robert Cox, "Structural Issues of Global Governance: Implications for Europe," in Stephen Gill (ed.), *Gramsci, Historical Materialism and International Relations* (Cambridge, U.K.: Cambridge University Press, 1993), p. 263.

17. See, for example, Jean Chesneaux, "Ten Questions of Globalization," *Pacifica Review*, vol. 6, no. 1 (May-June 1994), pp. 87-93.

18. Ibid., p. 89.

19. The term "constitutionalization" of the neo-liberal order is employed by Leo Panitch, "Globalization and the State," *Socialist Register 1994* (New York: Monthly Review Press, 1994), p. 76.

20. For an incisive review of this debate see Panitch, "Globalization and the State," pp. 60-93.

21. Ibid., p. 23; Cox, *Production, Power and World Order*, pp. 254-255.

22. This is a variation of the argument made in ibid., pp. 254-259.

23. See the discussion on hegemony in Gill, *Gramsci, Historical Materialism and International Relations*, pp. 41-45.

24. Cox, "Structural Issues of Global Governance," pp. 259-268.

4

The Visible Hand

Capitalism past and present — and, in all likelihood, future — requires a rudder, that is a force capable of mitigating the cycles and anarchic workings of the market, often to the short-term detriment of capital itself but needed to offset the effects of socio-economic polarization. In an age of transnational integration of corporations and capital markets on the one hand, and of greater social uncertainty with a propensity toward violence on the other, a non-economic global authority becomes all the more necessary. Yet because there is no recognized global political governing entity, control and regulation continue to flow from the more powerful states. This is in order to provide market forces with the degree of regulation, direction, and the defense that they themselves are incapable of generating.

Given the need for social and economic enforcement, neither at the national nor international level can the State afford to become lax — or totally privatized, or dispense with a political and military apparatus. Before dealing with that apparatus, it first must be shown that the global economy is incapable of governing itself, and that globalization has only highlighted and accentuated this incapacity.

The point of contention is not whether to interfere in the "free market" but how much and with what priorities. There are no principled guiding lines: the same corporations opposed to governmental boundaries that interfere with their expansion — principally abroad — favor home governmental measures designed to promote exports and secure markets.

Global "integration" accelerates the uprooting and displacement of workers and entire communities; existing socio-political arrangements, including modalities of control, are destabilized. Some segments of society demand that the State intervene in order to make globalization and integration take stock of social ramifications. By and large, these actors have been only partially successful in Europe, and virtually not at all in the United States. European Union, NAFTA, GATT, or World

Bank-IMF deliberations, not to mention corporate ones, take place in a secretive, non-accountable, and truncated fashion. At these levels an integration of another sort comes to the surface: the qualitative increase in the interlocking of capital and commerce, of corporations and bankers, both within and across national boundaries.

Democracy is the chief victim of the territorial expansion and centralization of capital. At this level at least, the hand of the market is far from "invisible" as it proceeds to shift resources and shape technologies with great implications over people's lives. At the same time, institutional forces such as the media reinforce an ideology that allows people to assimilate and internalize the resentment provoked by unrealistic expectations of quick economic success promised by the market.

And as technology becomes a market transformation force in itself, it too, as in the past, demands state guidance and public subsidies. Thus, the world market forces are fed by powerful governments. There is no automatic incompatibility between the two. Indeed, an interdependent relation between the global-economic and the national-political may be a more accurate analytical description.

The need of market-hungry, technology-dependent corporations to destroy what gets in their way must be channeled effectively and rationally by the State: such is the illusion. Even when corporate interests effectively control the State, when privatization simply entails the transfer of goods from a bureaucratic elite to its cousins in the entrepreneurial elite, when private corruption and official subsidies financially tie one to the other, the distinction between the private and the public cannot be a moot one, for each has its own particular dynamics and role to play, pay-offs notwithstanding.

The winner-take-all nature of the modern marketplace — that is to say, corporate "competitiveness" taken to its logical extreme — accentuates the capitalist tendency to demand order at the expense of reason and justice, principally on account of the ensuing unfair and inefficient distribution of economic resources. For the State to improve competitiveness means opening up foreign markets and reducing domestic production costs. The former means imposing structural reforms abroad that reduce or eliminate barriers to the export of corporate capital, and the latter means keeping unions weak and the social wage low. This feeds a contradictory cycle that pushes down long-term demand and feeds the compulsion to open new markets and secure privileged access to them. NAFTA is the ideal set up to yield these objectives, including a built-in preferential position for U.S. corporations at the expense of their rivals.

Global market cohesion does not entail free competition nor the neutralization of non-economic influences. Larger states retain a capacity to manipulate markets that is unavailable to the smaller ones; they can also resort to non-economic levers. In this context, corporate elites in Japan and Germany have much less influence over a global system that on account of its own crisis-producing propensity cannot afford to separate the global economic from the global military-strategic. Germany and Japan may have something to say about the former, but not much about the latter; while the United States has much to say and do in regards to both. True, the virtual exclusion of Japan and Germany from the military-strategic field since 1945 contributed in many senses to their present economic might, being allowed to concentrate their resources on non-military items. The question is whether that source of past advantage is now a source of disadvantage in a post-Cold War scenario characterized by economic rivalry as well as rivalry in dealing with outbreaks of violence. As argued in greater detail below, the basic post-Cold War reality is that the German and Japanese state elites lack the military strategic reach, or even a presence on the United Nations Security Council; France, Britain, China, and Russia, on the other hand, may be nuclear powers and permanent members of the Council, but their lack of international economic clout also takes them out of the superpower category, leaving the United States as the sole global superpower. This, however, does not mean that the United States can act alone, that its economy can dispense with European or Japanese capital and markets, or that it can, at every opportunity, freely impose its recipes for global peace-enforcement.

But even presupposing a grand capitalist alliance, is U.S.-harnessed world power capable of becoming the visible hand that would assist the market in the sublime task of organizing human affairs the world over? The system still appears to lack the necessary rudder to prevent or contain economic crashes, social explosions, and ecological destruction, which in many ways are the products of the system itself. Social, economic, and ecological indicators all point to continuing and deepening disaster on a global level, to a seeming inability to tackle the fundamental causes, or even to alleviate the immediate manifestations of the global crisis.

If the task of arresting inhuman and self-destructive tendencies is supposed to be in the hands of states, we also conclude that not a single government or group of governments seems up to the massive task of defending the planet's indispensable human and ecological resources. A global police force is nowhere in sight. According to two former high ranking United Nations officials, "At a time of ever more urgent need for coherent macro-economic strategy and policy for the *whole* world, no such strategy or policy exists either in the United Nations or outside it. There is much talk in meetings of the industrial countries about the global economy, but on close examination this turns out to be overwhelmingly concerned with their North-North economy." [1]

In effect, some quarters in the North may be insensitive to the global crisis in the South or in the environment, but they cannot afford to ignore the repercussions of disorder on profit-making abilities and human migration. Corporate leaders despair over scandals in banking and security industries, stock market price collapses, frenzied speculation in international currencies, or the recurrent outbreaks of economic clashes between the major trading nations. While "free market order" is elevated to the category of religious dogma, the same elites privately and sometimes publicly admit that "deregulation" has its limits and cannot continue to be viewed as an ideal, neither nationally nor internationally. Chaos in the South or East may also spell social disruption at home.

Under capitalism, market self-regulation is a contradiction in terms. Oligopolistic practices dominate both the market and the international political economy, subject, however, to recurrent battles for improved market positions. Whereas orthodox neo-liberal theorists would claim that "market reordering" reflects the work of the invisible hand to optimize individual and collective benefits, the reality is that even in the North the "public sector" tends to impose its own corrective mechanisms — an external ordering, or regulation, on the market.

GLOBAL FINANCE

Trade and investment issues are just as inseparable in economics as in politics. In the rich nations, bureaucratic elites are well aware that corporate investment abroad is becoming an increasingly important source of profits. This helps explain why foreign markets become more important and profits increase even while domestic economies and basic wage levels stagnante. The processes of globalization and impoverishment are one and the same, revealing the extraordinary capacity of the capitalist system to increase wealth without diminishing poverty.

Notwithstanding massive increases in the amounts of U.S. foreign investment since 1985, the U.S. share of total foreign investment has fallen from nearly 50 percent in 1960 to about 25 percent in 1990.

Other countries, particularly Japan, have increased their foreign investment at a much more rapid pace. Such competition, grounded in the corporate search for higher profits in overseas settings, translates into more contentious intra-imperialist relations, already troubled by other side effects of globalization, such as rising nationalist and racist tensions at home and abroad.

Deregulation, integration, and globalization take the form of more than a trillion dollars of foreign exchange being privately traded daily. The amounts and the speed of these movements could not have been predicted even by the most sanguine some 15 years ago. In the face of such mobility, most central banks are effectively sidelined, although less so in the principal capital-exporting countries. Capitalism remains caught between the prospect of potentially destabilizing speculator-driven transactions and the need to develop new regulatory authorities and procedures with global reach.

But it is deregulation that is in vogue, and dominant political philosophy insists that freer markets and greater marketization are by nature desirable, beneficial, and irreversible. How then to deal with the need to regulate or at least curb speculative money movements that could provoke panics and recessions the world over?

Supposedly, this is the job of central banks. Supposedly, in most countries they are independent from government. Although contradictions are frequent between banking and political authorities, experts tend to concur that no central bank operates in a totally depoliticized environment: public understanding and governmental apprehensions also weigh in. Interestingly enough, however, nowhere is a possible trend away from banking autonomy clearer than in the United States. Recessions and inflationary spirals evidently generate greater governmental involvement in central bank decisions, save where the supranational institutions have already assumed that role.[2]

During the 1940s, those who conceived of the need for an international financial regulatory body supported the creation of the International Monetary Fund. But few could have foreseen the capacity of big capital to be oblivious to the financial cop. The global economy seems to have become a free-for-all, as massive amounts of funds move about in search of higher profits, escaping the "guidance" of corporate managers, governments, the Bretton Woods institutions, and even investment banks.

Few countries were as adept in generating governmental tutelage over the national economy as Japan. Still, the guidance was not able to prevent the $6 trillion losses on the Japanese stock market in late 1991. It proved just as easy to blame corrupt practices among security firms, banks, credit unions, and bureaucrats. In the end, the Finance Ministry had to rush in to prop up the banks and the stock market by sending $15 billion of government-controlled savings into the market.[3] This probably helped explain the minimal repercussions of the crash on other financial markets, but it also reminded other capital-exporting nations that their governments, unlike the Japanese, were in a poor position to mobilize that amount of funds and inject them into the economy without provoking an inflationary backlash.

Some, however, felt that global capitalism had been brought to the verge of chaos, and that Japan should mend its evil ways. The *Economist* took the Japanese to task: "[These scandals] make the eye spin like a fruit machine. Add more noughts to the figures, find scams in every financial firm in the land, and no Japanese would any longer be surprised. It is dawning on many in the West, too: Japan is up to its neck in dirt .... Scandals are sewn into the fabric of Japan's financial system, its corrupt politics and even of its business ways. They are systemic not only in nature but also in the risk that they pose: the world's largest single source of capital and one of its three top financial centres is riddled with crookery, has been supervised by the blind or the complacent, and could be — not is, but could be — facing collapse. Japan's dirt is dangerous stuff."[4]

Whether the dirt was only endemic to Japan or to financial markets in general was beside the point for the moment, but there was little doubt that a Japanese market collapse, given the integration of markets, would send shock waves throughout the international financial order. Without recovery in the $4 trillion Japanese economy, worry was that the rest of the world would have an even more difficult time pulling out of the slump. There was, therefore, no rejoicing among Japan's competitors over its woes. To the contrary, pressure mounted from Japan's "partners" in the G-7 to undertake serious restructuring that would reduce huge trade surpluses and stimulate the internal market, so that Japan could become a bigger and healthier purchaser. Corporate sectors in Japan were also aware that the Japanese bureaucracy was increasingly limited in its capacity to intervene without offending its major trading partners.[5]

Independently of the origins of this specific systemic breakdown, its consequences were global in nature. Japanese capitalism is no exception to the recent trend found in the principal capital-exporting nations to develop multi-layered financial organizations relatively divorced from productive activity and dedicated chiefly to speculative activities. Perhaps the difference was that the "nod and wink" from political authorities is more open in Japan than elsewhere.

The problem is not to do away with "managed competition," but rather to allow outside entities to become part of the management and restructuring effort.

In this way the global order does not emerge spontaneously, but is shaped in accordance with the general interests of the powerful, and more specifically of the most powerful of the elite. Throughout, however, the justification is the "public interest" and the general welfare of all nations and people. Some regulatory measures do reflect a degree of political sensitivity and corporate self-protection, in the face of rampant corruption and sharp drops in stock market prices. But the fact that turmoil and crisis continue to reappear uncontrollably leads one to conclude that "reform and regulation" are more often geared to managing appearances and sustaining "confidence" than in tackling underlying factors.

As early as 1942, John Maynard Keynes insisted on global capitalism's need for what he termed an "internal stabilizing mechanism" that would exercise pressure on any country whose balance of payments with the rest of the world was departing from equilibrium, in either direction. At one point, some of the founders of the United Nations contemplated that the World Bank and International Monetary Fund, originally conceived as specialized agencies of the UN, would undertake such functions. By discreetly intervening in the economic policies of countries, both institutions were supposed to be democratic and multilateral instruments to help achieve and reflect coherent global macro-economic policies.

The Fund was intended in fact to function as a virtual central bank and regulating authority for the entire international community, promoting monetary coordination, trade expansion and exchange stability, as well as assistance to member countries with balance of payments problems. The Bank, originally termed the International Bank for Reconstruction and Development, was to act as the non-commercial lending agency of the United Nations. In a word, the Bretton Woods systems had the ostensible objective of helping member states achieve the UN Charter's economic and social goals in a way compatible with the principles of respect and cooperation on which all United Nations development activities were to be based.[6]

Very soon, however, the Bretton Woods institutions began to organize themselves in a manner independent from the UN, and more in accord with the recommendations of the great powers. Weighted voting according to members' shares (wealth) became the norm, as WB and IMF authorities at the time feared that being subject to the principle of one-member one-vote would subject the institutions to "undesirable" political control or influence and hurt their credit rating on Wall Street. Both the Bank and the IMF renegotiated their relationship with the UN to secure complete independence free from external coordination. The final texts of the two Special Agreements were strongly opposed by many member states in 1947. Norway stated that the special exemptions and privileges being accorded to the two institutions could undermine the authority of the United Nations and even jeopardize international cooperation.[7]

Indeed, under G-7 control and subject to the influence of Wall Street, neither the World Bank nor the IMF came to act as the mechanism of equilibrium and redistribution, including the promotion of social development with the capacity to influence economic decision-making in the core countries. The United Nations was denied its role as a forum for agreeing on global equitable macro-economic strategies, and in the final analysis, so too were the IMF and the World Bank, as their intimidatory power was directed almost exclusively against the deficit countries of the South. Two respected observers warned, "The world will remain at severe risk while its only universal multilateral institution [the IMF] does not include the kind of mechanism that Keynes outlined in the midst of the last world war as an essential institutional safeguard against a repetition of the 1930s."[8]

Of course, no one can say whether truly global financial and trade instruments could have averted the world economic crisis by acting upon some of its immediate causes such as unstable commodity prices, debt accumulation, interest rate manipulations, eroded terms of trade, and the vulnerability of national currencies to unscrupulous private speculation. Nonetheless, to state that global economic governance is not in the hands of the UN is not to imply that it cannot emerge elsewhere, albeit for the purposes of "stabilizing" an unjust system as opposed to radically reforming it.

Corporate and government leaders in the United States and its principal allies need not be convinced that the absence of minimal regulation in trade and finance can have disastrous consequences for profit-making and social stability. But multilateral institutions, including new ones such as the World Trade Organization, are deliberately made independent of the United Nations system or of any need to coordinate with UN development activities. The point is that the majority of states in the world, not to mention its citizenry, are not to be trusted with such vital matters affecting their daily life and future. Transnational democratic control over the free flow of capital for the sake of equitable development is simply unacceptable to capital.

In flat contradiction to the United Nations' original blueprint, and following the declarations of independence on the part of the Bretton Woods organizations and GATT, the United States and its economic allies now persistently assert that the negotiation of macro-economic policies must take place exclusively under the umbrella of the IMF, the World Bank, and WTO, all of which are under the effective control of the North. On debt issues, for example, U.S. delegates at the UN argue that "progress" being made through the Bretton Woods institutions should not be "undermined [by] imposing generalized formulae" at the UN. Meanwhile, the total external debt of developing countries has multiplied fourteen-fold since 1970, from $100 billion to some $1,400 billion in 1993.[9]

Such an undemocratic transfer of power to the multilateral financial and trade institutions, therefore, must be understood as part of a U.S. policy to foster, control, and uphold a global environment in which big multinational corporations can flourish and U.S. influence can be extended. Linkages between these bodies and official Washington form part of a power structure also extending to the "allies" and devised to maintain a position of privilege and disparity between South and North, but also within the North itself.

A manifestation and result of economic "globalization" is the increasing power of the Bretton Woods bodies and the new and old trade bodies, to better serve and reflect the interests of transnational capital. But logically the authority to regulate and intervene is largely defined and practiced in terms of the South, and not in terms of the North. In other words, the major economic powers and corporations can afford to flaunt the rules they insist that others abide by. Witness, for example, the breakdown of UN efforts to develop a code of conduct for multinational corporations, or the endemic weakness of UN economic bodies such as UNCTAD (UN Conference on Trade and Development), or the U.S. flouting of the World Trade Organization in regard to its trade conflict with Japan. Yet "order" is also required for the sake of the free flow of capital; the trouble is that the United States will accept no other order which it cannot aspire to control. Such are the prerogatives of hegemony, but also its price as one nation-state proposes to dictate the transition from one set of rules to another.

Not that the U.S. corporate-bureaucratic elite denies it has a responsibility to the global market order, but rather it interprets the self-given mandate through the prism of its own material interests and internal political dynamics. Given recurrent crisis and periodic social outbursts, those elites are convinced that the most powerful capitalist state must assume the duties of socio-economic management — duties that may also entail the projection of strategic and military power.

How then to extend management beyond the nation's borders and if possible over the transnational private agents? How can governments continue to act as problem-solving agents, mediating between markets and corporations, or crushing rebellions against the market order, this time on a global level? The answers are not clear, but what is impressive is the extent to which the United States has been successful in imposing changes in social values and political behaviors in fulfillment of its aspirations to this role: to engage in global social engineering assisted by the Bretton Woods institutions, but also by "peace-enforcement" and "nation-building" under the UN flag.

In all, the global expansion of the marketplace — capitalist colonialism — continues to be the dominant feature in defining relations between advanced and "less developed" nations as well as the principal explanation for the pattern of growing inequities and social polarization that provoke violence. The accelerated transnationalization of trade, investment, enterprise, technology, communications, and travel — also known as globalism — undermines the capacity of the nation-state, North and South, to stabilize its economy, U.S. efforts notwithstanding.

The emergence of a world economy simply has not (yet) been matched by the appearance of a single world polity; the only supranational state distantly on the horizon is the United States, although it remains to be seen whether such a state could broaden the scope of its national decisions and institutions to take account of and control over the still autonomous components of the global economy, while at once establishing the strategic parameters in which other large capitalist states would cooperate. Ironically, the same process of globalization, accompanied by recurrent crisis and stagnation, has accelerated the formation of regional blocs engaged in trade disputes in total disregard of the neo-classical notions of harmonious market relations.

An untutored global economy could spell chaos, but on the other hand disaster could also come about by heavy-handed attempts to impose "coordination" on rival powers in the North or by attempting to crush dissidents in the South. Attempts to impose discipline spell further disorder, both North-North and South-North, as well as internally in the South. Capital demands that the periphery as well as the other poles of economic power be subordinated and stabilized. In principle, such a paradox entails efforts in the North to strengthen the State as an instrument for the international expansion and stabilization of the market system. In current historical terms, this perhaps translates into the functional need by the most powerful nation-state

— the United States — to assume the role of chief regulator and protector of the system as a whole, yet to do so in a way that will minimize costs and maximize gains.

Washington therefore assumes global hegemony in a custom-built fashion, hoping that the domestic "costs" of competition and expansion (lower wages, higher unemployment, budget cutbacks in social programs) are transferred abroad as much as possible, while its principal benefits (profits) accrue at home and extracted as much as possible from abroad. Hegemony also means imposing state-weakening policies on other nations and insuring open doors for capital. Yet governing elites in the North will cling to the illusion of exports and foreign investment as the salvation for national economic well-being. The result is an increase both in North-North tensions and North-South exploitation, while at home the jobs fail to materialize and economists invent such terms as "structural unemployment," blaming technology and globalization for the new social ills.

Some suggest that capitalist polarization and expansion have reached their limits. This could be the case, particularly if one is to judge on the basis of prevailing neo-liberal dictates, with their insistence on the unfettered marketplace as the source of all hope. This short-term profitability criterion is inimical to the long-term interests of capitalism itself, and is bound to generate increased national assertiveness and explosive global imbalances. But even if we were to conceive of a cohesive political tripolarity, or a G-7 strategic command and control, it remains to be seen whether it could control or even cope with the intensity of the conflicts generated in the South, much less impose unconditional acceptance of market institutionality and ideology; that is to say to make globalization acceptable to one and all.

There is no escaping the fundamental paradox at the level of the State. It must gravitate toward closer international economic and political integration on the one hand, and yet face stepped-up demands at the level of civil society for government to sustain minimal, if not expanded, social programs such as health and education. Thus, not only national budgets and macro-economic policies, but also social, diplomatic, and environmental decisions are the subject of a tug of war between democratic constituencies on one side, and corporate demands for privileged global economic integration on the other.

Power in this regard is fundamental in determining whether an individual state can attempt to have its cake and eat it too, that is to say to impose policies of global coordination that can best complement, or be least harmful to, its particular citizenry and non-multinational enterprises. The contradictory nature of the respective impulses would seem to indicate that weak and especially undemocratic states, particularly in the South, are in no position — and have little inclination — to resist the transfer of economic decision-making to the global financial institutions.

But the more powerful states in the North are unwilling to surrender sovereign power to those same bodies that oversee Southern economies, retaining also a distrust of regional bodies. Witness, for example, the inability of the European Union to be trusted with full fiscal or monetary authority from member states. By and large, the building of an integrated Europe has been limited to the progressive widening of the market. Domestic and foreign security concerns remain tightly in the hands of the national governments.

As we will see, economic integration reaches a political threshold in the realm of monetary policy. Monetary union entails the acceptance of externally defined budget and credit policies, which in turn have a fundamental bearing on social policies and the capacity to unilaterally attack unemployment and poverty at the national and local level. Should the EU continue to succumb to the corporate competitiveness doctrine, the social and political strains will place the entire unified Europe project in danger.

From the standpoint of most of the South, the pressure to conform to transnational market logic is not purely economic, and more often than not, particularly in the case of wealthier markets, tends to be accompanied by big power political pressures. As the scale of "competition" becomes global, it becomes impossible to divorce it from "state" considerations; even more so when politicians and salespeople, along with businesses pleading for protection, join in the picture. At this point, the competitive impulse acquires a political dynamic that transcends the framework of corporate boardrooms, financial markets, and "pure" market competition. International politics and international trade become increasingly intertwined, perceived in government quarters in rather mercantilist fashion, with growing foreign and domestic efforts to attain an "edge" for respective exporters of goods, services, or capital.

It is in this context that we can measure the new dynamics of intra-capitalist or North-North competition based on the dangerous gospel that the economic and social problem facing modern nations is essentially one of competition on world markets. President Clinton views each nation "like a big corporation competing in the global marketplace." Some economists have now begun to question modern corporate and governmental obsession with competitiveness, terming it both wrong and dangerous.[10] Regardless of its justification and whether indeed it is the modern expression of long-standing capitalist logic, the competitiveness obsession is at the root of state policy and decision-making, the by-product of an elite tendency to associate national welfare with corporate well-being. Thus trade deficits and unfair competition on the part of rivals are conveniently projected not simply as causes of unemployment, but as indicators of national weakness. In neo-liberal fashion, social problems then are explained as a function of economic ones, and these in turn are the expression of an inability to compete in the marketplace: workers are pushed out of jobs on account of imports and unfair trading practices by rivals. The true root of the problem — capital's propensity to move to where more profits can be extracted — is then heralded as the solution, further shifting the center of gravity of wealth and power from the many to the few, from the rest of the world to the U.S. state oligarchy.

U.S. hegemony is thus disguised as the end of history and the triumph of globalization. The concern of imperialism — the chief imperialist power as well as fellow colonialists, including sectors of the effectively colonized — will be that the only change or development acceptable is one that precludes any substantive alteration of the capitalist system. It is not necessary therefore to directly control decision-making in other countries or in multilateral institutions, if formal and informal structures of influence already envelop decision-making procedures, setting their guidelines and securing safe outcomes generally favorable and accountable to the collective interests of the U.S. elite and its global allies.

MEXICAN MELTDOWN

Beginning in the late 1980s, the principal bankers, corporations, and governments in the North took the view that the post-Cold War world, symbolized by the liberated markets in Asia, Latin America, and Russia, spelled a new cycle of prosperity and the emergence of newly rich countries with boundless appetite for foreign capital, services, and goods. The same investors that demanded unfettered access to new "emerging markets" were the first to demand why no one was "in charge" when panics broke. An unexpected devaluation of the Mexican peso in December 1994 provoked financial mayhem in dozens of countries, undermining the illusion that consistently growing emerging markets were the new engine and guarantee of global prosperity.

Investors blamed the IMF and the U.S. government for not having intervened earlier and deeper in the management of the Mexican economy. Others pointed to the absence of an early-warning system that could have alerted markets and pressured the Mexican authorities. Calls went out for new regulations, not only over Mexico and all other capital-importing "emerging nations," but also over the financial markets themselves which, to some, were simply overreacting and multiplying the crisis.

For global capitalism, the Mexican crisis was potentially more serious than the panics provoked by the debt crisis of the 1980s. In those days, arm twisting by the IMF and bank syndicates could insure "sound" financial management of the economy and the use of foreign capital. But as small investors got into a much faster-paced market, dealing through powerful portfolio fund managers making their first foreign outings, the governmental authorities in countries in the South grew rash in deal-making and fiscal management, expecting no end to the flow of outside capital to feed the free market growth machines.

What one banker termed the first mutual-fund crisis in twentieth-century international finance began when in 1994 some $225 billion flowed to the boom economies of the South, three-quarters of which was private capital (mostly in securities), while only $55 billion was official assistance. The flow of private capital to "emerging" economies went from $41.9 billion in 1989 to an estimated $172.9 billion in 1994. Nearly half of this amount represented corporate direct investment, as opposed to portfolio investment — both, however, were exuberant capitalist reactions to the liberalization-privatization waves in the South. All this made the picture different from earlier years, when the private and "official" capital flows had been evenly divided.

Even U.S. pension funds ventured abroad, seeking higher returns contributing to the formation of so-called emerging market mutual funds.[11] In the Pacific region alone, the number of "emerging market" mutual firms went from 9 in 1990 to 44 in 1994, with total assets going from $775 million to $12 billion in that time.[12] For a time profits were handsome. Returns on Latin America had gone from about 14 percent in 1991 to 55 percent in 1993, as the principal U.S. investment banks led the pack in winning lucrative advisory and underwriting assignments in that region, as in East Asia.[13]

Most of that new capital flowed to Latin America, and to Mexico in particular. That country became the symbolic locomotive, as Washington fed expectations that if only other countries deregulated and opened as swiftly and deeply as Mexico had, then they too could be offered favored access to U.S. commercial and financial markets.

Building "investor confidence" was as much a political as an economic task, logically entailing no small amount of overselling, overlooking not only macro-economic considerations but also social ones. Washington and Wall Street, along with the Mexican elite (but also other elites in the South), had to sell themselves, their public opinions, and their markets on the benefit of NAFTA-type agreements.

It was on this basis that Mexico sold tens of billions of dollars in stock and debt securities in U.S. markets throughout the early 1990s, triggering a 50 percent surge of the local exchange index in 1994 alone. Security houses and brokers, some engaged for the first time in foreign undertakings, eagerly swallowed up propaganda and government junk bonds yielding up to 50 percent as compared to the meager 3 percent returns available at home. Days before the crash, Mexico was still the darling of investment bankers and security firms recommending its stocks and bonds.[14]

One explanation for the crisis was that the emerging nations no longer had to depend on banks and bank lending in order to tap funds. Local stock and bond markets sprang up in Latin America, Asia, and Africa directly attracting foreign (and local) capital. Average yearly flows went from some $10 billion in 1989 to $60-80 billion in 1993 and 1994. Values of listed shares or total capitalization in "emerging country" stock markets, calculated at $100 billion in 1985, reached $2.1 trillion by 1995. The flow of capital to Latin America, which had been negative as late as 1989, went from $100 million in 1990 to $45.5 billion in 1994, of which nearly two-thirds flowed to Mexico.[15]

Massive flows of "hot" money reduced the traditional leverage of governments and Bretton Woods institutions in the North over governments and borrowers in the "emergent economies" of the South. When Mexico unexpectedly devalued the peso, the other emerging markets immediately felt the effects. The picture was further complicated by speculators coming into the picture seeking to play off investor panics and attacking vulnerable currencies in order to gain from driving down their values and forcing governments and central banks to come to the rescue. Once again it became clear, as during the currency frenzy in Europe in 1992, that the IMF, the World Bank, and the major capitalist governments were barely able to contain, much less direct, the anarchy and raw power of private capital. No longer was a wink or a signal from a single powerful bank or government sufficient to smooth over market turmoil.

But until the new monies could be brought under the management of fewer hands, governments and corporations could only blame themselves and their sacrosanct deregulation philosophy. This was, after all, the free market at work, as new concentrations of capital engaged the "new" open economies on a world scale. Bureaucrats and bankers, along with the financial media, provided lengthy explanations of the enormous differences between the economies of Spain, Hong Kong, and Mexico, and why investors should not beat an overly hasty retreat. Still, the ripples continued to be felt, as financiers and dependent governments in the South asked how long it would take for capital to "recover" confidence in the "global" economy.

How then to tame financial markets for the greater good of the capitalist order, if existing institutions failed to prevent major and minor busts? The assumption had been that like-minded bankers in the North and technocrats in the South working together would insure the stable expansion of free market profiteering. Officials in Washington had become fond of pointing to Latin America, and Mexico in particular, as showcase examples of neo-liberal partnerships. According to the U.S. under-secretary of commerce, Washington could trust Latin America's U.S.-educated ruling technocrats, "one of the very important links that exists between the United States and economic teams in virtually all Latin American countries. Under no circumstances can that be anything but a great advantage."[16]

Nonetheless, neither shared orthodoxy nor shared profiteering proved a stabilizing match. It was investors and smooth technocrats playing the free market that had helped bring about the fiasco. The usual panic-prevention mechanisms had not worked, and grumbling was heard for the creation of ruthless global financial cops. Some mechanisms were already in place: a "shadow" G-7 group of 14 fund managers met twice a year to review world financial developments, including market and country behaviors; a "20-20" group consisting of 20 fund managers and 20 giant corporations also attempted to regulate investment and trading norms.[17] After the Mexican crisis, the IMF was no longer trusted in Northern power circles — it had failed to force changes in Mexican policy or to intervene quickly enough to prevent a generalized loss of confidence that spelled billions of dollars in losses for foreign, chiefly U.S., investors, as well as the prospect of a new wave of immigration over the Rio Grande.

Toward the beginning of 1995, Washington and Wall Street pundits began discussing new mechanisms to "improve" global market functioning and at the same time allow financial elites to prevent losses and make handsome commissions by better directing rich country savings into the foreign markets. But the crisis could not wait for long-term market solutions. The Clinton administration set aside the objections of both the U.S. Congress and its allies in the G-7 in order to bail-out the Mexican economy.

The extraordinary nature of the rescue package and the largely unilateral procedure employed both underlined the need and ability of the U.S. government to come to the rescue, not simply of Mexico, but of the global financial system. The objective was not simply to bolster confidence in the Mexican peso, but to uphold the value of capital invested in other "emergent" markets also affected by the panic. President Clinton was quite blunt in warning skeptics that: "If we fail to act, the crisis of confidence in Mexico's economy could spread to the other emerging countries in Latin America and Asia, the kind of markets that buy our goods and services today and that will buy far more of them in the future."[18]

But capital movements and political rationality do not go hand in hand, nor are such massive flows to be left strictly in the invisible hands of the marketplace or of cautious government authorities. A group of powerful speculators and money managers had the power to bet against currency movements in such dimensions and at such speed as to neutralize equally persistent government efforts to prop up any major currency. Administration officials admitted in May 1994 that they were intervening in markets that had become too "disorderly" — to the point that even the dollar was under attack.[19]

A skeptical U.S. public believed their taxes were being used to bail-out greedy millionaires on Wall Street and in Mexico at a time when several U.S. municipalities were themselves fiscal emergency zones. "This loan will only prop up Mexico's corrupt elite," said one Congressman.[20] NAFTA critics recalled the much publicized win-win arguments put forth by the corporate elites in both countries predicting a continental economic boom. The truth was that it was more than simply bailing out a few investors, or simply Mexico alone for that matter; the Clinton administration felt the system as a whole was at stake.

The administration felt it had no choice but to grab the bull by the horns and override public and congressional opinion in order to take the side of the system, including key corporations and banks in Mexico, particularly Citicorp. Big investors claimed that the U.S. financial system would be damaged if Mexico were allowed to slide into financial chaos, affecting the U.S.'s own financial and political credibility. For them a marriage contract could not be broken. And of course there was the overriding goal of keeping Mexico stable in order to stem domestic political fallout from the influx of new immigration in key electoral states such as Texas and California.

European banking and political elites protested U.S. unilateralism. Six Western European nations — Britain, Germany, Denmark, Holland, Belgium, and Switzerland — abstained from approving the Clinton plan in what the *New York Times* called "a rare rebuff of American leadership in the handling of the emergency."[21] The Europeans complained that the package was pushed through too hastily without regard to whether it would dry up IMF funds for other countries with debt problems, particularly in Eastern Europe.

Congressional critics shared the same concern with regard to procedure. They too pointed to other priorities, such as the crisis in Orange County in California or the equally bankrupt local administration in Washington, D.C. Failure to muster support in Congress for a $40 billion package in official loan guarantees forced the administration to tap emergency presidential funds and to force an extraordinarily swift and unprecedentedly large emergency loan — some $17.8 billion, several times larger than Mexico would have qualified for under normal circumstances. European officials and Capitol Hill pundits concurred that the precedent was dangerous.

If the high degree of unilateralism was unusual, so too was the episode feared to be the opening act of a new wave of world debt and currency crises that would make past ones look tame in comparison. Not only "developing" countries but also industrialized nations could find themselves in the same boat as Mexico, as investors now looked for any sign of potential debt default in any country, touching off chain reactions of interest rate increases, bond defaults, and currency turmoil in other debt-laden countries, including Canada, Belgium, Sweden, and Spain. According to one analyst, "With more than $1 trillion looking for a home in the foreign exchange market every day, even a slight deviation from the straight and narrow can invite a savaging."[22]

And if it could happen in Mexico, perhaps the most coddled Third World economy in the world and the only one "integrated" with a rich country, then what could be in store for others in the South? $40 billion in external help was still not able to reverse the skid of the peso. But the United States government felt it had no choice but to act.

At home and abroad the Clinton administration resorted to unusual high-handedness in order to come up with the funds. Some officials admitted that the root problem for Washington was the disjunction between the speed with which markets reacted and panicked on the one hand, and the slow pace with which deliberative bodies such as Congress or the IMF could decide on action. Global investors turned the tap of funds on and off by punching a few computer keys. Portfolio investments in particular were the most volatile, leaving as quickly and massively as they came, sending stock markets into spins, undermining currencies, and, in the investors' nightmare, provoking default.

No time to consult and/or no ability to control? Or worse yet, from the standpoint of unipolar-minded strategists, no capacity to "lead"? Clearly there was fear in the Clinton administration that global liquidity could not deal with more Mexicos and at the same time, for example, provide a $13 billion IMF loan package to Russia. Some warned that an international financial crisis was in the making if one emergent market after another began requiring bail-out assistance.[23]

Top U.S. officials proposed the organization of a formal working group with bankers and investment managers in order to assume some watchdog and bail-out functions originally assigned to the International Monetary Fund and the World Bank. Some even began drawing up plans to bring together high-level government representatives, financiers, and investors (including portfolio managers) in order to create a new governing body that would also invite representatives of the IMF and the World Bank.

Most of the responsibility was assumed directly by Washington and Wall Street. The objective was to work out a global management system, similar to the century-old one dealing with domestic issues, to handle directly the allocation of capital and insure that recipient countries met United States-set political and economic standards.[24] In other words, to impose order and conditions on both investors and recipients, but especially the latter because this was easier and simply meant greater micro-management of societies and politics in the South. This in order to prevent the recurrence of conditions that prompted private capital to withdraw en masse, setting off panics that could turn into global recessions. In Mexico's case, this meant forcing the government not only to tighten up economic policies but also to crack down on the Zapatista insurgency in the state of Chiapas, the original detonator of capital's crisis of confidence.

The question remained whether sufficient imposition — or organization and communication, as the marketeers prefer to term it — could be articulated in order to prevent financial meltdowns or social backlashes. There was no choice but to insist. A new wave of oligopolistic consolidation in the North seemed to be in evidence in the mid-1990s, as U.S. firms and foreign investment firms teamed up to multiply the export of capital and therefore to tap and expand global markets. Wall Street gurus prepared for major mergers of banks and mutual fund companies in order to create new financial services global powerhouses able to swiftly tap savings in one part of the world and channel them to another, with controlling interests at both ends, and large underwriting fees in the middle.[25]

But such marriage proposals, across national boundaries and business specialties, were not easily consummated. The very idea of bankers and fund managers sharing market information seemed anathema in a highly competitive horserace to reach illusory bonanzas. Moreover, there were profits to be made on busts and turmoil in the currency markets, going in when markets were deflated in order to reap the benefits of later recovery, or betting on one country, currency, or industry against another. Hence the continued need for watchdog bureaucratic technocrats in representation of political authorities.

Even if the private and governmental sectors could agree on new regulatory terms, including more stringent accountability and intervention in the economies of the South, this did not necessarily assure the much wanted profit-making stability. Technocrats and investors preferred to avoid social questions, such as whether Mexican workers would accept their government's call for huge cutbacks in the standard of living when real wages in 1994 were already 10 percent below 1980 levels, or whether the Chiapas uprising had anything to do with the NAFTA integration scheme. Indeed, so long as the benefits of globalized investment could not be democratically shared, so too could social rebellions such as the one in Chiapas fire off shots that would be heard around the world.

If global corporations required continued access to and expansion of "emerging markets," it followed that the United States and its allies, including the multilateral financial institutions, had to step up intervention in order to guarantee that governments as well as societies, indeed all potential recipients of foreign investment, adhered to the global corporate agenda. That is to say, if local governing elites could not secure the "confidence" of corporations and adhere to "sound" management standards, then the United States government itself had to assume greater political and economic tutelage. This meant going over and beyond the orienting macro-economic policies, but also pushing concrete political agendas oriented to defuse and demobilize socio-political challenges that could touch off investor panics and migration waves.

The IMF, long impotent and marginalized when it came to financial crisis in the North, played a marginal role at best in the initial stages of the Mexican crisis. Eventually, the Clinton administration forced that institution to act massively, without member consultation and within a matter of hours. Some analysts came to the conclusion that Mexico's near-default meant that the IMF could not be of much use to countries that drew too heavily on undisciplined private capital. A free market system could be a victim of its own "success."[26]

Some blamed the Mexican episode on greedy U.S. investors or an administration overly concerned with its political image, following its forceful endorsement of the Mexican regime and the fanfare over the NAFTA agreement. They felt that the market itself would have sorted itself and Mexico out, if politicians in Washington had not panicked. But the fact is that politics and economics could not be separated: the same low-keyed European critics were the first to insist that the IMF take a gamble on Russia by granting it a $13 billion stabilization loan while setting aside the usual fiscal preconditions, in order to shore up the regime.[27]

For a moment, there was doubt whether the IMF could bail-out Russia and Mexico at once without facing a liquidity crisis of its own, unable to lend more money with the speed demanded by the instant domino effect of a currency value drop or a political crisis. In any case, the amounts increasingly or potentially required put the ball squarely in the court of the few rich states that could afford to contribute sizeable amounts of capital; yet along with the capital would come more political considerations, along with politically influenced decisions about who should be aided first and for how much.

Governments, therefore, both North and South, remained crucial players in the quest for systematic stability. Sounder fiscal stances implied sounder political ones, which in turn fed direct corporate state intervention from the North in the South as well as greater privatization of the State in the North. Still, the global economy was more vulnerable and more state-dependent than at any point in the post-war period: the Washington-Wall Street axis had to assume a greater role to steer portfolio capital movements, to make them less volatile, placing them as much as possible under the control of establishment bankers and corporations. By the same token, the same axis assumed the micro-management of the wealthier emerging market nations, while ignoring the fate of the other impoverished South.

But there is no guarantee that greater external control over domestic policies will insure stability; the profit-orientation remains the same, and one set of oppressive extraction and intervention mechanisms may simply be displaced by another. No degree of colonialist tutelage of or control over world financial markets seems sufficient to contain and isolate one crisis in one part of the system from the other. Yet the United States government dreams of a stable global order where management and timely intervention offset downward cycles, where all states follow the same corporate agenda and model, where private capital is constantly revered, rewarded, and reassured, and where people — particularly peasants and polititians — learn to behave.

Certainly not admissible to the U.S. is any nationalist attempt to protect societies from untamed global capitalism, particularly if large potential markets are involved. One elementary lesson of the Mexican fiasco, for nationalist capitalists at least, was that basic governmental controls were increasingly necessary in order to reduce exposure to love-hate foreign investor behavior. Unfortunately, any retreat from the prescription that the solution to the problems of the free market is greater market freedom is likely to provoke a forceful political and corporate response from the North. In either case, with or without free market policies, further social and economic turmoil, along with intervention, will remain on the horizon — at least until the time when the state-corporation relationship is fundamentally challenged in both North and South.

DAMAGE CONTROL

At the height of the Mexican crisis, Wall Street managers and their government allies prepared for the worst disaster scenario: a full-fledged peso collapse, the freezing of dollar accounts and profit remittances, currency controls and outright default on billions of dollars in debt. This would have triggered a swift financial pull-out by investors from the dozen or so emerging markets deemed central to the future of global capitalism. A "global financial apocalypse," as the *New York Times* characterized Washington's nightmare, would result from the setting off of a chain of stampedes from other foreign financial markets provoking similar market-restricting responses the world over. "This isn't the old days where there are three rich market manipulators in a back room threatening to pull the pin," lamented Robert Rubin, a multi-millionaire and himself a former securities trader at Goldman Sachs, and secretary of the treasury in the Clinton administration: "Now, its everyone."[28]

There was never any question in official circles as to the need to come up with "non-market" responses to the market crisis. The "free" market had to be protected against itself, principally against currency speculators and nervous investors. Bailing out countries and investors was a job for government — to provide the loan guarantees now demanded by the market but which the market itself was unwilling to provide. Characteristically, the threat of Mexico defaulting on billions of dollars invested in that country sparked a cry for U.S. government intervention just as loud as that which earlier demanded that bureaucrats get out of the way when the market was promising endless plenty.

This was no ordinary crisis, because, as explained, it was not ordinary money that was in movement. But, just as important to the U.S. government and Wall Street money managers, nor was Mexico simply an ordinary country. It was the United States' neighbor and third largest trading partner, whose economic and political stability was crucial to important corporate interests, and of course to the economies of border states, which did not look forward to new waves of immigrants escaping the effects of devaluation-provoked unemployment and depreciated wages. In somewhat exaggerated fashion, U.S. officials warned that some 700,000 jobs in the U.S. depended on Mexico, and that the U.S. economy would be unable to cope with an anticipated increase of half a million illegal immigrants fleeing over the border if full chaos broke out in Mexico.

The threat may have been blown up for the sake of skeptical legislators in the United States, but it was real in other respects. Wall Street and Washington strategists had larger concerns at heart and felt it imperative to hold up a model that was the symbol of the global economic order being constructed in the interest of corporate America, and as such could not be allowed to fail. The United States could not afford to remain on the sidelines in the face of the possibility that this unique carefully constructed prototype, nurtured from the beginning to be emulated worldwide and to defeat skeptics at home, could now provoke a full-scale domestic and world stampede away from the global corporate agenda.

Mexico provoked a catalytic effect one way or the other, either as living proof of the benefits of the free market model, or sparking a panic among governments and investors who had dared invest in emerging markets and jolting the entire world economy with sudden pull outs. All eyes were on the Mexican economy and on Washington's reaction, and if markets characteristically impatient had voted thumbs down, Washington injected itself forcefully in order to reverse the verdict. Once the system was saved, however, the Mexican economy could be quietly allowed to slip back into a slump.

At the time, saving the Mexican model was both a domestic task and a global imperative for the Clinton administration. Throughout the hard and bitterly fought campaign for ratification of the NAFTA treaty, the Clinton administration, like its Republican predecessor, joined by the U.S. and Mexican corporate elite, hailed Mexico as an engine for the growth of U.S. exports and jobs. According to them, there could be no finer example anywhere of a country practicing no-nonsense liberalization, aggressive privatization, tough enforcement of intellectual property rights, low inflation, and more privatization in store. In general, an investor's paradise with locked-in irreversible commitments to an open economy and integration with the United States.

NAFTA even more than GATT/WTO was the blueprint of what the United States hoped to achieve for itself in its commercial and political interactions with all nations, particularly in the South. "It is the linchpin, the model," pleaded Rubin in congressional testimony, "and I don't think any other country plays such a pivotal role." Inaction, he warned, would be taken as a withdrawal of U.S. participation in emerging markets, backtracking from the world's move toward more open economies and toward reform. "Fixing this now is cheap," he threatened, "fixing it later may be very expensive."[29]

This was post-Cold War capitalism's first major economic crisis: major because the Mexican breakdown threatened to derail the next wave of capital's expansion into the so-called emerging economies. Expansion entailed marshaling more capital and production toward new markets and investment opportunities; and if the opportunities were not quite there, then they could be invented, and still sold, as long as "confidence" was maintained.

The stakes were enormous. Until the Mexican episode at least, calculations were bantered about indicating that up to 30 "emerging countries" in the South would be demanding an extra $300 billion per year to finance their new investment plans over the next decade — about three times as much as the total net flow of capital from developed to developing countries in 1993. This suggested an unprecedented outflow of capital, exports, and services from the North, with proportional profit opportunities.[30] Bursting the bubble would hinder expansion and place the corporate-dominated economies of the North at risk.

For their part, "developing" countries seemed to have moved from dependence on volatile commodities to dependence on volatile investors. Banana republics became sweatshop republics as part of the global market reorganization. But in order to keep the adjustment process flowing, the United States government felt a duty to contain breakdowns, even if much of the problem was related to the bust and boom nature of capitalist expansion itself. It was always easier, however, to blame economic mismanagement than the market itself. But having played down the risk of investing abroad, the corporate-government elites now had to restore credibility in a hurry.

The emphasis was not on why the patient had become ill, or on the nature of the illness itself, but rather on how to keep it from spreading. And characteristically, the answer offered to the ills of intervention and free market capitalism was more intervention, more borrowing, and more privatization. Nonetheless, because governments were now rescuing corporate investors, some embarrassing questions were bound to crop up. How to convince the skeptics that "frontier capitalism," with all its risks, offered big pay-offs in the long run? How was it the top financial officials in Washington and Wall Street had been caught flat-footed — or had they really had access to information that they kept to themselves for fear of upsetting the global financial apple cart?

Some 80 percent of those polled in the U.S. opposed the bail-out. They were not impressed by the global logic and instead believed that saving Mexico was less a matter of saving the West than of rescuing greedy investors and corrupt politicians.With much fanfare, the Clinton administration had been selling the need for the U.S. public to think "globally" while demanding that other nations "act" globally also: that is to privatize to the hilt. But the December 1994 events in Mexico threatened to throw the entire effort into reverse, with drastic effects on the future of corporate American itself. Elites in the South also worried that a massive outflow of investor capital and confidence in Mexico City could provoke the same in their own foreign investment-dependent countries. They too rushed to liberalize even further.

Investment contraction and a run on the currencies could lead to defaults and political turmoil. People would also react to further devaluation, inflation, cutbacks in domestic spending, and jumps in unemployment. All this would endanger the type of reforms and regimes in the South and East increasingly demanded by the North. Rubin warned that such "interconnectedness" could provoke a global meltdown. Europeans at first believed this to be an exaggeration, at least until news of congressional resistance to the Mexican aid package provoked a new batch of sell orders affecting stock markets from Poland to Hong Kong.[31]

More than simply rescuing a handful of reckless investors who had made a bad bet, financiers claimed the United States had no choice but to hold back a potentially grave setback to the strategy of securing market access regimes, and of shutting out non-liberal, statist regimes. The Mexican crisis came at the same time that the left was making electoral gains in Eastern Europe, reflecting widespread resentment of the social burdens of orthodox free market policies. As a result some "market" reform processes were already in trouble, as were the politicians who defended them in Lithuania, Hungary, Bulgaria, and Poland.

If the United States stood by as the markets pounded the "emerging" economies, the anti-reformers everywhere would be provided with new arguments. Events in Mexico did nothing to boost the already diminished East Asian confidence in "free trade" and integration schemes promoted by the U.S. and others in order to lessen the appeal of state-centered and export-oriented capitalist development models. Mexico therefore could not be allowed to stand out as a lesson to others of what could happen if they repeated the mistake of totally embracing corporate capital, the free market, deregulation, and the United States. This would have amounted to playing Russian roulette with an already rattled global economy.

Nor could the domestic U.S. economy de-link itself from the fate of global markets. Corporate and administration strategists believed that domestic fiscal policy was no longer sufficient to spur profits and growth; there was no room in the budget to allow sizeable government spending on industrial or technological programs, particularly as even the defense budget was also being checked. The implication was that if the U.S. economy and corporate profits were going to grow, they would do so through expansion in the South, where the placement of investment, goods, services, and information did not by and large face the obstacles and competition encountered in Japan and Western Europe. For its part, the U.S. public was told that millions of jobs would be created by breaking down export barriers — insuring market access regimes, particularly in Latin America and Asia, with Mexico leading the way.[32]

If the Mexico crisis could now provoke a reverse domino effect, endangering present and potential corporate profits, then no price could be too high for saving that country. Hence the swift, high-level governmental response in reaction to a strategic challenge regarded as no less serious than that posed by the Soviet Union during the Cold War. Only this time, the president called on the heads of the United States Treasury and Federal Reserve Board more than on the secretary of state or of defense. Clinton had created the National Economic Council to deal with economics the same way that the National Security Council had dealt with strategic questions — but now the strategic became economic.[33]

The entire episode pointed to the United States government as the savior of last resort of the world economy. Not least because officials managed to force new "reforms" in Mexico deeply resented by nationalists, to override U.S. domestic public opinion, to ignore Congress, to disregard financial and political allies in Europe, to force an enormous IMF package loan through in record time, and to assuage the demands of big U.S. investment firms demanding blood (and oil) from Mexico as collateral. This was hardly the free market at work, nor was it a collegial G-7 affair. It was Washington's doing, the product of White House midnight meetings at the highest level and frenetic telephone calls to different parts of the globe in close coordination with Wall Street tycoons.

Some asked whether the United States could afford to be seen as capitalism's bottom line guarantor or indeed the grand savior of any major country whose leaders borrowed too much and failed to "discipline" their own booming economies. Where and when could such offers stop, when even the dollar came under attack as the result of the bail-out? Was Mexico unique, or did Russia and other nuclear holding ex-Soviet states also qualify? When asked to draw the line, Rubin said he could not. Had not foreign investors and U.S. government officials been forewarned of "overheating" in the Mexican economy? Were they not, out of greed or out of electoral considerations in Mexico itself, also chief oversellers of the Mexican model? Was the U.S. government itself to enter the money managing business, and if so would political considerations not tinge recommendations more than usual? It was true that the administration had not been able to come up with all the necessary cash on its own, but it did provide the major part and the rest probably could not have been assembled without a very visible directing hand.[34]

The truth was that the Mexican market was increasingly critical to the very well-being of corporate America. And because corporate America and Washington were central to global capitalism, then so too was Mexico important to the other major capitalist powers. It was the same logic that prevailed in regard to the dollar: domestic economic "mismanagement" could be criticized, but in the final analysis it was in the interest of the system as a whole to prevent the dollar from collapsing. Growing pains of a globalized economy, said the optimists: but all the core countries and the multilateral agencies felt forced to participate to keep the United States from being drawn into what one termed "the fiscal equivalent of Vietnam."[35] This also entailed imposing "reforms" on world markets, particularly the larger ones, as a matter of need, not choice.

Confidence in Mexico, in the dollar, and in the United States all seemed necessarily interconnected. But precisely because no currency was poised to take over the dollar's role as premier world currency, and if Germany and Japan wanted to boost dollar values to keep their goods competetive, then support for the "peso bloc" was required. If Mexico and the dollar collapsed, so too might the world financial system, bringing political chaos in its wake. After the Mexican-sparked drop in the dollar's value, officials in Washington quickly prevailed on their counterparts in Bonn and Tokyo to engage in concerted currency purshases and interest rate modifications in order to contain the surge in the value of the mark and yen against the dollar.[36] Again, not a matter of choice but of need. Both the yen and the mark lacked the dollar's status as international safe haven with built-in safety guarantees, a savior of the last resort status required by the system as a whole: that is, a political and military superpower with the will and capacity to project force to deal with rebellion. The dollar could continue to erode, the United States government could contine to run massive deficits and borrow its way out for itself and now for Mexico — and yet the chief reserve currency in world central bank vaults was the U.S. dollar, a faithful reflection of dependence and adherence to U.S. power. The degree of domination could vary, but its essence did not.

Washington's increasing recourse to aggressive and unilateral global "leadership" could not be divorced from the transformations suffered in world finance, whose nature, if one can discern from present trends, necessitate political authority to hold the system together. But as the "emerging markets" became a more integral part of the system, then too came the need to engage in interventionist micromanagement, not simply for the sake of individual investors, but also to assure the stability of the apparatus and uphold the sanctity of the free market reform model. Globalization increasingly required the U.S. to move from stage-management to stage presence. And with each crisis and new competitive wave of capital demand and offerings, with more rapid introduction of new technology, more volatility and more Mexicos were to be expected, increasingly taxing not only the financial and political capabilities of the United States, but of global capitalism as a whole.

On the one hand, there were the enormous amounts of surplus capital demanding higher returns, and on the other, the equally huge amounts demanded by the so-called emerging markets fueled by $1 trillion-a-day currency markets. Liberalization and deregulation at both ends spelled a greater capacity to match supply with demand, casting aside governmental, social, or environmental impediments, the pace dictated largely by the handsome returns offered to capital and greedy commission collectors at each end, all exacerbated by the sheer speed with which capital flowed in and out of modern financial markets.

Given the speed and amounts, vintage institutions such as the IMF and the World Bank cannot cope adequately with developments. Even governments and central banks were pressed, but it was the U.S. government that picked up most of the tab. For Mexico, the U.S.-assembled package included $20 billion in medium- and long-term loans or loan guarantees from the Treasury's dollar-exchange stabilization fund (which the president could use without congressional approval), $17.8 billion from the IMF, $10 billion from the central banks of leading nations through the Bank for International Settlements, and $3 billion from commercial banks. Clearly the rescue was chiefly a governmental-multilateral affair, and of the United States in the first place.

Germany and Britain objected that Russia was being short-changed in order to bail-out a major trading partner of the United States.[37] In effect, governments and multilateral institutions in the North have not been able to articulate the required level of power to shape priorities and set common political and market regulated standards. But private corporate and financial entities have not fared better, also unable to transform themselves in tandem with globalized market structures and functioning.

Corporate heads and government strategists search for new strategies and mechanisms to generate new wealth, to educate investors and better scrutinize volatile portfolio investments, to find new means to "liberate" business from governmental and social controls the world over, and to reduce the costs of labor also on a global basis. They feel compelled to respond as both customers and sellers to the demands of "emerging economies" supposedly clamoring for Western goods and services, and offering cheap wages and fat profit margins in return.

But rules are required because markets, just like governments in the South, cannot be allowed to engage in behavior that can produce generalized pandemonium. Growth expectations have to be sustained as an end in themselves, perpetually insuring and increasing "investor" confidence and consumer credit. In this way, the same Wall Street and Washington experts that should have detected Mexican economic mismanagement were too busy selling NAFTA and Mexican securities to sound an early warning. Perhaps nobody wanted to know for fear of piercing the bubble. Nor was it a question of non-interference in market dealings. Bankers had no objection to state intervention, and indeed were dependent on it in many senses: government opened doors and government came to the rescue when the free market went haywire.

This was not therefore a smoking gun scenario posing the question of who knew what and when in regards to Mexican monetary policy, and why didn't they act sooner to prevent or warn. The "miscalculations" were more structural than political or economic, the assumption among bureaucrats and brokers being that the peso, the Mexican economy, and indeed emerging markets as a whole, could indefinitely continue to rake in foreign capital, to deregulate the economy without provoking a social backlash that would provoke the massive retrenchment of investors.

The signposts in this regard were not to be found in balance books or current accounts, but in the free market-induced impoverishment of vast sectors of the Mexican population, and consequent political and military rebellions. In deeply polarized societies such as Mexico, no amount of "correct" political management, or of foreign investment, could neutralize the social effects of neo-liberal economic policies; on the contrary, greater state democratic sensibility could only spell trouble for the market "reform" process. The crisis was not new, it was only greater than many had imagined, much less prepared for, transcending financial problems and reflecting the inability of globalized neo-liberal market policies to foster socially just economic development.

Notes

1. Erskine Childers and Brian Urquhart, *Renewing the United Nations System* (Uppsala, Sweden: Dag Hammarskjold Foundation, 1994), p. 55.
2. Sam T. Cross, "Following the Bundesbank," *Foreign Affairs*, vol. 73, no. 2 (March/April 1994), p. 132.
3. "Fixing Japan," *Business Week*, March 29, 1993.
4. *Economist*, August 17, 1991, quoted in Shigeto Tsuru, *Japan's Capitalism: Creative Defeat and Beyond* (Cambridge, U.K.: Cambridge University Press 1993), p.1.
5. "Fixing Japan."
6. Childers and Urquhart, *Renewing the UN*, pp. 82-83.
7. Ibid., p. 79.
8. Ibid., p. 83.
9. Ibid., p. 56.
10. The assumption is challenged by Paul Krugman, "Competitiveness: A Dangerous Obsession," *Foreign Affairs*, vol. 73, no. 2 (March/April 1994), pp. 28-44.
11. "Going with the Flows," *Economist*, January 28, 1995; "All Shook Up," *Newsweek*, January 23, 1995, p. 10.
12. "The World's Emerging Markets All at Sea," *Economist*, January 28, 1995.
13. "Humble Pie," *Newsweek*, January 16, 1995, p. 12; "On Wall Street: This Too Shall Pass," *Business Week*, January 9, 1995.
14. "A New Mantra for Investors: Picky, Picky, Picky," *Business Week*, January 23, 1995, p. 15.
15. "The Education of Robert Rubin," *New York Times*, February 5, 1995.
16. "Humble Pie."

17. "All Shook Up."

18. "More Trouble for Zedillo," *Newsweek,* January 30, 1995, p. 39.

19. *New York Times,* May 3, 1994.

20. "More Troubles for Zedillo," *Newsweek,* January 30, 1995.

21. *New York Times,* February 3, 1995.

22. "The Currency Casualty List Could Get a Lot Longer," *Business Week,* January 16, 1995.

23. *New York Times,* February 3, 1995.

24. "All Shook Up."

25. See, for example, the article on Mellon Bank Corporation negotiating for the acquisition of Dreyfus corporation in "Tense Scenes from a Marriage," *Business Week,* January 16, 1995.

26. "A Fork in the IMF's Road," *Economist,* January 28, 1995, p. 170.

27. Ibid.

28. "The Education of Robert Rubin."

29. Ibid.

30. "The Global Economy," *Economist,* October 1, 1994, p. 30.

31. "The Education of Robert Rubin."

32. The evidence from Mexico, however, indicated that while U.S. exports had increased some 20 percent from 1993 to 1994, reaping handsome profits for corporations, there had been no corresponding increase in the number of jobs. What the administration preferred not to state was that high-tech factories could increase exports and profits with fewer and fewer laborers. Nor did it remind the public that even cheaper Mexican labor costs and exports would further imperil certain categories of employment in the United States. See "NAFTA's Unhappy Anniversary," *New York Times,* February 7, 1995.

33. "War, Peace, Aid: All Issues Are Trade Issues," *New York Times,* January 15, 1995.

34. *New York Times,* February 5, 1995.

35. See the report on Rubin, "A Cool Customer — But Is He Tough Enough" *Newsweek,* March 20, 1995.

36. "Surprise German Rate Cut," *New York Times,* March 31, 1995.

37. "U.S. Allies Soften Criticism of Plan to Rescue Mexico," *New York Times,* February 5, 1995.

5

The Transnational U.S. Empire: How Washington Manages Its Super Powers

In the mid-1990s, despite increasing complexity and competition among the global economic powers, the United States remains the sole superpower, whose global reach, both economic and strategic, continues to dominate the world's political economy. Washington's overarching power is more than the body of the U.S. government institutions themselves. Power grows out of the increasingly multi-faceted web of interlocking governmental, corporate, and U.S.-led multilateral financial institutions that stretches not only from Washington to Wall Street but across the oceans and around the globe. It is this interlocking web that dominates the international economic order. It is, in short, an empire, albeit of a new and different sort, and it is not one aimed at ruling territory as much as it is ruling over the cyberspace of transfers of money, credit, goods, production technology, military hardware, images, and information.

Market-generated inequities, if they are to become sustainable, require political-security apparatuses. Not only a coercive apparatus at the national level, but also a corollary or complementary one to dominate other nations. Increasing globalization means new and newly empowered supranational institutions as well; a mega-State, as it were. Yet tensions will remain, as different state apparatuses still attempt to assume this regulatory and supportive mission of controlling the market on behalf of local elites.

The tasks of organizing the system are distributed among states in the process of market expansion. Transnationalized capital may demand either consensual agreements between states, or outright imposition of control by one state over others, which takes the form of colonialism. Most striking toward the end of the twentieth century is the propensity of the imperial core state (the U.S.) to uphold the pre-eminence of the "market" order (even more than its own political domination) against any challenges, whether from allies, rivals, or subjects. Imperialism also means filling in gaps and correcting disorders that the market alone has been unable to fix.

Political power or hegemony cannot be understood solely in pure market terms. Nor can it be measured in relational terms alone; that is, through a check-list of geopolitical, technological, and military attributes. Our framework of analysis must combine both political and economic components of the modern global system, to show how each interacts — or is perceived to interact.

Relational power means the ability of one actor to secure desired behaviors from another by way of direct or indirect coercion — when those behaviors would not otherwise take place. Structural power, on the other hand, is not a one-time lever, but an ongoing framework within which one actor has the capacity to determine the overall behavior of the others. Further, the system itself rewards cooperative behavior and punishes acts of (real or ascribed) resistance. In the international arena, structural power extends beyond the traditional nexus of state-state relationships or state-centered economic or political institutions. It also embraces thought, culture, and usages.[1]

Such a system presupposes a social-economic framework, parameters of thinking about problem definition, process, and solutions. That is, the framework provides an ideological and material scaffold that limits the ability of participants (whether willing or coerced) to challenge or even identify fundamental issues in a non-systemic manner. It shifts attention and analysis away from root problems and underlying power relationships, and propels them toward set facile explanations and symptomatic, rather than systemic, expressions of "crisis" to be analyzed and handled in ways that further reinforce the system. This entails the creation of what some have termed "capitalist cosmopolitanism"; that is, transnational socio-economic groupings that share in the political-ideological task of imposing discipline on other social forces, principally though not exclusively in the South, in order to deepen acceptance, as well as the global reach, of transnational capital.[2]

In general, structural power in the 1990s has less and less frequently been the province solely of the governmental apparatus, even in the most powerful states, but rather requires simultaneous involvement by government authorities and national economic forces. One could argue that the international market regime itself constitutes a form of structural systemic power through its comprehensive influence on states, societies, and individual behavior. The imbalance of power is inherent in the modern market system, but it still lacks a clear center of political authority. Both are needed in order to resolve persistent conflicts and move periodic crises toward solutions that reflect the interests of, and in fact strengthen, the more powerful forces. In the real world of the 1990s, structural power takes the form of the United States using its predominant influence over global market structures. That control is conceived in an interactive form, however, in which neither the State nor the market mechanisms can completely overpower the other. Instead, market and policy-making influence and empower each other, politically, economically, and institutionally.

Susan Strange defines four basic components of the international political economy: security, knowledge, production, and credit. Power in one tends to reinforce, although not necessarily coincide with, power in the others: control over one or the other translates into global influence. Structural analysis necessarily entails studying the interaction between political and economic authority: the use of economic power by political authorities, and the impact of economic imperatives on political decisions. "Only by structural analysis is it possible to develop theoretical propositions regarding the impact of political authority (for example, states) on economic transactions in markets, and conversely of the impact of transactions in markets upon states."[3]

The division of power in the international system is best understood in terms of each country's relative capacity to participate in and influence the political economy in which states and corporations operate. Nationality and location of production matter less, ultimately, than the influence a given bureaucratic elite has over the structures in which bankers and corporations make their decisions.

As Eastern European and Soviet state socialists found out, there was little room for independent economic authority vis-à-vis the pull and expansion of global capitalism. Increasing proportions of goods and services were available only within a world marketplace subservient to transnational corporations. Technological and foreign exchange needs increasingly forced the socialist countries to sell in the market and borrow money from financial institutions over which they had little or no influence. This escalating economic gravitation toward the West contributed to the political, as well as the economic, dislocations that spelled the end of state socialism in that part of the world and elsewhere.

These developments were not all the result of abstract market forces or of simple reflections of the law of supply and demand.

Strategists in Washington and other Western capitals closely monitored developments and made the principal decisions regarding credits and access to markets and advanced technologies. Structural power meant control over decisions on credit and, to a large extent, over knowledge in the form of technological know-how. In this way the West, and especially the U.S., was able to extend influence over production within the former socialist countries, and eventually preside over and claim credit for the collapse of their bureaucratic structures. The result brought the West a greater margin of "security" than previously existed.

What is produced, how it is produced and distributed, where and how it is marketed and financed, and increasingly what is "in demand," are not decisions made entirely by the "market" or even exclusively by huge transnational corporations. Political factors accompany and shape market supply and demand — not devoid of elite-defined "national interests" over and beyond the interests of corporations or even of the economy as a whole. There is no automatic relationship or direct line of causation between economic and political crisis, yet one will impact and shape the other.

U.S. power cannot be measured solely in terms of factors under its exclusive national control, or only in terms of wealth generated within its own borders, or by corporations owned mostly by its own nationals. Nor can the modern United States empire be solely conceived as being made up of a central enforcer attempting, as in the ex-socialist countries, to "command" or micro-manage the world market. Its power rather reflects predominant, although not exclusive, influence, even hegemony, over the global political economy. It is a power shared by centers of governmental authority in Washington and financial authority in Wall Street. Those parallel centers themselves, which more often than not will see eye-to-eye, still on occasion disagree over the terms and nature of regulation and expansion; the effect of such disagreements is a further diffusion of structural power expressed as incoherent or indecisive world "leadership."

As explained elsewhere, no major exporting nation, world financial investment firm, or multinational corporation with global aspirations can afford to ignore the United States market, and therefore, the political and commercial authority of the United States government. Such a concentration of wealth — be it in the form of a huge consumer market, capital markets, and research and development — forces a gravitation toward the United States in the same way that its military deployment capacity and predominant influence over multilateral lending agencies force governments around the world to follow, or at least take serious account of, Washington's position. Even other wealthy capitalist nations are not immune to Washington's gravitational pull.

The evidence does not appear to uphold the argument that we have witnessed the emergence of a powerful transnational bloc of forces, symbolized by the Trilateral Commission, in which the national economic and political elites of the U.S., Europe, and Japan actually merge their competing interests in response to the crisis of the old hegemonic structures.[4] But the globalizing and concentrating thrust of capitalism does not automatically translate into international cooperation or smooth global "partnerships." Tasks and tabs may be distributed among big governments or international bodies, just as corporations may share market access. "Leadership" may be a collective facade but true authority is not, particularly in periods of keen competition and crisis.

Nor does hegemonic globalism entail the emergence of a single mega-state authority and international civil society. Rather, it can take the form of a single state exerting an increasing influence over other states and national societies the world over. It uses a set of transnational organizations, norms, and values determined by, and ultimately responsive to the interests of, the core countries. According to Robert Cox, hegemony is a structure of values and understandings about the nature of order that permeates states and non-state entitities.[5]

Taken as a whole, what appears is a massive and unforgiving structure of global power. The question is whether one state's dominance in such a structure is sufficient to create hegemony. The answer may be positive only to the degree that that state has the capacity to rise above itself, so to speak, and govern on behalf of the entire market system in a way that the elite in other nations benefit from and thus also support. Full hegemony would imply success in winning credibility and acceptance of a U.S.-dominated capitalist framework in all quarters of society throughout the world.

Herein lies the importance and contradictory contribution of transnational capital. It is a cohering force that unifies diverse national elites, as well as harmonizing their opposition to the local resistance activities of those marginalized by the hegemonic process. As part of that process, television imagery become ethical smokescreens disguising the real effects of structural adjustment or other globalization programs. Majorities in the South must be convinced through propaganda that United States "leadership" and the expansion of market economies serve "universal interests," and that someday they might even get to share in those benefits. The wealthy minorities in those same countries, however, demand down payments on such promises — they demand at least token shares in the global corporation in return for giving up sovereignty.

Exceptions could be found, but they tend to confirm the reality that globalization is an uneven process, which accentuates the asymmetry of power and wealth apportionments both among and within nations North and South. It therefore represents a reconfiguration of process more than of substance: in a word, the modernization of capitalist dynamics. Still, the adjustments tend to complicate attempts to measure the extent of U.S. power. While the U.S. economy may be considered the overall motor force of the entire international economic system, specific indicators focused on particular "national" territories, governments, or societies are less useful in analyzing the logic, organization, and projection of power. The exercise of United States authority in the world must take account of the numerous governments, markets, and corporations impacted by U.S. policy decisions and the behavior of its domestic economy and financial markets.

LEVERS OF POWER

While the United States government does not absolutely control world financial markets, its decisions, for example on domestic interest rates, have significant impact. In this way the U.S. government becomes what might be called the "flywheel" of the world economy, by virtue of the enormous leverage exercised through this particular manifestation of power over the financial structures of the world economy.

For example, the 1994 Mexican crisis demonstrated that the amount of credit to be provided by governments, by international organizations, and by banks, to whom and on what terms, is often chiefly determined by government policy-making circles in Washington. The cases of Russia or Poland further indicated how big power political decisions override "pure" market considerations in order to pull together massive financial packages for countries at moments deemed strategic to the stability of the system. Yet it would be doubtful, by contrast, whether France could have on its own secured acceptance of its unilateral political and security considerations by the IMF in order to obtain extraordinary loan guarantees for Algeria. Only the U.S. maintains the requisite economic and strategic sway over IMF decision-making for such campaigns.

Much less publicized but equally forceful is the overseeing by U.S. embassies over the internal workings of many economies in the

South. The task is as much structural as bureaucratic. Not that every faceless bureaucrat in Washington is bent on micro-managing every component of local decision-making, but for example with the global integration of financial markets, the tightening and the loosening of capital availability or the value of principal currencies are decisively influenced by the value of the dollar and U.S. Federal Reserve system decisions over interest rates.

Perceptions may exist that governments have lost power to banks, corporations, currency values, and financial markets, but this is true only in the short-term context of limited deregulation and contemporary reluctance of governments to intervene.[6] But an interventionist imperative could materialize virtually overnight, drastically reversing liberalization trends, if these trends threatened to upset the economic stability and global influence of the United States.

Furthermore, production and credit decisions presuppose the existence of processed information that determines the strategic thinking, perceptions, and demands of producers, borrowers, and sellers. Control over that information means power. Another form of structural power takes the form not only of competitive access to information, but to the system which will be used to process that information. Once again, U.S.-based management consulting firms dominate corporate and financial decision-making the world over.

Power takes the form of influence over how and when the information will appear, but also over where it will be accumulated and how it will be processed, to whom it will be communicated and on what terms — that is, influence over the systemic terms of corporate and national competition in the global economy and society. It is not simply a question of monopolies or even of the inside track: the United States does not object to the proliferation of nuclear weapons know-how if it can trust the potential users (i.e., Israel) to behave within the system; but where overall structural guidelines are violated, meaning non-acceptance of market-oriented U.S. leadership (Iran, North Korea), the punishment may be severe. The Clinton administration's targeting of "rogue states" as its most recently created collective enemy provides a telling example.

More conventional expressions and instruments of U.S. dominance in the global knowledge structure are U.S. corporations that dominate critical high-technology industries; U.S. banks and investment firms involved in capital dealings and imposing forms of capital management; the U.S. media giants in global news; Hollywood in entertainment; U.S. management styles eagerly accepted and assimilated abroad; U.S.-educated native elites in control of governments and non-U.S. corporations and universities; the dominance of U.S. consulting firms; U.S. defense and private industry in communications; the widespread use of American English as the lingua franca of the political, business, and cultural world. Again, it is not a question of direct control over industry and nations, nor of dominance over every sector of economic life and technology, but rather dominance over globally-configured structures and systems in which non-U.S. components find it virtually impossible to resist the magnetic pull of the United States policy and power apparatus.

The same picture appears with greater clarity in regards to security and military affairs. Unlike economic-technological competition, the United States empire cannot afford to yield key fields of military capacity to any other nation and still retain its hegemony. Since World War II, the United States has been the determinant force in the establishment and the ruptures of the balance of force. It created that role through direct military-industrial-financial engagement during World War II, and continued it by nuclear deterrence and a massive arms race with the Soviet Union.

Having prevailed in both battles, the United States is now positioned more powerfully than ever to shape the framework of global engagement for the new century. Its approach involves transforming the post-World War II order, based on a neutralized Germany and Japan on the one hand and a Soviet nuclear and ideological rival on the other, into a new post-Cold War order featuring a disintegrated Soviet bloc and an economically competitive Germany and Japan. By and large, the post-WWII framework achieved its fundamental objective of rolling back any Soviet efforts to replace U.S. world power with its own. The U.S. objective now is to adjust the framework to deal with new economic competition from strategic allies, while maintaining an unrivaled military apparatus that will insure continued U.S. control over who will and who will not be brought under the security blanket designed to repel any threat to the market's ideological and economic stability.

The sum total of predominant influence in the realms of security, ideas, production, and credit determinations — all part of a single international political economy — translates into an historically unprecedented degree of hegemony by any power over so much territory in so many ways. Having more power than at any point in its history, or than any other nation throughout history for that matter, still does not translate into absolute power. The same market processes that lend themselves to the concentration of political power also impose limitations on those forces, economic and political, which would seek absolute command over the market. Hegemony means predominant influence over the choice of options available to others, and therefore the capacity to influence, but not define, outcomes. And while U.S. hegemony remains accountable to a national core of corporate interests, it also shares its benefits more broadly, allowing, as the market itself does, non-U.S. corporations and major non-U.S. capitalists to exercise that hegemony outside and within U.S. territory.

This is what Strange terms a "non-territorial" empire, with its imperial capital in Washington, D.C. drawing lobbyists from countries and corporations the world over, projecting itself over foreign groupings, jurisdictions, cultures, and mentalities, exercising authority on economies and peoples.[7] Neo-liberal policies and practices need not be imposed by the United States in classic colonial form, or even through the now-antiquated narrowly political formulae of 1970s and '80s neo-colonialism; preferably power is exercised broadly and ideologically, not simply on heads of governments but also on and through businesspeople, teachers, technocrats, and journalists.

The result is an emerging homogeneity that seems to be becoming the norm because the principal macro-economic policies implemented in the vast majority of countries — deregulation, liberalization, privatization, deflation — began in the United States and were followed by others. In many cases the ruling elites were willingly convinced; in others they felt unable to resist; but in both cases they were responding to structural encroachments that easily overcame national frontiers.

The impact of the U.S. empire in this context is neither a social nor a territorial based phenomenon. Not everyone in the U.S. stands to gain from imperialism, any more than all those outside the 50 states emerge as losers. Global structural analysis must also concern itself with class divisions and especially the concentration of economic power within countries in corporate circles with evident transnational interests. Herein lies a source of state incoherence or unilateralism, as even very corporate-dominated governmental elites in the rich countries must also face some domestic electoral and social consequences of market-induced dislocations. That tendency toward unilateralism is further enhanced by the relative weakness or passivity of many international institutions ostensibly designed to mitigate the effects of market-driven adjustments. Clearly the richest governments and corporations have failed to diffuse nationally oriented competitiveness, and with it the potential destabilization of the world political economy.

In many senses, the empire has broadened, and with it the privileges of citizenship. Those perks have been extended along transnational lines determined by considerations of wealth, location, and race. English-speaking and U.S.-educated power brokers, including scientists, economists, consultants, soldiers, and educators as well as government officials, long to be part of their respective U.S. peer groups, in the same way that governments long to be in the good graces of Washington. But in a more fundamental way, there has been a parallel process of interconnected disenfranchisement, in which the economically superfluous and socially discarded of the First World become part of the global majority long disempowered in the rest of the world. Those who run the empire appear to believe these outcasts, devoid of social or economic security, represent no serious threat to the globalized free market.

Empires, past and present, are full of incoherences and contradictions, particularly when they pretend not to exist. Disputes often take place over the pecking order assigned to other countries and fractions of capital. In matters of military policy or sensitive technologies, we find that there is not much room for consensus decision-making. Nor is there always time, as the speed in communications and sensitivity of markets accentuate competitive pressures among nations and corporations. Here is where the superpower factor comes in: more than in any other country, U.S. domestic decisions routinely strain the elite bonds of shared transnational corporate-government interests, or incite rebellions of broader forces in countries outside the U.S. core.

Since U.S. corporate-governmental partnerships dominate Western market structures, U.S. globalism should spell ample shared benefits for all "Western" (including Japanese) elite constituents. This rosy and generous view presumes a constantly expanding global market economy, which in turn is supposed to translate into an improved livelihood for all of the world's inhabitants, while reserving, naturally, the lion's share for the United States elite, with handsome rewards for its partners abroad. But the question then arises: why did U.S. structural power, so successful in assuring economic expansion, fail throughout the Cold War to insure market stability? And if the overriding strategic competition with Moscow was a factor, why are markets (not to mention the world at large) still in turmoil after the Soviet collapse? Why is there no single identifiable Keynesian policy of demand management to stabilize a disorganized world economy? Where is the international banking system capable of preventing financial markets from spinning into panics and collapses? Is it not the historical task of the nonterritorial empire, embodying the highest political form of capitalist development, to act as the supreme political regulatory and punishing authority? Can the internationally powerful nation-state known as the United States transcend its own state-centric selfishness?

There are two different, though not totally contradictory, answers to these questions. The first is that the United States has not achieved the degree of structural power required to enforce global stability. The second possibility is that as long as U.S. power tends to be brandished in nationalist, unilateralist, short-sighted fashion, it will not serve the broadest interests of the changed world political economy, acting as it does with insufficient regard for components of the system.

Either explanation would imply an actual or potential state capacity to impose stability on a global market and social structures. In the first instance, it is a question of time and insufficient concentration of power; in the second of short-sightedness or an incoherent hand on the global rudder. Superior power does in fact exist; the variable seems to be to what degree it will exert influence internationally. The coherence of its impact on global economic developments seems to reflect the pressure brought to bear on the national policy-making establishment — among others, by actors in the domestic political arena who face being sacrificed to the forces of globalization. Democracy or sensitivity to the plight of the poor becomes destablizing. The greater United States government allegiance to corporate globalization, the smaller the degree of democratic accountability to its own population; unless, of course, the victims of the market at home can be convinced they are all winners under global capitalism.

A third hypothesis would be that the global political economy has become so complex and fluid that the governing capacity of any existing national, supranational, or imperial political entity is simply inadequate to bring the system under control. Under that premise, raw political Darwinism, both within and between states, would be the likely result. A mitigating possibility, from the vantage point of the core countries, would be to create regional partnerships to at least regulate market competition and coordinate efforts against dislocated peoples or marginalized states that might rebel against their disadvantaged place in the world economy.

In any case, present-day U.S. structural power appears to generate a cooperative structure that would make stable, all-sided, democratic global governance a possibility. The currently unrivaled structural power allows the United States to make or break multilateral rules with impunity while imposing them on others, to shape global constitutions and structures to fit its needs, to reap maximum national benefits on the international market order and pass the costs of adjustments and manipulations on to others, including the disempowered among its own population.

THE AGE OF NEO-MERCANTILISM

Political and media elites in the United States tend to repeat that, in the face of political and economic turbulence, the strongest power on earth cannot be forced to choose between acting alone or not at all. There is some truth in such an assertion, a clear indication of the will to rule on the one hand, and on the other a recognition of constraints, internal and international, fiscal and military, placed on the exercise of power.

We are told that the United States has no option but to remain the key player in the construction of a "multilateral" security system designed to protect a "global" interdependent world economy, to direct the use of coercion in a collective fashion against the "backlash states" and protectionist minded economies in general. In the name of the protection of living standards, the United States increasingly demands "burden sharing" from its own "allies," including internal economic measures deemed necessary to U.S. and global growth.

Supposedly, crisis and conflict could be avoided by way of the sustained expansion of international trade, whereby each of the nation's exports would find ready purchasers. The trouble is that in the context of a general economic contraction, consumers are also short on purchasing power. And following massive debt accumulation in most of the rich countries over the past 25 years, there is not much scope for deficit spending and new borrowing to counteract economic recessions. Thus each of the economic powers insists on exporting its way out of recession, feeding new competition for markets. The U.S. would also demand that its competitors manipulate credit and interest rates so as to shift those sizeable national economies from export-led to a more domestically centered growth. Japanese governmental and corporate authorities resist such pressures, while the German Bundesbank has repeatedly made clear its unwillingness to cut interest rates for the sake of alleviating European and global unemployment. Currency speculators, including the banks, can profit handsomely from the ensuing turmoil in financial markets.[8]

One way out favored in certain Northern quarters (principally Japan and France) would entail dividing up markets among contenders in order to avoid a full reversion to protectionism. But such recommendations are anathema to Washington, which insists upon commitment to an open trading system, notwithstanding a long record of self-interested departures from the norm. In the global macro-economic sphere the United States is still unable to repeat what it does in the security sphere: effectively impose its will and standards on its "allies."

The assumption in Washington is that the greater the leadership, the greater the stability: hence the need for state intrusions in the marketplace. But unlike governments in the South, powerful states in the North also follow the U.S. example in employing political muscle to increase national or regional shares of expanding global markets. But politically backed corporate competition feeds preferentialism and systemic instability. When financial panics break out, or a major "emerging" economy or bank faces the prospect of default, then governments and corporations are forced to engage in "stock market diplomacy" in often vain attempts to rein in the speculation, which risks further collapse in investor confidence, affecting currencies and entire banking structures.

Nor can the hegemonic state always effectively neutralize challenges from other major political actors bent on securing preferential market access and protected zones of influence. The result is the present-day move away from "free trade" toward "managed trade," in which power politics increasingly influences patterns of global commerce and investment flows.

For example, the Clinton administration often argues that its commercial foreign policies are geared to playing "catch-up" with its rivals now that the Cold War is over. Each economic power center has its own bureaucratic policy for the promotion of "strategic industries," be it the powerful Ministry of International Trade and Industry in Japan (MITI), "industrial policy" in the U.S., or "competition policy" in the European Union. State authorities encourage the already tightly interlinked conglomerates that control each country's economy to engage in more national and regional mergers in order to better compete abroad yet lessen the competition at home.[9]

As this practice grows, so does the overall power of government over trade and investment, deregulation theories notwithstanding. Thus we witness how the U.S. is demanding that the Japanese government intervene so that the "market mechanism" can work in favor of U.S. corporations in the Japanese economy.[10] The principal industrial nations all face internal political pressures to adopt some version of Clinton's "Fix America First" program or to adhere to a "social charter" as idealized in the European Union scheme. These programs all aim to provide, to some minimal degree, economic and social protection for the livelihoods, health, and education needs of the domestic workforce. Governments of the South and East, however, whose workers face far worse conditions, are virtually banned from even trying to undertake similar socially protective schemes. The restrictions, tied to access to crucial credit and loans, are all justified in the name of free enterprise.

An unusually rebellious note was sounded by Japan in 1991, when it criticized the World Bank for its simple-minded faith in the free market. In a press conference, the head of the Japanese delegation to the World Bank conference that year said that many of the policies that East Asia followed are precisely those that the Bank prohibits other countries from adopting. Japanese and East Asian government policies in many cases were, he said, "market friendly," but when necessary had also included inexpensive credit, protection, and state support for key firms.[11]

Such tendencies reflect growing skepticism in official government quarters with regard to the benefits of unfettered "free trade." Politicians find that their ambitions could also suffer on account of an economic transnationalization which also impacts national businesses and industries unable to compete with their global counterparts, forcing thousands out of jobs and generating new political pressures. Reflecting and capitalizing on the discontent, official Washington doctrines are being scrutinized as "moderate free traders" or "fair traders" insisting that modern competition is not free by nature or by politics in Japan and Europe, and therefore should also not be free in the United States.

Japan's MITI is famous for an industrial policy based on a combination of governmental guidance and subsidies designed to promote key industries. Some economists debate where the interventionism stands up to its reputation, citing statistical measures indicating the Japanese government actually intervenes less than its rivals in Europe and about the same as in the United States. Still, other MITI coordination and pressure tactics cannot be quantified.

There is little doubt, however, that large MITI subsidies to the semiconductor industry in the late 1970s allowed Japan to temporarily overtake the U.S. in the chip market, which led the U.S. to pressure Japan into promising U.S. firms 20 percent of the Japanese market for semiconductors, while the U.S. retained a lead in microprocessors. MITI promoted aerospace, but not with much success. In the energy sector, MITI controls everything from investment plans to retail fuel purchases.[12]

Governments in the North usually cannot afford to openly ignore the plight and pressure of specific industrial sectors. In the United States, the growth of imports from Japan and the Pacific, while augmenting profits for larger, more diversified multinationals, has created problems for certain industries or firms in the advanced capitalist countries. Both labor-intensive industries and now high-tech industries are under pressure to adjust by the NICs (newly industrializing countries), as fears have grown that "de-industrialization" is the destiny of countries such as the United States and the United Kingdom, feeding a "diminished giant" syndrome.

U.S. trade legislation is designed to strike back at this trend, harassing foreign suppliers who would compete with national production, but also pressuring foreign governments and producers on their home ground to accept more U.S. exports. Such indeed is the content and intention of the infamous Section 301, also known as "super-301." This legistation obliges the administration to produce an annual list of foreign "unfair" trade practices that may incur retaliation. Its alleged intention is to pry open markets that have not liberalized sufficiently according to GATT or structural adjustment norms. It can serve as a means to secure better deals for U.S. corporations that might not otherwise materialize without the recourse to threat. But it also stands as a reminder that the United States will not trust to multilateral institutions the defense of what it perceives to be its national interest, nor, as Japan is aware, will it renounce the right to impose unilateral sanctions.[13]

Europeans have similar legislation. In this bilateral game, the weak become the victim of the strong, as the strong enter into a dangerous struggle with each other, resulting also in a greater reliance on managed trade. Giant corporations, for their part, play both sides of the fence, profiting from both protection and free trade wherever convenient. General Motors (Europe) bought the Polish automobile company PSO with the unwritten condition that government provide it with a 30 percent tariff duty. A similar prerequisite was made by Korean Goldstar Electronics for its establishment of a television assembly plant in Hungary.[14]

The U.S. government and its principal rivals provide support for research and development, in effect providing subsidies to selected corporations. Purists object that categories of permissible subsidies (environmental, regional development, research and development) could be exploited by other countries that might pour huge sums into these areas.[15] However, they also must take into account that governments are impacted by local political forces and cannot remain oblivious to mounting unemployment and job insecurity.

In this way the ruling elites become the victims of their own rhetoric. Fear of unemployment and competition from East Asia and elsewhere has made the task of selling free trade harder than ever, especially in Europe and America. As social discontent rises, so too does the search of the rich for non-corporate scapegoats, along with the argument that true "national" self-interest lies in stimulating and invigorating your own economy and getting away with maintaining as much protection for job-sustaining industries as possible, no matter how uncompetitive abroad.

Each nation fears that it is giving too much away in trade negotiations. Some critics in the United States claimed that the U.S. could not afford to sign market-opening agreements on account of growing overproduction in Europe and Japan which could be dumped in the U.S.[16] However, elite economists will insist that everyone stands to gain from the general market liberalization, but governments refuse to accept curbs on their statutory power to protect or subsidize, as well as to retaliate commercially against foreign producers.

THE BATTLE FOR THE SOUTH

"Developing economies" are increasingly important to the rich countries, perhaps now more on account of their capacity to consume than to produce the proverbial raw materials demanded by the North. This means that while many parts of the South are simply written off, some are becoming indispensable and hotly contested markets for the export of goods and capital from the North. Between 1990 and 1993, countries in the South increased their total imports by 37 percent, considerably above the increase in world trade — yet their exports rose by only 22 percent. "In other words," observed the *Economist*, "for the first time developing economies were acting as a 'locomotive,' helping to pull the rich world out of its recession of the early 1990s."

In trade alone, some 42 percent of U.S. exports, 20 percent of Western Europe's (47 percent if intra-European Union trade is excluded), and 48 percent of Japan's go to the "Third World" or to countries of the ex-Soviet bloc. EU countries export over twice as much to the South and East as they do to North America and Japan combined. The U.S. in turn also exported more to the South than to Japan or Western Europe; during those same three years, U.S. exports to developing countries grew at an annual average of 12 percent, while those to other rich countries rose by only 2 percent a year.[17]

The increase in consumption of capital and goods was not distributed evenly within societies of South or East, or among all countries as a whole. Most was concentrated in selected states of East Asia and Latin America, as the world's fastest growing markets. Making the best of the market expansion, corporate investment (but also drug cartel earnings in Latin America) set up production facilities to take advantage of liberalization and privatization. Yet such profit-centered corporate decisions did not always dovetail with the "national economic interest," in so far as the corporations, and not the workers in the rich countries, could also benefit from stepped up intra-regional trade centered upon the more dynamic markets. Thus, for example, the proportion of Asia's non-Japanese exports that went to other Asian countries increased from 26 percent in 1986 to 37 percent in 1992.[18]

Supposedly, modern trade, particularly in the high-technology area, is already government-managed in most of the advanced industrial world, as high-tech companies require a relationship with their governments with exemptions to the free market rule and to the general liberalization of commerce. According to Laura D'Andrea Tyson, head of the Clinton administration's Council of Economic Advisers, government sponsorship of advanced industrial activity is necessary and desirable on account of the "special contribution" to the long-term health of the U.S. economy, particularly in regards to effects on employment, productivity, and research. Free trade in this context is a false ideal, highly inappropriate in a world of managed trade, particularly in technology. Because policy intervention is certain to be practiced by others, Tyson concludes that the United States can no longer afford the soothing yet irrelevant position that market forces alone should determine the industrial and social outcomes of nations.[19]

Indeed, by the early 1990s the massive growth in public debt and budget deficits left even rich governments limited in their internal fiscal capacity to stimulate new economic upswings. This forced retrenchment from Keynesianism led core governing elites in the North to stimulate private spending by way of providing corporate capital with unprecedented facilities and opportunities, invading what had become traditional areas of the public sector but also attaching greater importance to the export of goods, services, and capital; in short, to generate profit by privatizing and seeking out, increasingly at a global level, higher labor productivity at the lowest cost.

According to Mickey Kantor, U.S. trade commissioner, "the U.S. economy is now intricately woven into the global picture. Where we once bought, sold, and produced mostly at home, today, over a quarter of the U.S. economy is dependent on trade."[20] Much the same sentiment was voiced by Leon Brittan, EU commissioner for external economic relations, who demanded a "user-friendly post [Uruguay]-round world." The reasons are not to be hidden: EU merchandise trade accounts for 20 percent of the world total, while absorbing over 30 percent of total world trade in services. One job out of ten in the Union was directly generated by exports, according to Brittan.[21] In Kantor's opinion, "the United States is well-positioned economically, culturally, and geographically to reap the benefits of the global economy."[22]

But where are these markets for the competitors? One calculation is that developing countries will account for two-thirds of the increase in world imports over the next 25 years, as the increased export ability of some key countries in the South provides more money to spend on imports.[23] But corporate interests will not simply stand and allow the market to allocate shares; instead they put their respective governments to work to become engaged in what the *Economist* termed "a brazen, mercantilist battle for markets in China and the Middle East, twisting arms and bending foreign policy to grab commercial contracts."[24]

The question was whether U.S. would shoot itself in the foot if it persisted with the pressure policy. Some U.S. bankers worried about the economy's dependence on Japanese capital to make ends meet at home. None of these objections, however, changed the U.S. governing elite perception that U.S. foreign policy was economic policy, that the "national interest" was inextricably intertwined with the global economy in general and with the securing of export markets in particular. Foreign policy therefore translated into a strategic imperative to shift the internal make-up of other countries — North and South — in order for the U.S. to prosper.

Of course, the issue was not posed in these terms, but rather in the form of a simplistic discourse of market opening for the sake of avid consumers and in order to stimulate global growth and competition.[25] But there was no mistaking the importance of foreign markets to the principal United States corporations: international sales by U.S. multinationals (exports, direct investment, or joint ventures) stood at $1.2 trillion in 1991, representing 29 percent of all corporate revenues. Foreign purchases as a proportion of total sales represented 51 percent in non-electrical machinery, 59 percent in computers and office equipment, 37 percent in manufacturing, 22 percent in services, 44 percent in autos and parts, 43 percent in construction and mining machinery, 39 percent in chemical products, 37 percent in electrical equipment, 34 percent in petroleum, 34 percent in non-automotive transport equipment, 30 percent in food and beverage products, 22 percent in construction, and 16 percent in non-bank financial services.[26] The U.S. remained the leading exporter of commercial services, in 1991 some $148 billion compared with $84 billion for France, $60 for Germany, and $46 for Japan, as well as the principal exporter of merchandise: $447 billion in 1992 as compared to $428 billion for Germany and $340 billion for Japan. All these figures reinforced the vision of an export-led economic recovery and expansion.[27]

From the European-North American perspective, Japan's post-war strategy ran against the grain of liberalization. According to them, government-supported Japanese conglomerates exported as many high-tech goods as possible, while excluding foreign competitors and investors from the home market, forcing Japanese consumers to pay higher prices which further subsidized exports. Japanese manufactured goods were claimed to overwhelm Western markets, yet manufactured imports accounted for only about 6 percent of the Japanese market, as opposed to 15 percent in the U.S. and Germany.

"Such a mercantilist system is no longer tolerable now that Japan's economy is the world's second most powerful," clamored *Business Week*.[28] Washington's denunciations, however, lacked moral authority: top U.S. government authorities, including the president, did not hesitate to resort to arm twisting in order to secure benefits for U.S. corporations. A $6 billion order for U.S.-made commercial jets was secured from Saudi Arabia after the intervention of the president himself. A French airline official was quoted as saying that "the way the Saudi order was obtained shocked people in Europe," warning that the Europeans would not accept "defeat" quietly.[29] European officials threatened a trade suit against both the United States and Japan if European interests suffered as a result of any Japanese agreement to accept the U.S. demand to set numerical targets for increased exports of U.S. cars.[30]

LOCKING IN THE NEW ORDER

According to standard liberal thought, politics is largely divorced from economics, political power is chiefly directed to security concerns, and the world economy advances unfettered and naturally toward a single market. If "external" market forces are seen as separate from internal and external political ones, then indeed one can presume that integration into the marketplace, submissive or not, is also the inevitable culmination of an historical process of economic modernization.

Political forces in the North help shape order in the South and determine the submissive nature of the integration. But if the world market forces are purely economic, then there would be no point in resisting them. To admit the past and present capacity of a few capitalist states to assert their political power over the world market would invite other states to entertain similar notions with respect to their own national economies. Hence the North's need to keep such power hidden, to present the Bretton Woods institutions as the technical non-political organizations which act as consultants to governments in the South and East. The G-7 for their part would be a council of elders of sorts which meets periodically to respectfully comment on the evolution of the world economy. The entire argument denies the centrality of the role of the United States government, and dismisses the possibility that colonialism is a past and current feature of global affairs.

Yet most government officials in the North do not, in practice at least, buy the notion of the depoliticized world market. In their view, governments in the South and East should commit functional suicide for the sake of the new "depoliticized" order. States are to abandon prerogatives, peoples are to give up on the notion of creating sovereign democracies, because the open door world, entrusting police powers to the higher authority which also oversees the single world economy, no longer requires local official doorkeepers for other than menial and repressive tasks. Governments can no longer be trusted to abide by multilateral trade or financial agreements, more functions and more authority must be delegated upward, states must deliver their partially closed societies to higher authorities, amorphously known as "the market," as a contribution to the U.S.-directed endeavor to create a new global framework. Governments, as well as people, are therefore to be convinced that they have the obligation to uphold a new market-driven global order and that there is no room for democratic forms of collectivism or nationalism.

In this theory, the "market access" or free trade international regime undercuts protectionism ostensibly by letting all competitors share in the profits conferred by the universalization of market-oriented structural adjustment policies. This ignores the historical fact that market integration and market expansion for most key industries, from automobiles to semiconductors, have been and continue to be the subject of active governmental protection. The new economic orthodoxy also ignores the new industrialization paradigm appearing most prominently in East Asia, in which the State once again assumes a prominent role in regard to the market operations.

Whether admitted or not, governments of the industrialized countries continue to skirt multilateral free trade rules when it comes to defending their national corporations against foreign ones, contesting each other's "right" to expand into each other's national markets. As social pressures mount around employment and welfare issues, the advanced states become all the more jealous in protecting their industrial base, sometimes to the point of interfering with the short-term profit considerations of the multinational actors. The tendency, however, is not toward confrontation nor opposing international corporate alliances, but rather the seeking of new forms of state-industry collaboration, in which Japan in particular has excelled, seeking to keep the "best" if not always the "most" jobs at home.[31]

New corporate alliances as much as new modalities of government assistance represent complementary means by which transnational capital secures access to, or maintains, new markets and technologies. Indeed, under "managed trade norms" it is up to governments to secure political agreements for market and technology sharing. Here again, however, some governments enjoy a more privileged bargaining position than others for reasons that have little to do with economics.

Such market sharing bilateral accords, like those signed between Japan and the United States, fly in the face of free trade theory and post-WWII multilateral trade rules, not to mention the recipes imposed by the Bretton Woods institutions on the South and East. Nonetheless, Japanese, European, and to a lesser extent the United States authorities retain final discretion over which foreign companies or items may enter their markets as well as the power to discriminate and retaliate.

Colonialism is of course a question of making one or several powers exempt from the rules which apply to smaller nations. Power explains why certain countries can demand exemptions from obligations that would otherwise be called into question. And power is reinforced in an order that permits government intervention or tampering in order to further accentuate the benefits of free global market "competition." Thus integration agreements (not to mention rhetoric) will go in one direction while national economic measures march in another. Unlike earlier historical rounds of ultra-capitalist competition, there is no reversal from interdependence. Which is why the United States, free from Cold War alliance shackles and pressed by negative economic trends, does not feel willing or able to cooperate with economic "partners" whose own national economic measures threaten to wreak havoc on Washington's prescription for global order.

By the same imperial logic the often cited globally-destabilizing features of the United States (budget deficit, low rate of national savings, structure of capital markets) can be addressed at Washington's own leisurely pace and timing, if at all. While Asian and European governments feel beholden to the United States military apparatus, Asian and European corporations are similarly dependent on access to the U.S. market. Most of the world provides the U.S. with interest-free loans when they purchase or hold U.S. dollars for international reserve or for savings. Furthermore, and while paying lip service to multilateralism, the U.S. vision of a global order is built piecemeal as key issues are negotiated bilaterally where the imbalance is most acutely felt and exploited. All these forces reinforce each other and manifest themselves in the U.S. tendency to demand and receive concessions on all fronts.

Such hegemonic procedure, however, spells long-term global disorder as the U.S. gets caught up in its own web of often contradictory bilateral or regional arrangements, which tend to weaken the same multilateral political and economic quasi-constitutional framework necessary to insure the principle of market access and political submission, and to keep others from following Washington's example. In terms of neo-classical economics, a hybrid is in the making, but in geopolitical and historical terms it is quite consistent with hegemonic aspirations. The United States logically has no interest in taking multilateralism seriously in either its security or economic world contact, that is, to push for the transfer of all state authorities into multilateral instances. The challenge is for Washington to achieve global governance without giving up its state-centrist prerogatives — or better yet to combine them. Any other idealist scheme for world order would be incompatible with a drive for hegemony.

Multilateralism and trans-oceanic alliances served Washington in the Cold War period when economic rivals were absent, and could even be allowed exemptions to the free market rule for the sake of further impeding "communist expansion." But in the post-Soviet era and in the face of the economic transformation of once destroyed nations, there is less tolerance for national exemptions which threaten the "competitiveness" of the U.S. economy itself.

At the same time, multilateral trade institutions are being revamped, from being simple depositories of trade agreements, unable to block bilateral deals and indirect protection, in favor of IMF or World Bank instruments providing safeguards and penalties for noncompliers. Insistence on government commitments to "economic fundamentals" is crucial in order to sustain the argument that the new world order is built upon common political values that require the existence of international interventionist vigilantes.

U.S. attempts to restructure the global order are nothing less than an acceptance by Washington and Wall Street that it will not or cannot rely on the global marketplace to redress its internal socio-economic problems. Nor do they trust the market to deliver to the United States the "leadership" mandate to which it feels morally entitled. Of course, no government willingly entrusts "national well-being" to the pristine marketplace, but politically many feel in no position to contest Washington's market leadership, at least without a massive democratic, revolutionary mandate on the one hand and major international allies on the other.

Although new world order policy in Washington is still being sorted out, there can be little doubt that in practice at least, the U.S. is forging a strategic response to the changing global scenarios. The tendency for now is still one of simplistic and dangerous rationalizations for incoherent approaches to the various facets of a new and unexpected world picture. NAFTA, APEC, NATO, or the UN, or aggressive multilateralism, are all bandied about in Washington and in the U.S. press as formulas of quick relief for the anxieties of the economy and globalization. Economic forces will continue to battle with governmental treaties on the one hand and rebellious peoples on the other, as the U.S. strives to impose order and orderly behavior on a reluctant globe.

This is not a question of catching up, but rather of rigging the rules, creating the national, social, and global conditions to sustain U.S. hegemony. No longer would corporate managers look with envy at Japan's *keiretsu* system or at Germany's social compact. The norm is to restructure, U.S.-style. Breaking unions at home (flexible workforces) and aggressive diplomacy (enlarging democracy) are the two sides of the same coin. "Competitiveness" requires low wage, nonunion, part-time jobs at home, and structural adjustment abroad.

Not everyone will play by the new rules, although corporate apologists of all nationalities have assumed the privatization logic. While the principal governments in the North will probably not abandon their preferred recourse to managed trade and threats of bilateral retaliation, governments in the South are not allowed to do the same. Hence Northern insistence on introducing irreversible "adjustments" to state structures that would lock in "market reforms," including punctual debt repayment and re-indebtment.

Indeed, IMF/World Bank programs are more active than ever before in promoting project borrowing as a means to maintain policy "leverage" over client countries. Working together with U.S. and other government official lending agencies, the World Bank and IMF will make loans and grants to induce nations of the South to articulate their own development strategies and policies to the demands and needs of international capital. "Modernization" entails acceptance of neo-liberal development, chiefly the enshrining of the principle of free flows of trade and investment. The objective is to seek the most "competitively" possible integration into the "global market," orienting development to the satisfaction of the external rather than the internal market.

Structural adjustment programs openly advocate restructuring national economies into "free market" ones open to free trade and unimpeded foreign investment and repatriation of capital. In short, the programs are designed to secure unconditional, irreversible, and subordinate integration of states and attractive sectors of their national economies into the global system.[32] As one observer noted: "In coming years, America's far reaching economic interests and the intertwined nature of the global economy will require that American diplomats more and more get under the hood of other countries .... When American foreign policy becomes economic policy, the work of diplomats doesn't stop at another country's borders ... to the contrary, it starts there and moves inward."[33]

The point is that governments in the North, and the United States first among them, unfettered by political-strategic restraints imposed by the Cold War, and plagued by internal economic woes, are resorting to unprecedented levels of aggressiveness in their international economic diplomacy. There is no solid power bloc either among or within the principal economic powers, but rather a complicated network of internal contradictions along with allying interests. Studies of the power elite groups within and outside the Trilateral Commission give numerous examples of such conflicts.[34]

Since Soviet disintegration the "management of interdependence" has become more complex, and recession further contributes to the deterioration of trilateral unity. Unless a new "common enemy" is soon defined, allowing the U.S. to reassert its hegemony, North-North frictions could turn into conflicts. One temptation may assign that role to Japan, but elite theorists are furiously engaged in sustaining the trilateral consensus by insisting that European, U.S., and Japanese interests are identical in a globalization process now threatened by the clash of civilizations in this "post-ideological age."

The commercial dispute between Japan and the United States is a case in point. Washington's top foreign policy priority is to force the Japanese government to reduce its trade deficit by restricting its exports and providing guaranteed access to its domestic market. Government intervention on behalf of their respective corporate structures had been evident for some time.

The Japanese government is now accused of reneging on vaguely-worded commitments to reduce its trade surplus and specifically open its market to foreign automobile units and parts, insurance and telecommunications and medical equipment. "Foreign" in this case meaning "U.S.," as the Europeans have loudly pointed out. In this day and age of liberal free trade and deregulation, however, Washington is demanding that the Japanese government dictate the purchasing decisions of "private" industry. Sanctions have been imposed, and according to the *New York Times*, "such sanctions also invite retaliation from Japan against American companies and could trigger a trade war between the world's two biggest economies."[35] At stake is the very capacity of Japan to sustain its post-war alliance with the U.S. with demands for structural reforms in its political economy. As the then U.S. secretary of the treasury stated, the objective is to insure that Japan does not pursue "recovery based on exports to the U.S."[36]

But what happens if the same logic is extended across the board? The situation could be out of the hands of the corporations, as many of them would be the principal losers in the event of a commercial war. Yet another example of politics overtaking economics. Tensions are multiplying among the principal economic powers. They may all agree to use global institutions such as the World Bank, the IMF, and the WTO to impose open markets on the South and middle powers; they are all in favor of insuring access to cheap labor; but among themselves they are increasingly resorting to economic warfare, trying to build competing regional blocs with built-in cheap labor zones, and disregarding trade rules.

One wishful interpretation of United States hegemony argues that, in the face of the prevailing chaos of unregulated world capitalism, Washington is merely providing the indispensable means to impose order on the more unregulated components of the international capitalist economy. This, of course, is a self-contradictory strategy, because the U.S. will not sacrifice its own economic recuperation for the benefit of the world economy, much less that of the domestic political and economic needs of its rivals.

Furthermore, in order to remain in the driver's seat, the United States is not above employing the leverage that its military role and market size affords it, in order to impose and redefine the rules of the economic game, both in regard to the multilateral financial institutions, but also by increasingly demanding a voice in national economic policy-making.

Such is the essence of the notorious structural adjustment programs imposed on countries of the South and East, relegating the nation-state to near observer status in most fields of social and economic policy, keeping chiefy its police abilities intact. Structural adjustment entails greater dependence on foreign capital and assistance, leaving U.S. aid-dependent countries in Latin America, for example, (or French aid-dependent countries in Africa) prey to conditioning on trade preferences, or security policies, or voting in the United Nations, in conformity with the interest of the metropolis. A clearer indication of North American hegemony, and the attempts to sustain it indefinitely across the board and the world, is the imposition of similar adjustment demands and the threat of commercial retaliation on the other major economic powers, principally Japan, forcing it to break down what are spuriously called structural impediments — a euphemism for the bureaucratic-monopolistic character of Japanese capitalism, which, at the expense of the Japanese consumer, has given that nation a relatively powerful and autonomous center of accumulation and technological prowess.

Much the same heavy-handedness once reserved for the Third World — also termed "aggressive multilateralism" in Washington power circles or "strategic trade" among the Clinton administration's academic advisers — reveals itself in regard to Europe in the form of direct pressure on the German government and banking system to lower its interest rates, or on the French to renounce its long-standing insistence on defending national culture against Hollywood onslaughts. The Clinton administration has been relentless in pushing foreign governments and bureaucracies to increase the purchase of U.S. goods, services, and investment.

In the face of a sluggish market demand, we can anticipate that the principal economic power centers will gravitate toward a new mercantilism while espousing free trade multilateral doctrines. Each will seek to gain the most abroad and give the least at home. Yet the "mercantile" picture is not totally accurate, because it would obscure the reality that corporate elites on both sides of the pact may benefit from their bilateral "free trade" arrangements.

Any gravitation toward bloc commerce and intensified tri-polar competition will be just as damaging to the poorer and weaker countries that are left out of the false "free trade world order." The Cold War continues, its original version best understood as an attempt to defeat "communism," then the salient expression of departure from free market based socio-political organization. And because such a "communist" virus continues to exist, nations of the South and the East must be obliged to adhere to the rules of the free market if they indeed are to be recognized as nations in this golden age of capitalist globalization. The question then arises: can the U.S. transnational empire be challenged successfully by other means, drawing on alternative bases of power?

Notes

1. These definitions employed are adapted from those presented by Susan Strange, "Toward a Theory of Transnational Empire," in Ernst-Otto Czempiel and James N. Rosenau (eds.), *Global Changes and Theoretical Challenges: Approaches to World Politics for the 1990s* (New York: Lexington Books, 1989), pp. 165-75.

2. Stephen Gill (ed.), *Gramsci, Historical Materialism and International Relations* (Cambridge, U.K.: Cambridge University Press, 1993), pp. 31-32.

3. Strange, "Theory of Transnational Empire," p. 166. See also Strange, *States and Markets* (New York: Blackwell, 1988).

4. Gill, *Gramsci, Historical Materialism and International Relations*, p. 35.

5. Quoted in ibid., p. 42.

6. Strange, "Theory of Transnational Empire," p. 168.

7. Ibid., p. 170.

8. Rudi Dornbusch, "Europe's International Policy Agenda," *Politik und Gesselschaft*, no. 1 (1994), pp. 20-21.

9. "Taming the Chaebols," *Economist*, January 22, 1993.

10. *Far Eastern Economic Review*, January 20, 1994.

11. Alice Amsden, "Beyond Shock Therapy," *American Prospect*, Spring 1993, no. 13 p. 101.

12. *Economist*, January 24, 1994.

13. "The Two-Door Policy on Trade," *Economist*, October 1, 1994, pp. 63-64.

14. Amsden, "Beyond Shock Therapy," p. 95.

15. *New York Times*, February 1, 1994.

16. *Business Week*, January 10, 1994.

17. "The Global Economy," *Economist*, October 1, 1994, p. 13.

18. Ibid.

19. Laura D'Andrea Tyson, *Who's Bashing Whom: Trade Conflict in High-Technology Industries* (Washington, D.C.: Institute for International Economics, 1992). For an analysis, see James K. Galbraith, "Who's Bashing Tyson," *American Prospect*, no. 13 (Spring 1993), pp. 142-147.

20. Mickey Kantor, "Reaping Benefits for the Uruguay Round," *New York Times*, April 15, 1994.

21. Leon Brittan, "A User-Friendly Post-Round World," *New York Times*, April 15, 1994.

22. Kantor, "Reaping Benefits."

23. "The Global Economy."

24. "Beyond Bretton Woods," *Economist*, October 1, 1994, p. 27.

25. See, for example, the arguments made in *Business Week*, February 28, 1994.

26. *Business Week*, February 10, 1994.

27. *Economist*, December 4, 1993.

28. *Business Week*, February 28, 1994.

29. *New York Times*, February 20, 1994.

30. "Europe Threatens Trade Suit," *New York Times*, May 25, 1995.

31. See the example of the semiconductor industry in Peter F. Cowey and Jonathan D. Aronson, "New Trade Order," *Foreign Affairs*, vol. 72, no. 1 (1992/1993), pp. 187-189.

32. Dot Keet, "Regional and International Factors and Forces in the Development Perspectives for Southern Africa," *Southern African Perspectives* (Centre for Southern African Studies, University of Western Cape), no. 29 (November 1993), pp. 16-19.

33. *New York Times*, January 30, 1994.

34. Stephen Gill, *American Hegemony and the Trilateral Commission* (Cambridge, U.K.: Cambridge University Press, 1991), pp. 89-121.

35. *New York Times*, February 12, 1994.

36. "Washington's Ire," *Far Eastern Economic Review*, January 20, 1994.

6

Regionalism, Globalism, and Asianism

Fortunately for the United States government and global corporations, there are few nationalist states bent on radical policies of democratic income redistribution, and no dissident regional associations at all. But the threat is there, perceived perhaps more vividly in Washington than on Wall Street or among corporate executives. However unlikely its realization may be in existing globally-dominated regional blocs, the great Pentagon nightmare is that of closed economic regionalism giving way to strategic political challenges accompanied by the building of independent military alliances, directly challenging Washington's global behavioral guidelines.

Is the announcement of geopolitical "threats" simply a self-serving scenario cooked up to defend Pentagon budgets, or is it a realistic scenario given the workings of contemporary capitalist development? Are regional blocs in the making and, if so, do they constitute effective obstacles — economic as well as strategic — to the construction of the global consensus that Washington seeks to impose?

Most states take on the task of adjusting shifting domestic political power frameworks to fit into molds demanded by dominant economic interests. When that task is taken onto an international level, the result has often been war. The modern corporate claim, however, is that wars have become obsolete. Given the interdependence and the multinationalization of modern production and finance, CEOs claim, violent conflicts among like-minded capitalist states would prove counterproductive. But it doesn't always work that way. It cannot be assumed that the local political frameworks "recommended" by the United States for adoption the world over will in all cases be submissively accepted by all governments and all peoples.

The point is that U.S. law stops at U.S. borders. The U.S. government challenge is to extend norms of U.S. corporate governance beyond current international limits, which multinational corporations find exceedingly arbitrary. Not all U.S. laws, norms, and regulations — of course — because part of the corporate objective is to escape profit-detracting provisions. Major U.S. utility companies are delighted to find in Argentina, for example, a chance to do business in a market which is, at least by U.S. standards, unregulated. There producers can charge whatever the market will bear, and obtain monopolistic protection from governments to boot, as compared with an environment at home which often tends to set rates and fix profit margins. U.S. companies "like the rules of the game in Argentina," said the managing director of the Chase Manhattan Bank in charge of Latin American project finance.[1]

Washington and Wall Street may not agree on every nuance or definition of "national interests," but they coincide on crucial questions. The occasional profit-driven discrepancies also emerge in U.S. relations with other friendly governments, but the point is that the policy/economic divergence, both within and between North and South, increasingly takes place within a broader code of allegiance to the "free market" economy and the corporate agenda in general.

Regionalism, grouping a number of states for external protection and internal free trade, thus stands either as a potential stepping stone or obstacle in the path toward universal liberalization.

It may reflect the interests of associated national elites, trying to block their economies off from the world economy, or seeking to influence the evolution of globalization in self-serving ways. That logic would in principle apply to all regional efforts. But in fact it is the United States which most actively resists such tendencies (especially if the regional effort takes shape outside the U.S. umbrella) because it is U.S. corporations and the U.S. government that have the greatest vested interest in dictating the framework of the entire global political economy.

Most governments have accepted neo-liberal "market economy" recipes. But this does not spell universal harmony. There is an implicit challenge to the U.S. by any group of states with capital-exporting power that establishes internally integrated but externally protective economic market zones. That external "wall" hinders the exploitation of the same liberal regimes by external powers.

Nor can every nation play the regional game on equal terms. It is basically a game of the strong, with the rules set largely by the owners of global capital. The initial tendency is for weaker countries to benefit, as their export commodities gain at least limited access to the industrialized country markets. But the price is the full-scale acceptance of corporate governing norms over local political and economic decision-making: the "internationalization" of internal markets and the removal of remaining opportunities for autonomous development. The result is the strengthening of the international division of labor, along with the widening of gaps between rich and poor within the South.

Wealthier states must often mediate between their corporations' compulsion to integrate in order to benefit from economic "globalization," and the domestic political demand to segregate in order to protect sectors from the same process. Conceivably, a regional scheme offers a middle way out, entailing smaller losses of accountability to local communities: For Western Europeans to be able to choose Brussels as opposed to Washington (although an anti-EU referendum in Norway did order the government to retain accountability at home). It is possible, as in Europe, for discussion of common (even if minimal) labor and social standards to accompany discussions of internationalization, thereby strengthening regional bodies, either multilateral or non-governmental, committed to social concerns. That would represent, to some degree at least, a firmer line of defense against the soulless U.S. model of globalization which "equalizes" social and environmental safety nets downwards — to the lowest standard, or out of existence altogether.

National and regional governing elites, backed by corporations, will also argue that in the face of austerity-induced decreases in worker living standards and unemployment, local demand drops. Thus, they say, profits increasingly depend on exports, which in turn demand regional strategic policies, in order to better compete with the export-oriented strategies of other national or regional economic blocs. In this context, governments and corporations band together regionally in order to insure the strengthening of the local corporate sector.

The obsession with international competitiveness and achieving "efficiency" in the global market conflicts directly with any effort to make basic human needs a component of development thinking. Neo-liberal ideology and the profit motive combine to divorce the needs of the most vulnerable from predominant schemes for national, regional, and global governance.

Progressive social values can form part of emerging regional models only if social struggles in metropolitan countries insure the incorporation of minimum standards of democratic accountability and egalitarian approaches. The conception would be a form of regional state welfare capitalism as a counterweight to the self-serving ultra-liberal transnational governance schemes of the U.S., modeled on NAFTA and characterized by the virtual absence of a social dimension.[2] Under NAFTA, no democratic intervention or effort to even the drastically unequal playing field is allowed.

One must come back, however, to the nature of the regimes themselves and whether these in fact have been lost irreversibly as social instruments to mitigate the ravages of the "free" market. Securing government support for market access is critical to corporate profit-making. That principle is preached, exported, and imposed on the South, but in the North all sorts of exceptions are contemplated. This in turn feeds the need to find new external outlets, while increasing political tensions at home. Corporate states assume the duty of helping to meet desperate capitalist demands for flexibility, but if the flexibility is generalized then the advantages of particular uses of the power of one state or a specific coalition of states are diminished, making the competitive complications only worse.

Political governmental strategies for securing market access (like regionalism) more often than not contain some component for protecting the home market against competition, securing some preferential "flexibility," or at least assuring access on a reciprocal managed basis. Furthermore, if corporate operations tend to expand regionally before going global, Washington's globalist aspirations must take into account both national and regional attempts to control the rules of their own development, including securing preferential treatment for their own.

This does not translate into die-hard U.S. opposition to regional economic groupings per se: this would depend on their character. As long as their purpose is to further enhance and uphold neo-liberal domestic policies eliminating all distinctions between foreign and domestic capital, then indeed support can be expected for all "open" trading arrangements further committing members or signers to pursue internal and external liberalization. To the degree, however, that a regional bloc maintains anything like a protectionist instinct aimed at the U.S., let alone an independent development agenda, it can expect to be smacked down.

As one bloc appears, another must be set in motion to counter it, especially if dangerous protectionist or closed market tendencies manifest themselves which could be the stepping stone to the creation of new centers of strategic power. Autonomy, even relative autonomy, from the Washington or Wall Street axis is not acceptable.

In terms of commercial foreign policy, the U.S. appears to play all sides: the national, the regional, and the global, establishing particular sets of rules most advantageous to expansion at any given moment. If the rules then require moving the goal posts, then so be it. This means playing off Latin America (NAFTA) and Asia (APEC) against each other and against Europe (EU). Invoking the specter of NAFTA and APEC offering exclusive privileges to U.S. corporate needs, for example, the Clinton administration brandished threats against Europe to further prod open the EU's economies to U.S. production and capital, as well as to drop protectionist positions in regard to GATT.

As by far the biggest kid on the block, the U.S. can afford to make its own rules. To take advantage of the singular weight of the U.S. domestic market, and of the availability of U.S. financial markets to channel investment abroad, the rest of the world, divided into governments, local capitalists, or sub-regional blocs, compete with each other under self-serving U.S. regulations. Thus, during GATT negotiations, the U.S. team warned recalcitrant Europeans that as the result of Asian and Latin American concessions, the U.S. would give priority to interlocking with the economies of those two fastest growing global sectors, leaving Europe out and behind. U.S. trade representative Mickey Kantor warned that Europe should therefore follow the South's example in liberalizing to suit U.S. demands: "The U.S. will have an active role in Europe for as long as we can see. Our desire in Europe is to have greater access for U.S. goods .... If Europe blocks efforts to expand trade, it will be hurting itself most. U.S. trade will continue to expand to Asia and Latin America, and Europe will be left out."[3]

In other words, if the post-Cold War economic order is to be structured around zones of competition or regional blocs, the United States is to have a foot in every one, but its competitors might not. The goal is to play Europe, Asia, and Latin America against each other as a means of achieving not regional blocs, but the open door order demanded by transnational capital in general, and U.S. corporations and strategic interests in particular. Within a month, President Clinton could proclaim the building of free trade areas across the Pacific or from Anchorage to Tierra del Fuego. Hastily organized summit meetings gathered leaders fearful of regionalist trends abroad in order to proclaim their own regional liberalization goals. With the U.S. government directing the respective Asian and Latin American orchestras, nervous governments and regions vied with one another to lower trade barriers and further open their economies to corporate investment, all at the risk of being left out of the "gains" of the regional and global liberalization party.

Washington's diplomacy of competing liberalization or global structural adjustment consists precisely in invoking the dual threat of countries being restricted in their access to the U.S.-NAFTA-APEC markets on the one hand, or of living without access to foreign investment and technology on account of non-neo-liberal economic policies on the other. Perhaps in most senses, the prospect of keen economic rivalry among Asia, Europe, and Latin America is exaggerated on account of the huge differences between their economies. Nonetheless, the panic of not being able to "integrate" further into the world economy continues to drive national (and regional) economic policy-making, with devastating effects on those sectors deemed marginal to the all-encompassing drive for "competitiveness."

THE EAST ASIAN ENIGMA

As was the case with Germany, Japan's post-war economic recovery was largely a by-product of the Cold War. In Asia, the Chinese revolution and the Korean War reinforced the U.S. determination to make Japan a bulwark against "communist expansion." This entailed major changes in previous U.S. occupation policy, principally that of expediting economic reconstruction, reversing reparations, and reassembling in modified form the pre-war *zaibatsu* corporate groupings. The banks, resurrecting the name of the old *zaibatsu,* once again became the core of the business groups, assuming an even higher degree of influence than before the war.

In this way the U.S. participated actively in the rejuvenation of authoritarian Japanese capitalist practices: the three best-known pre-war *zaibatsu* groups — the Mitsui, the Mitsubishi, and the Sumitomo — which had earlier tended to specialize, now vied with each other in leaping into new technological fields. Assisted by an extremely favorable yen-dollar rate artificially set during the early pre-war years, the Japanese groupings experienced an upsurge in their exports. Between 1955 and 1975, Japan's exports expanded 27.7 times, in terms of dollar volume, with steel products and motor vehicles leading the way.[4] To a large extent, the overall economic growth rate during these years was export-driven. Thus Japan's share in world export markets went from 2.4 percent in 1955 to 10.1 percent in 1985; in terms of manufactured goods in those same years from 4.2 percent to 15.5 percent, and in machinery and equipment from 1.7 percent to 22.0 percent.[5]

Explanations abound for the Japanese economic "miracle." Western scholars often cite factors such as low wages, reduced defense spending, high savings, skilled corporate management, Confucian work ethics, or a submissive non-individualistic ethos. Some even claim that Japanese capitalist production methods — "flexibility," quality circles, team concept, just-in-time, export-led manufacturing — were somehow part of an historical category of their own which operates in a way that neither Adam Smith nor Karl Marx could have understood.[6] But none of these factors would have proven important in the absence of a high degree of concentration and interpenetration of corporate and state power, under a U.S. umbrella, all of which allowed a more effective marshaling of resources toward elite-defined strategic objectives.

Specialists point to the Japanese surge in resource concentration and an effective government policy of managing economic and human resources.[7] Under the watchful eyes of the United States, Japan's post-war leaders used the institutions of a strong, centralized state and old monopolistic corporate structures to devise a development strategy in which state protection promoted production innovation and private investment. Making the internal market difficult to penetrate, and facilitating the conquest of overseas markets, were central components of a strategy that served Japan well. Indeed the "Western" alliance profited, as rising Japanese economic prowess was accompanied by a subservient, low profile, and unswervingly pro-U.S. foreign policy.

Probably to a larger extent than in other advanced capitalist nations, national industries benefited from government initiatives, yet in the case of Japan the West's tendency was to focus instead on the cultural and institutional role of Japanese society in building economic success. Certainly the statist monopoly system of pre-war Japan had not thrived on military expansion alone. Rather, a paternalistic administrative guidance that, while supposedly guaranteeing competition at home, concentrated on providing support for sales abroad, played a much greater role. Such "guidance" was in itself a form of power inasmuch as it was accompanied by the ability to provide or withhold access to grants, subsidies, tax breaks, official contracts, foreign exchange, as well as approval of cartel arrangements.[8]

Industrial policy has long been prevalent in Japan, taking the form of direct MITI (Ministry of International Trade and Industry) involvement in corporate strategy. Whether each government intervention has met with success is the subject of debate, but there is little doubt that learning from the "Japanese model" was, in the early 1990s, practically an article of faith among U.S. politicians, particularly in the Clinton administration, and in key business circles.

MITI's powerful protection of Japan's domestic electronics market during the 1950s was an important factor in Sony's development, forcing a number of major U.S. multinationals to license important technologies to Sony and other Japanese firms. Similar MITI moves against Ford, General Motors, and Chrysler, among other forms of direct assistance to national automobile firms, were also critical in the build-up of the Japanese motor vehicle industry.[9]

Yet contrary to common belief, protectionism is not the principal factor in Japan's huge trade surplus with the rest of the world, and the U.S. in particular. Rather, the surplus reflects a domestic political economic structure in which capital accumulation and investment does not translate into higher consumption of imported goods and services. Japan is warned that the lack of "reciprocity" and of market access affects the well-being of the other core economies, which also constitute its major markets.

One Western conclusion, shared by some Japanese politicians and industrialists, is that the "reform" of Japanese capitalism is crucial to its own survival and indeed that of the global capitalist economy. As the *Economist* warned, "the question about Japan is no longer why one of the world's most successful economies should change its ways, but whether it can change fast enough to meet its own aspirations."[10]

Economists argue that, in the case of the United States at least, the trade deficit is a sign of relative prosperity, and that technically it is not a problem but simply an expression of the fact that the U.S. market spends more because it produces more, and the difference is made up in imports and credit. Even if a free trade heaven were to prevail on earth, the argument goes, it does not follow that the Japanese-U.S. trading account would undergo substantial modification. The real problem is that economists do not make policies, politicians do, and they in turn are not above simplifying the facts in order to provoke or reflect a public opinion which would prefer to blame others — particularly the Japanese — for the "export of unemployment." At the heart of the matter is the tendency in the United States, shared also in other economic power centers, to view trade or competition in adversarial terms.

The argument is only superficially one of principle, and in substance one of historical and contemporary practice in the advanced capitalist world: no country manages its trade more than Japan. The U.S. is not interested in ending such a practice, neither at home nor abroad, but rather wants to modify the use of such a weapon on its own behalf. That is, the U.S. doesn't want the Japanese government to stop managing its economy, but to do so in a way more consistent with U.S. and Western corporate norms.

Thus, the United States has little interest in assuming a joint negotiating position with the European Union vis-à-vis Japan (with a view toward increasing the share of all foreign manufactures in the Japanese market). The goal is to assure specific market shares for the U.S.

— or a "trade by numbers, quotas, or restrictions" — that is, forcing people to buy goods and services they otherwise would not buy, a travesty of the very free trade principle being asserted.

U.S. foreign policy toward the ex-allies is increasingly perceived as a set of bilateral bargaining and bartering relationships. Government-induced agreements guaranteeing market shares in Japan for the U.S. car parts industry, for instance, were protested by European automobile industries and the European Union's trade commissioner, who expressed concern "that such activity should not lead to discrimination against Europe."[11]

Both U.S. and Japanese elites are aware that it is not simply a question of reducing Japan's trade surplus with the U.S., or with the rest of the world, but also of restructuring the economy and implementing fiscal policies that will further "integrate" what some mistakenly call Japan's "Robinson Crusoe economy" into the global system under the U.S. socio-economic engineering framework. Even when the political will could be muscled in Japan, little changed.

The heart of the "problem" is not, as some claim, the groupings of powerful unrelenting bureaucrats, but rather the particular nature of Japanese capitalism. The export drives might have been accepted by Japan's competitors, but not when combined with practices tending to exclude foreign competitors and investors from the huge domestic market. Were it not for the fact that the Japanese economy is the world's second most powerful, the anger would simply remain at the level of principle. Manufactured imports account for only about 6 percent of Japan's domestic market, as compared to 15 percent in the U.S. and Germany. This is perceived by U.S. and European corporate elites as grossly unfair, and what is worse, grossly detrimental to their own domestic economic stability and the global system.

Free trade in the abstract is not the issue; preferential access to the Japanese markets and a restructuring of the Japanese political economy is. In the short term, the U.S. is looking for a share of the Japanese market to be guaranteed by the Japanese government to U.S. firms and no one else. Both the U.S. and Japan say they want free trade, but the first would insist on numerical targets and the second will continue to route its economic decisions through the Ministry of Finance.

But imposing preferential structural adjustment on Japan is not a simple task, however vital U.S. governments regard it for the universalization and stability of the capitalist order. This may well translate into an eventual confrontation with the bureaucratic-corporate cartels that the U.S. helped put in power in the first place, but that are now supposedly blocking the change demanded by Washington. The assumption is that the Japanese political economy has more to lose than the United States from an outright commercial conflict, that Japanese corporations would eventually feel the pinch strongly enough to push the bureaucrats into a liberalization arrangement.

Such logic induced U.S. officials in 1993-94 to wage financial war on Japan by allowing the dollar to depreciate radically against the yen. That is, to refuse to intervene on financial markets to prop up the value of the dollar, and therefore make Japanese exports more expensive and U.S. exports to Japan more attractive, squeezing the profits of the Japanese conglomerates.

The game, however, is a dangerous one, both in political and financial terms, as the U.S. puts at risk other components of its hegemony. By May 1994, financial officials in the U.S. were forced to call on the principal central banks of the world to intervene in the financial markets because the dollar was dropping faster than calculated, and not only against the yen but also the mark. The European Union chastized the U.S. for irresponsible financial manipulation and demanding self-serving import quotas under the threat of trade sanctions that could unhinge global markets. Exchange rate manipulation turned out to be a double-edged weapon, as markets and bankers began to lose confidence in the dollar. Furthermore, there was little progress on the trade front: the 36 percent rise in the yen's dollar value between the end of 1989 and the beginning of 1994 did not bring the Japanese economic system to its knees — predictions of a surge in Japanese unemployment rates and in the level of export competitiveness proved wrong.

As for commercial sanctions, U.S. officials were able to line up precious little corporate support for these politically popular tactics. On the whole, sanctions tended to hurt U.S. companies almost as much as they did Japan: nearly half of the U.S.-Japan trade imbalance consists of components imported by U.S. companies to make their own products. Corporations were concerned less about arguments over free market principles, than whether a retaliatory cycle would engulf investments and profits. When President Clinton signed an executive order giving him authority to impose up to 100 percent tariffs on Japanese products (Super-301 authority), an impulse was generated to use that authority. Prominent officials, including the head of the Council of Economic Advisers, had to remind the administration that a trade war would ultimately harm American companies.[12]

The U.S.-Japanese stand-off was becoming qualitatively different and more serious than previous rows: minor tinkering could alleviate the tensions but the contradiction remained between the two different national capitalist models unable to coexist peacefully under the same roof of the global economy, or more precisely, on the growing dependence — or perception thereof — of the U.S. economy ("jobs") on the international marketplace. The target was the "buy Japanese" system, upheld by laws and customs that made it very difficult for foreign capital to penetrate, and at the same time would have been considered illegal in the United States. Such was the point: to make it illegal, or at least untenable, internationally. In this context, doing business in Japan, opening markets, is a political as much as a market exercise: every "win" has a political component.

While in no capitalist country are corporate interests easily split off from their government partners, politics often acquires a dynamic of its own. A trade stand-off could degenerate into a conflict that would transcend the individual fortunes of U.S. or Japanese corporations, or of global financial stability as a whole. The problem of the U.S. trade deficit is not necessarily a problem for every major U.S. multinational, much less for financial conglomerates.

The transnational character of major corporate operations across the North tends to diminish the impact of sanctions, and may even make them counterproductive. Many Japanese conglomerates are tied in to their U.S. counterparts, and thus they have a powerful lobby at their disposal: Matsushita Electrical Industrial Co., a ready target of U.S. mobile phones sanctions, has protective partnerships with AT&T, General Motors, and IBM, while AT&T subscribes to a semiconductor agreement with the NEC corporation.

Also, many Japanese brand products sold in the U.S. are not in fact made in Japan, and some important U.S. exports to Japan (such as auto parts) are actually manufactured by U.S. branches of Japanese corporations. Prospective U.S. investors in Japan are also warned off by the rising cost of the yen, which was designed to cheapen the entry of U.S. goods and increase the price of Japanese exports. But the currency factor only stimulates the transfer of manufacturing operations from Japan.[13] As important was the diminishing tendency of Japanese corporations and investment firms to recycle their dollars directly into the U.S. economy, in effect financing the U.S. debt over most of the 1980s.

All of this meant that securing changes in the Japanese internal model was becoming increasingly vital to the well-being of the U.S. corporate economy. But systemic stability was also imperative, particularly to most U.S. corporations. Washington therefore would proceed to gamble, hoping to make gains on both fronts while risking disaster.

AN EAST ASIAN BLOC?

Many influential opinion-makers consider Japanese mercantilism the chief threat to domestic living standards and the global principle of open market access. Furthermore, there is an obsessive fear on the part of some U.S. officials that countries in East Asia may join forces in defense of the relatively closed export model, thereby thumbing their collective noses at neo-liberal multilateral trading rules as well as the U.S. presence in the region. "Don't think for a second these other countries aren't watching the outcome of this stand-off closely," warned one senior administration official.[14] Such a tendency would be reinforced by the shifting of Japanese domestic manufacturing capacity to lower-cost nations in the region, in order to escape the effects of the high yen, rising labor costs, and the possibility of U.S.-imposed sanctions.

But in fact, for all the talk of an East Asian bloc, there remains a fundamental ambivalence among Japanese policy-makers with regard to Asia. Some analysts attribute the ambivalence to a deep-seated intention of never repeating the mistake of the 1930s, when Japan made enemies of the U.S. and Britain in pursuit of its mission to establish a "co-prosperity sphere" free of Western influence. Such catastrophic "Asianism" is not to be repeated, and the constant reassurance by Japanese politicians of their special security ties with the United States is supposed to evidence Japan's unwillingness to lead Asia against the West.[15]

Making Japan dependent on the United States was a central part of Washington's post-World War II strategy. This entailed creating an economic sphere with facilities to draw Japan away from its dependence on East Asia. Oil, foodstuffs, technology, capital, as well as an open market were now to be provided by North America in an attempt to better shape the post-war economic and political development of the entire region, with Japan acting as linchpin. In effect, much of the East Asian boom has its origins in the U.S.-Japanese Cold War alliance, as U.S. military power and political influence help create conditions in which Western and Japanese corporations could invest in the region.

Economic buoyancy in East Asia, however, and the demise of Cold War security logic, spell a reordering in Japanese and United States linkages. In essence, the U.S. continues to be fiercely opposed to the development of an independent trading or security bloc in Asia. Japan was to assume a greater economic and security role in the world and in the region, but not in an independent fashion.

In the face of a changing political and economic relationship with the United States marked by increasing differences and growing "loathe America" sentiment, historical policies are also being reassessed. Some see a middle course being sketched out of a new U.S.-tolerated Japanese Asianism, one in which the U.S. maintains its police role and acts as counterweight to China. That is, a "lite" bloc could be created, but not allowed to become exclusive.

One critical problem with this scheme is that Japan itself would have to lead the way and restructure its own market system, and, in the light of the same pressing U.S. internal economic situation, also take up a greater quota of "burden sharing." Japan therefore would be expected to resist proposals calling for bloc formations exclusive of the U.S., opting for the U.S. vision of an inclusive "Asia Pacific" grouping as opposed to the competing concept of "Asia."

Impressive statistics indicating the sharp growth of trade between the U.S. and East Asia are taken by some to herald the advent of the "Asia Pacific century." Commerce, however, is not a reliable indicator of power shifts. And in a region as vast and diverse as "East Asia," sub-regional fragmentation and an overarching United States presence are two factors that must be taken into account when considering the rise of single or multiple trading blocs.

Of course, U.S. policy-makers prefer not to dwell on the military and political dimensions of the relationship and instead point to the hundreds of millions of potential credit card-holding consumers ready to pounce on U.S. goods and services. Thus the Clinton administration attributes to the once-obscure Asia Pacific Economic Cooperation (APEC) group a new level of strategic importance. This would all be part of an integration of the U.S. economy into a larger Asian grouping. For their part, some Asian officials play up to the rhetoric, inventing trans-Pacific voices allegedly terrified at the prospect that NAFTA should discriminate against their products.[16]

But greater expansion does not necessarily mean freer or fairer trade in the new U.S. lexicon, as Asians are forced to come to terms with the U.S. zeal for managed trade targets, and the adjustment of their national economic models to suit a global prescription laid down by the U.S. Some foresee a collective East Asian rebellion against managed trade backed by strong-arm pressure tactics, but this is not in the making. At present the inclination is still toward a greater distrust of Japan than of the United States. The argument is often heard that the United States wishes to withdraw strategically from the region but that a pressure to stay persists on the part of the countries in the region as a "guarantee" against a revival of Japanese militarism. What remains unchanged, however, is the maintenance of U.S. politico-military dominance in the Western Pacific in which Japan plays a continuing yet carefully measured role.

Although this situation could vary in the light of aggressive commercial behavior on the part of Washington, it would not change the fact that, by and large, U.S. capital and multinationals in general continue to be preferred in Asia over their Japanese counterparts, on account of alleged greater willingness to share skills, management, and technology. More importantly, the East Asian economies are not in a position to cut themselves off from the U.S., the first or second largest single market for their exports and a principal source of foreign investment. Japanese financiers are far from being able to match the ability of their U.S. counterparts to tap billions of dollars of U.S. institutional monies.

There is no "yen bloc" now or in the making and it is in fact the U.S. and the West as a whole, not Japan, that are drafting the rules of economic intercourse in the region, and specifically the rules of the booming capital markets. Japan, once touted as No. 1, has lost economic momentum, suffering in the aftermath of one of the deepest stock market and property value plunges in recorded history, amounting to some $6 trillion by 1994.[17] Its entire political structure has been rattled, which means that, for the near future at least, it is unlikely to challenge its role as a pliant junior partner of the United States.

The life-time employment system has been undermined. Japan has all but lost the crucial race for supremacy in the chip, aerospace, and high-definition TV fields. And the corroded Japanese financial system threatened to be overwhelmed by the same U.S. investment firms that were steadily outflanking Japanese financiers by pouring billions of dollars into the East Asian economies and even assuming the management of that region's own exploding wealth.[18]

To be sure, there is little happiness among non-Japanese Asian capital groupings in relation to Japan's chronic trade surplus and its hesitancy to open its domestic market. But governments in Australia, Malaysia, and South Korea have critized U.S. insistence on managed trade, and setting quotas favoring U.S. market penetration in Japan. "Politically-correct" purchasing in Japan entails diminished markets for similar imports from third countries: Japanese "Buy American" campaigns apparently have affected the sale of Australian-made auto parts, South Korean computer chips, and European luxury automobiles. Japanese officials accept that such is the case, perhaps exaggerating it somewhat. Nor are they above portraying themselves to China as that country's most reliable partner, never dreaming of mixing business with human rights questions.[19]

The Australian prime minister, Paul Keating, accused Washington of using a "heavy-handed sledgehammer to crack the nut." In reality, the nut is perceived in the United States, correctly or incorrectly, as central to the vitality of the U.S. economy — an issue which more than justifies the use of the sledgehammer. All the rhetoric of the Seattle APEC summit held in November 1993 does not hide the ambivalence felt among the East Asians.

The Malaysian prime minister, Mahitir Mohamad, refused to attend the summit out of anger at U.S. attacks on his proposal to create an exclusive Asian economic grouping. He warned that if APEC became a formal trade grouping, U.S. dominance would be detrimental to Asian interests.[20] Certainly, Asian corporate interests could suffer on account of unilateral U.S. insistence on guaranteed access for U.S. products and services to local markets, but many of those same interests would likely agree that the liberalized structural adjustment of internal national economic systems, also being demanded by the U.S., would afford greater costs than benefits.

The summit message, in this context, was much the same as that sent out after the NAFTA ratification to all nations, especially the EC: access to the U.S. market and admittance to the club depended on the adoption of the "right" economic policies as well as de facto recognition and acceptance of U.S. self-serving infringements to the free trade rule. Europe was thus pressured to ratify the GATT agreement on U.S. terms or else U.S.-led NAFTA and APEC would both turn hostile.

On the other hand, countries far advanced in the adherence to "open economies" and accommodation to the U.S. rules, such as Chile, which first initiated its economic "liberalization" under General Pinochet in the wake of his bloody 1973 coup, were to be placed first on the list to join APEC as well as NAFTA. U.S.-supervised liberalization in the Asia Pacific region is the guarantee that, if indeed as some claim the turn of the century is witnessing yet another westward swing in the center of economic power, the United States should still be at its core.

"U.S. future growth is tied directly to dynamism in this region," said the deputy U.S. trade representative. "We have to make sure that the U.S. is positioned to take advantage of globalization," said her chief.[21] Apparently moving away from its obsession with Japan, the administration increasingly placed greater emphasis on the new "emerging markets" in Asia and Latin America as the world's greatest potential consumers of U.S. goods and capital. "We're not abandoning our efforts with Japan, because we can't allow the world's second largest economy to have sanctuary markets," stressed the U.S. trade representative, Mickey Kantor. "But when we looked at the numbers, we saw where the action is, and it is in our own hemisphere and in Asia outside of Japan." In the heady days before the 1994 Mexican crash, which threatened to turn all emerging markets into submerging ones, Kantor went on to predict that U.S. exports to Japan would grow by nearly 70 percent, to $80 billion, by 2010, but exports to the rest of Asia would rise 163 percent, to $248 billion, more than three times as much. For Latin America, the projection was an increase to $232 billion, as opposed to $128 billion with the European Union.[22]

It was not simply a matter of taking advantage of globalization or the explosive growth of the "emerging economies," but rather of steering the process to the benefit of U.S. corporations and strategic interests. Moreover, it meant focusing the pressure on those regions pressing for reduced trade and investment barriers so that U.S. corporations would not only benefit but indeed help conduct the "emergence" — producing not only profits, but an increase in domestic employment levels so central to re-election prospects. And unlike Japan, the new industrial countries were in no position to resist U.S. pressure.

Just as important was the fear in Washington that the fast growing markets would not necessarily gravitate on their own toward a convergence with U.S. interests. They could gravitate toward rivals in Japan or Europe, or worse yet into protectionist regional associations. Herein lay the importance of active diplomacy and pressure tactics in order to institutionalize the breaking down of trade and investment barriers, and to do so in such a way that U.S. corporations were the principal beneficiaries.

This was not something that could be left to GATT/WTO: U.S. business could not wait, and it was the U.S. government and not a deliberately toothless world body that could define not only the pace but the scope of liberalization. APEC or NAFTA in this regard could be fronted by the United States to counterbalance the European Union. But APEC, unlike NAFTA, did not have the rules and guarantees so precious to the United States. Here the United States could also play Europe and NAFTA against APEC, exploiting the latter's fear of a world breaking up into closed economic blocs.

In fact, U.S. global strategy faced no deadlier antagonist than a closed regional bloc. What Kantor termed "sanctuary markets," such as Japan's model, were simply out of the question, particularly if those markets were rich and perceived as necessary to the well-being of U.S. multinational corporations. Over and beyond being able to open the markets was the concern that the sanctuaries could be used as launching pads for an autonomous global projection of economic power. Herein lay the "lesson" of Japan: the United States government and top corporations were determined to break the monopoly Japanese firms had in their home market, not simply for the sake of principle and profits, but also to deny the competitor the home base to generate protected margins of profit and independent technology which in turn could finance independent expansion abroad. It was therefore essential to undermine a model which emerging economies tended to emulate, to the detriment of U.S. globalism. There was no question therefore of letting up pressure on Japan, or on China for that matter, if those nations refused to accept the new economic marching orders from Washington.

According to the U.S. neo-liberal agenda, the entire world would be persuaded or forced to do business under U.S.-set trading and investment rules propitious to U.S. investment and exports. Supposedly, a "free trading" APEC and NAFTA would help break down the construction of a Fortress Europe. Emphasizing Japan's competitors in Asia would supposedly also prove productive to Washington in its dealings with the insecure Japanese. But the administration had fears and reasons of its own in regard to any emergence of an independent bloc mentality among the East Asians. The more advanced countries in that region were perceived to be moving along the perilous bloc path, as local economies were becoming too big to grow by simply exporting to the United States and Europe.

Increasingly they were selling and investing in each other, threatening to leave the United States corporations out of the picture, particularly if accompanied by bloc-minded attitudes reinforcing long-standing protective and governmental interventionist tendencies. The six ASEAN countries, in particular, were rapidly moving to create an internal free trade region by 2003, but it was not clear how open or liberal it would be with external parties.

The Malaysian government for one was pushing the idea of an East Asian Economic Caucus which was to exclude the United States, Australia, and New Zealand.[23] Some of the biggest investors in China were ethnic Chinese entrepreneurs from Hong Kong, Taiwan, and Southeast Asia. Japan's exports to Asia exceeded its exports to the United States, and investment multiplied, stimulated by the rising value of the yen.[24] China, on the other hand, seen by some as a future economic superpower, turned a deaf ear to U.S. demands to lower trade barriers or enact uniform investment codes and enforce copyright protection.

The United States therefore could not simply depend on progress in the WTO and await the rise of "free enterprise" consciousness at the national level in order to remove global barriers to corporate trade and investment. More threatening was the possible emergence of European Union-type fortresses in different regions which could challenge or at least stand in the way of the desired global economic system. NAFTA and APEC were not the same; the first was more tightly integrated and under control. The U.S. has no Japan to contend with in the western hemisphere, nor were most Latin American nations in an economic position to seriously contest the new order.

Unity, however, also escapes the East Asia Pacific area, a much more diversified region than Latin America. As with the Latin Americans, there were misgivings over a rising protectionist streak in U.S. policies accompanied by blunt "trade advocacy." Some governments fretted that Washington was pulling out strategically from Asia, leaving the region alone to deal with China, Japan, and each other. Others complained of Washington's overly aggressive political embrace. At the heart of the misgivings was the new U.S. proclivity to brandish threats in regard to commercial, human rights, and nuclear questions, claiming that the "free ride" of the Cold War days was now over and that countries desiring access to the market and the security blanket of the U.S. would have to pay in the form of open markets and contracts for U.S. corporations. In many Asian quarters, such behavior rekindled attempts to form an Asian bloc protective of their own regimes and markets.

Arguments are made that economic regionalism may succeed only when rooted in "common civilization" and that different civilizations are prone to conflict. Supposedly, then, Japan, unlike Europe, faces great problems in creating an entity comparable to the EU because Japan is a society and civilization unique to itself. Japanese trade and investment links with other East Asian countries would, according to this argument, never be strong enough to overcome cultural differences, thereby perhaps precluding EU or NAFTA style integration schemes.[25]

But in fact, it is the United States government and not cultural differences that so far has kept Japan from taking the lead in forming an independent regional grouping. Such an option lies fully outside the reference framework of traditional Japanese politics, which at all costs seeks to preserve warm political ties and a close economic relationship with the United States. Choosing subservience to the U.S. in regional and global affairs stems from an accurate perception that the United States would regard any exclusive East Asian economic grouping as a direct challenge to its power in the region. Proof of this is Washington's hostility to the proposed East Asia Economic Caucus as well as official Japan's formal distance from the scheme, notwithstanding considerable "unofficial" interest in the concept of a grouping which could entail the development of what could be the world's most dynamic economic powerhouse with pretensions of strategic independence.

This also helps explains Washington's unease toward China and its feverish inducement of growth policies that will lock that country's economy to that of the United States, precluding the rise of a new ideological, political, and economic competitor. So far, Chinese authorities have been consistent in giving more attention to attracting Western capital and technologies than in attaining military modernization, preferring to forge regional commercial links over military ones. Shared also is a sharp resentment over human rights pressure from the West, viewed by many in the region as more modern colonial attempts to "civilize" the Asians. Authoritarian regimes call for the protection of "Asian values" as a way of separating their capitalist ties to the West, yet fight off sometimes spurious and sometimes serious human rights attacks from the North.

Still, neither shared values or regional groupings per se are the problem, but rather whether the culture and economies are open to Western capital or not: the dynamism and potential of the "Confucian" economies, if loyal to the West's neo-liberal economic guidelines, are then seen as a huge opportunity instead of a threat. Certain Asian "values" are conveniently invoked to justify capital-friendly authoritarianism, while other "values" such as the "free" labor market are adopted from the West. Labor groups in Asia call for support from the North against their own state apparatuses' failure to provide minimal protection. The idea that rapidly expanding market economies can be slowed down to accommodate democratization has no adherents among either rulers and corporations, and "trade-offs" by Western governments over human rights issues in favor of commercial ones are also indicative of the general balance of forces. The common objective is to destroy old and new attempts at socialism, and not to interfere with the capitalist market-oriented design of the new global order.

Any conflict, therefore, would be a product of the clash not of civilizations but of a regional drive for a strategic and ideological economic independence incompatible with the long-standing and renewed

U.S. drive for dominance and control. Governmental rhetoric aside, the real battle line is drawn more in terms of pro-market and anti-market forces than between competing models of capitalist development. Defining models, values, and rights is the self-attributed prerogative of the dominant world power. Thus there need not be an inevitable ideological-cultural clash between the U.S. and Japan, because in the alleged global defense of "market democracies," the emphasis is on the market far more than on democracy.

Notes

1. "The Great Argentine Sell-Off, Part II," *Business Week*, February 6, 1995.

2. Robert Cox, *Production, Power and World Order* (New York: Columbia University Press, 1987), pp. 292-294; Leo Panitch, "Globalization and the State," *Socialist Register 1994* (New York: Monthly Review, 1994), pp. 84-86.

3. Quoted in David Peterson, "From Dominoes to Dynamos," *Z Magazine*, January 1994, p.7.

4. Shigeto Tsuru, *Japan's Capitalism: Creative Defeat and Beyond* (Cambridge, U.K.: Cambridge University Press, 1993), pp. 37-65, 72-77, 83-86.

5. Ibid., p. 183.

6. Such arguments are made by, among others, Chalmers Johnson in *Japan: Who Governs? The Rise of the Developmental State* (New York: Norton, 1995), and Lester Thurow in *Head to Head: The Coming Economic Battle Among Japan, Europe and America* (New York: Morrow & Company, 1992), pp. 113-151.

7. Chalmers Johnson, *MITI and the Japanese Miracle: The Growth of Industrial Policy, 1925-1975* (Stanford, CA: Stanford University Press, 1982).

8. Tsuru, *Japan's Capitalism*, pp.96-97. According to Tsuru, as opposed to the tendency of the Western corporation toward the dispersion of corporate ownership, "what is increasingly happening in Japan is the inter-corporate ownership of corporate equity shares either through mergers and acquisitions or as the continued legacy of the erstwhile *zaibatsu* ties." Independent giants such as Toyota only later emulated the agglomeration tendencies already undertaken by their *zaibatsu* and U.S. corporate counterparts. Ibid., pp. 187, 190.

9. See Peter F. Drucker, "Trade Lessons from the World Economy," *Foreign Affairs*, vol. 73, no. 1 (January/February 1994), and response by Mark Mason in *Foreign Affairs*, vol. 73, no. 2 (March/April 1994), pp. 177-178. A contrary view is that of Karl Zinsmeister, "Miti Mouse: Japan's Industrial Policy Doesn't Work," *Policy Review*, no. 64 (Spring 1993), pp. 28-35.

10. "The Trouble with Japan," *Economist*, October 1, 1994, p. 17.

11. Leon Brittan, "A User-Friendly Post-Round World," *New York Times*, April 15, 1994.

12. *New York Times*, March 4, 1994.

13. *Business Week*, February 28, 1994.

14. Ibid.

15. Nihon Kezai Shimbum, "Japan Looks to Asia," *Far Eastern Economic Review*, December 16, 1993.

16. See *Far Eastern Economic Review*, December 24, 1993.

17. "The $6 Trillion Hole in Japan's Pocket," *New York Times*, January. 21, 1994.

18. "Clouded Sun: Japan, Economically and Politically Ailing, Is Sinking into Gloom," *Wall Street Journal*, December 29, 1993; "Outflanked in Asia," *Business Week*, November 29, 1993.

19. *New York Times*, May 2, 1994.

20. *Far Eastern Economic Review*, December 3, 1993.

21. "Clinton's Asian Game Plan," *Business Week,* November 14, 1994.

22. "More Growth Predicted for New Markets," *New York Times,* November 4, 1994.

23. "A Dream of Free Trade," *Economist,* November 19, 1994; "APEC Nuts and Bolts," *Far Eastern Economic Review,* November 10, 1994.

24. "Asian Nations Wary on Pacific Trade Zone," *New York Times,* November 11, 1994.

25. Samuel Huntington, "The Clash of Civilizations?" *Foreign Affairs* (Summer 1993). Sharp counter-arguments are provided by Chandra Muzaffar, "The Clash of Civilizations, or, Camouflaging Dominance," *Just Commentary* (Malaysia), no. 5 (September 1993).

7

The "New" Europe

In 1995, those who dreamed of a Europe on its way toward rapid unification, with enormous economic and political potential, awakened to cruel realities. A seemingly endless war raged in the southeast portion of the continent; in the north Norwegians refused outright to join the European Union; and several Central European governments were politely told that their membership applications would be welcomed later rather than sooner. The only European common ground appeared to be record levels of unemployment, financial turmoil, and continued dependence on the United States government for military action in Bosnia. Hardly the characteristics of a rising global power.

Some may have recalled the post-World War II scenario. During those years the United States entrusted newly created multilateral organizations, such as the IMF and the World Bank, to assume direction over the post-war economic reconstruction of the western part of the continent, while directly assuming control over Germany's future and the "containment" of the Soviet Union. There could be no camouflaging the reality of U.S. dominance over the strategic, political, and economic rebuilding of Western Europe.

THE POLITICS OF ECONOMICS

Publicly at least there appears to be little inclination in Europe or in the United States even to discuss, much less to deal with, the political implications of a new German-dominated Europe. But there could be no hiding, for example, from the fact that, following the fall of the Berlin Wall, the Franco-German partnership, linchpin of the Western European economic and military alliance, came under severe strain. No longer did the French bureaucracy feel secure in its traditional role of directing the European political orchestra while Germany tended to building up its economy.

Neither British nor French officials were able to disguise their lack of enthusiasm over German unification, nor with later German proposals to turn the European Commission into a powerful executive body or for a "two-speed" process that would allow a "hard core" group of EU members to push for greater integration, leaving others behind. Under this scheme, drawn up in an August 1994 strategy paper presented by the ruling German Christian Democratic Party, Britain and southern European members would be relegated to second-class membership, on account of their projected inability to meet the agreed criteria to join the monetary union (ceilings on the level of inflation, trade, and deficit rates). Other member countries, including France and the Benelux nations, would move ahead toward integration, tying their economies even further to the German mark and neo-liberal economic orthodoxy.

No longer was the French elite convinced that the "pooling" of European sovereignties into a federal super-state would work chiefly to expand French influence on the continent and in world affairs. Germany now appeared as the eventual leader, especially if more German-influenced states from the East were admitted. France, supported by Spain, Portugal, and Italy, feared the competition for financial resources and political influence represented by the Eastern petitioners. They hesitated, therefore, to speed up the process of admitting new members (as demanded by the Germans) and insisted on placing ceilings on the amount of economic assistance to the ex-Soviet bloc. Observers called on Washington to take a stronger position in order to "help reassure Mediterranean countries that German influence would be balanced and that their concerns over North Africa would not be slighted."[1]

With Finland, Sweden, and Austria now members of the EU, the French were anxious to keep Bonn from refocusing the European Union's political center toward the East. The British government, Euro-skeptic as always, criticized tendencies to construct a "centralist Europe," and promised to veto any effort to change the Union's constitution. They feared proposed voting procedures which would make it difficult for a British-led minority to block legislation. Nor was London happy about giving major powers to the European Parliament or assuming a firm commitment to a single currency. Britain therefore supported EU expansion toward the East as a sure way of diluting political integration.[2]

But the essential question was whether a German "gaullism" was on the horizon, entailing the emergence of Europe as both a political and economic rival to the United States.

Indeed, German efforts to fill the East European political and economic vacuum fed such suspicions. Following the collapse of the Iron Curtain, hundreds of German companies relocated their assembly lines on the other side of the eastern borders, assuming control of "privatized" industries, particularly in the Czech Republic, where wages were only a tenth of those prevailing in Germany. Differences soon emerged between Germany's eagerness to incorporate at least some of the Eastern Europeans into the EU, while France remained cool to the notion.

With some 17 million people out of work in 12 European countries, pushing the issue of membership for the poor cousins in Eastern Europe was not a popular stand to take. Only with much coaxing was Germany able to get French approval for "associative" status for six Eastern European countries (Poland, Hungary, the Czech Republic, Slovakia, Bulgaria, and Romania), along with an opportunity for a "structured dialogue" over the terms of freer trade. Limits were imposed on key products such as steel, coal, textiles, and clothing, precisely their most competitive products.[3] The EU in this context threatened to become a perpetuator of the old East-West divide, in part to restrain German influence, but also to keep the new "South" from destabilizing the other half of Europe.

Neither the Spanish nor the Portuguese governments felt enthusiastic about the German-led shift of EU attention toward the East. No longer were these countries the most capital-friendly providers of low wages and long work weeks. Average wages for skilled manufacturing in the East were only half those in Portugal. As expanding European multinationals discovered new hot spots, direct foreign investment in Portugal plunged to $1.03 billion in 1994, after peaking at $2.28 billion in 1991, according to the Bank of Portugal, while foreign investment in Eastern Europe and Central Europe more than doubled to about $7 billion, according to the UN Conference on Trade and Development.[4]

German government officials complained that their European partners were not providing sufficient financial support for countries such as the Ukraine and Russia. Moreover, few of Germany's western neighbors seemed eager to eliminate tariff walls against key East Eastern European exports such as steel and textiles. Authorities in Brussels encouraged their colleagues in Poland, the Czech Republic, Hungary, and Slovakia with stories of the "irreversible momentum" to bring them into the EU as a reward for their transition to market economies. In practice, however, no important specific steps had taken place by the end of 1994, leaving the impression that admittance to the Brussels Club would not take place before well into the next century.

The reassertion of German power was a logical by-product of floundering EU efforts to make itself the center of transnational authority, ostensibly accountable to all and not simply to its strongest members. But because European Commission policies had to be decided by consensus, the result was a political paralysis on fundamental questions, such as the incorporation of Eastern European nations or the adoption of unified foreign and defense policies. Some exasperated members came to insist that integration and unanimity could no longer be reconciled, that majority rule should govern EU decisions, so as to prevent Great Britain from stalling the march forward, and not allowing any member to aspire to an à-la-carte scheme of membership, inside the union on some matters and outside on others.[5]

A federated Europe as demanded by Germany, or a Europe of nations as promoted by France? When a European policy and when a national one? How to separate political discussion from economic-monetary debate, when both are increasingly intertwined? The truth was that national mindsets of governments were not easily abandoned, at least in part because national bureaucracies had an interest in their own self-perpetuation.

In the final analysis, the EU was only as strong as its national governments' willingness to act on its resolutions — even assuming those resolutions were being incorporated into each country's national legislation to make them binding instead of leaving doors open for opting out of "Europe" in the future. In fact, a December 1994 survey indicated that not a single member state had adopted all 217 relevant laws under the single-market program. Denmark scored the highest with 207, Greece was the lowest with 165, and second worse was Germany with 180.[6] On other matters — passport, educational credentials, insurance policies, and public works procurement — national guidelines continued to prevail over regional ones, indicating that the EU was still far from becoming a genuine single market.[7]

The multiplication of EU mechanisms reflected how different European bureaucratic and corporate elites had not agreed on what they wanted and how to get there. Electorate disillusionment combined in many countries with local factors: fear of turmoil in the East, or worry that a strong Europe would undermine national identity, culture, and independence. At some point one of the two models would have to prevail, the federalist or the associative. Right-wing politicians pointed out that the federal model could not work if indeed new members were being added to the EU. A majority voting formula would then have to prevail, which could mean, for example, that the five largest states, with most of the population and wealth, could be placed in an "unacceptable" minority position.[8]

If a Union of some 15 members proved difficult to manage, one of 20 countries would be impossible. Voting formulas would have to be revamped. For example, on the Council of Ministers and in the European Commission, Germany had the same number of votes and members as Spain did, notwithstanding the huge differences in population and wealth. Germany had one EC vote for every 8 million of its citizens, and Luxembourg one for every 195,000: would tiny Malta, if it joined, also enjoy such privileged proportionality?[9]

Many of these questions, along with Germany's isolation, would become clear at the 1996 inter-governmental conference of the European Union. Such a gathering, likely to last several months, would set the stage for the German drive to both expand the EU eastward and deepen integration at the center.

One solution would be a Union "à la carte," with each member choosing what it wished to adhere to and what not. European corporations already subscribed to much the same viewpoint, applauding deregulation and chastizing welfare. The European Round Table, a group led by the heads of 40 European firms, issued a statement calling for the drafting of the European Charter for Industry to stand as a counterweight to the Social Chapter of the EU Treaty. Countries would continue to be free to ignore the Social Chapter's labor and welfare protections, yet enjoy "corporate welfare" in the form of subsidies which could add to corporate profits.[10]

But European governments felt limited in their capacities simply to abandon long-standing notions of public social responsibility. Would the broadening of membership also allow new transnational social bodies protective of workers, or could the EU simply remain a glorified trading association — the preferred British and U.S. option? Was there enough will and capacity to reinforce political institutions and financial integration in the West, while bringing in Eastern Europeans at the same time? Jacques Santer, the president of the European Commission, believed that if both goals were not accomplished by 1999, including the establishment of a single currency, then the European experiment could prove an historical failure.[11]

Other Europeans held that Germany's hidden agenda was to tie political and defense union questions to the single currency implementation. Such a German-drawn blueprint for Europe assumed that the German public and the Bundesbank could only be convinced to abolish the national currency in favor of a European one if there were concrete political and security stability guarantees. That is, to abolish one-country-veto power in the European decision-making process. German conservatives admitted that, for the moment, Germany could only lead "with others" and that this required European financial and political structures responsive and respectful of German power — a position which embodied what one observer described as "the contradictory German desire to simultaneously exert influence and deny leadership."[12]

EURO-SKEPTICISM

In short, the EU cannot escape social contradictions and the competing demands placed on governments and European bodies. Tensions arose between the social democratic and the neo-liberal approaches, as each envisioned a different role for the State in the economy and in assuring basic equality of opportunity for its citizenry. This was further compounded by the economic plight of East Europeans demanding closer cooperation with and eventual membership in the EU.

In the East, the stampede to free market fundamentalism, aside from provoking severe disruption of the economies and bitter battles for power and property, was in some way parallel to the struggle being waged in the rest of Europe to salvage what was left of the reformist states. The hope of many was that the creative destruction of capitalism could give way to, if not the old form of communist welfare, then at least its milder social-democratic counterpart.

A 1993 "White Paper" on restoring European competitiveness prepared by then-president of the European Commission, Jacques Delors, went beyond the orthodox stress on labor market "deregulation" to also insist on the necessary role of government in the creation of employment.[13] Under the Maastricht treaty's Social Chapter, for example, all companies in Europe employing more than 1,000 workers, and with 150 in at least two member states, were required to establish information and consultation councils with worker participation. But this was against the grain of the corporate drive to escape labor market "rigidities" (i.e., worker protection).

Monetary union in this context was not simply a matter of dispensing with currency exchanges, it was a question of insuring low inflation as well as the power to prevent politicians from resorting to "costly Euro-socialist ideas" such as the use of fiscal policy, including devaluation, to stimulate employment and borrow or redistribute incomes in order to retain some form of social safety net. The Social Chapter remained enfeebled, and Britain opted out of it altogether.

Pointing to rapidly climbing U.S. and Japanese inroads into "emerging markets," European corporations and government officials claimed that the welfare state was a luxury that could no longer be afforded; that lowering social benefits and the world's highest wage levels were the only paths to catching up with their rivals. Otherwise, Europe could find itself excluded from the new emerging markets. For corporations the stake was already high: 9.7 percent of total European assets in mutual funds were already invested abroad (as compared to 3.4 percent for the U.S.). Accumulating more profit at home in order to move abroad became a matter of urgency.[14] "If we don't," warned the director of foreign economic policy at the German Economics Ministry, "we run the risk of being inward-looking and missing the chance to improve competitiveness."[15]

One employers' association in Germany argued that if German workers had time off only as often as U.S. workers did, Germany's gross national product would grow by $100 billion.[16] But it was not simply workers' demands that stood in the way of greater profits at home and abroad; corporations were also at odds with the propensity of government bureaucrats to continue to think "national."

Farm subsidies absorbed some 50 percent of the entire EC budget, with another $7.5 billion approved by Brussels for the bail-out of various national subsidy-dependent airlines.[17] In these as in other cases, regional free trade did not necessarily contribute to the global liberal trading order demanded by the United States, since the benefits of internal liberalization did not extend to all newcomers outside the region. In that case, the regional agreement became an obstacle to U.S. globalization, which preferred no such regional deals, except those of its own making (such as NAFTA).

On the other hand, capital-hungry European corporations were being forced to go abroad, and specifically to the United States, to secure financing for their operations. This introduced a new element of uncertainty because stock-buyers in the United States did not follow the pattern of traditional corporation-shareholder relations in Europe. So called "investor-activists," in the form of pension fund managers and others, were upsetting old concepts of corporate governance. New funding through new mechanisms, as explained below, threatened to expose European markets and borrowers to the same stresses that Mexico and other "emerging countries" had faced. In Britain, for example, U.S. investors held 20 percent of all securities. Therefore there could be no hiding or shielding from global, or U.S. provoked, shocks.[18]

In the final analysis, arguments over free markets and regionalism, when put to a vote or referendum, invariably took second place to local social and economic concerns. No small amount of governmental rhetoric over the benefits of integration and free trade was directed toward an increasingly impoverished home audience, which was still not fully convinced that drumming up more business for corporations spelled more jobs and improved living standards.

Visions of a global prosperity mysteriously synchronized to benefit all countries and all people were out of tune with reality. The social divisions are there, but they are not simply between low-wage workers in North and South pitted against each other, but exist as well within countries, pitting the living standard of the privileged against the basic human needs of the many.

Each tended to interpret globalization and integration from their particular perspective, as each economic crisis drove home the question of how to deal with deep-rooted economic problems. By late 1995, governments and corporations gleefully pointed to signs that "recovery" was on the horizon and that overall corporate profits were at an all-time high. But in Europe, that same year, at least 16 million continued unemployed with an equal number underemployed. "Jobless recovery" was therefore not limited to the United States; vast social and political problems persisted in Europe, yet the corporate elites insisted that wages and state-mandated comprehensive health insurance, welfare, and unemployment benefits were still too large, leading Europe to price itself out of world markets.

Restoring "competitiveness" seemed to be on every businessperson's and bureaucrat's lips assuming as gospel the notion that there was no longer any room in Europe for reforming the management of capitalist society. The "Americanization" of the continent was entering a new stage, characterized by defeated labor unions and massive privatization, accompanied by the virtual banishment of social-democratic values of social responsibility for collective welfare and job security.[19]

In Eastern Europe, many of the social movements which had brought on the transformation in the first place were being bypassed by the parties and bureaucrats demanding integration with the West. New elites espoused a near religious adherence to the "free market," even though it became patent in most countries of the region that market forces, far from addressing the real problems in the economy and society, were only provoking new dislocations along with polarization. The transition from state socialism to liberal capitalism, in the midst of severe recessions and skimpy support from the West, threatened to pull Eastern Europe deeper into recession, in effect make it part of the South. Of course, this was not an unattractive proposition from the standpoint of visionaries and corporations in the West eager to appropriate markets and mentalities, as well as to insure access to a vast new pool of cheap labor.

FINANCIAL DISUNION

With the demise of the Soviet Union, some questions were raised about the continuing presence of the U.S. A decade earlier the Reagan administration's own self-centered manipulation of the international financial system pushed European governments to step up the creation of pan-European trade and monetary policies.[20]

By this time national economic policies had also been moving toward liberalization, as European capital itself needed to expand unencumbered by borders and multiple national regulations. There was corporate uneasiness over how individual countries were at the mercy of interest rates set in Washington, affecting capital flows and currency values throughout Europe. A bloc, however, was to hold its own internationally against the dollar, and some foresaw Europe becoming the strongest financial bloc in the world, attaining genuine economic power on a global basis. Then too there was the need to attract foreign investment on more favorable terms by offering the perspective of being inside an integrated market.

Others worried that in the absence of tough and unified European institutions and policies, the old continent would simply become a receptacle for United States technology and culture, lacking independent competitive abilities and even an identity of its own. Freer trade was not good enough, the ultimate goal was to construct a pan-European harmonization of macro-economic policies subservient to big business, leaving behind once and for all statist national development strategies of the 1960s and 1970s. Europe was said to require a currency union, common economic policies, and a broad political union so as to not become an appendage of the U.S.

The corporate-driven integration process, however, did not envision giving labor and local communities substantive participation in economic policy-making. This process was driven more by market forces than by social ideals. The emphasis in any case was on the enactment of a single currency controlled by an independent European central bank. Governments came into the picture in order to insure the "harmonization" of different national approaches in industrial relations, technological policies, and labor relations, until these matters were transferred to the hands of a European Commission. EC recommendations were ambiguous in this regard, attempting to cater to both the deregulation corporate urge but also introducing longer-term regional "re-regulation," much to the displeasure of the Anglo-Saxon neo-liberals who preferred that Europe become nothing less and nothing more than a totally deregulated free trade zone.

But a purely economic Europe would not make the continent a central actor on the world scenario, the very goal of Jacques Delors, former president of the European Commission. Under his scheme the new Europe would be a federal "organized space" between nation-states and the global market, with European-level powers over trade, finances, social, environmental, regional, and industrial policies.

Europe was to become, through the EC, the center of a regional bloc to supplement, or better yet, replace the old national systems of regulation, no longer up to the needs of corporate capital. The European Parliament, for its part, would be gradually endowed with greater political powers.

With the end of the Cold War, some of the political questions politely set aside arose with new vengeance and in a dramatically new context. Was the Community ready to have its own foreign policy, especially if the post-Soviet power vacuum in the East was exacerbated by the perception that the United States would also be withdrawing from the European defense scene?

The intentions of a newly reunited Germany were at the heart of every debate. Would the now largest and richest country in continental Europe continue to act as a congenial team player in European affairs, working with and through the European Union, or would it reassert Germany's historical "drive to the East," constituting itself as the new power center of the European mainland? What use would Germany make of its enhanced economic and political power? Would German transnational capital give greater priority to new investment in the East, including the old GDR, at the expense of its political and financial ties to other European capitals? The German answer was to expand influence toward both the East and West — if possible, without antagonizing either.

Superficially at least, the momentum toward deeper and wider economic integration seemed unstoppable. In January 1994, the European Economic Area came into being, creating the world's largest free trade zone, that spread from the Arctic to the Mediterranean. And one year later, Sweden, Austria, and Finland joined the European Union, which then encompassed 372 million consumers with a combined annual gross domestic product of $6.6 trillion.

Corporate capital eagerly supported monetary union in order to reduce the costs of doing business in multiple fluctuating currencies.

Pro-EU politicians saw the single currency as a means to foster greater political unity and to position a new pooled currency to better escape the ups and downs of the dollar. To prepare for the single currency, the Maastricht Treaty imposed agreements that budget deficits would not rise above 3 percent of gross domestic product and that accumulated debt levels would stay below 60 percent of GDP.

Germany was the main force defending the strict guidelines, lest its own jealously guarded monetary policy become hostage to the more liberal inflationary practices of some its neighbors. But, by the end of 1995 even Germany could not meet the tests, although the treaty states that at least 15 countries have to meet those standards by the end of 1996 in order for the single currency to come into being. Soon after passage of the Maastricht Treaty, the first financial round of instability forced both the British pound and the Italian lira to drop out of the currency grid. One year later, speculators went to work again, pushing the value of one currency against another and forcing officials to widen the parameters to permit greater percentage swings in value for any one currency. And in March 1995, both Spain and Portugal announced new devaluations.

Notwithstanding lip service to the goal of a unified currency and fiscal discipline, the political realities in the countries were different, and national priorities tended to be placed first. This included Germany, whose political and economic obsession with reunification and expansion to the East entailed costs and domestic monetary policies detrimental to the rest of the economies of Western Europe. Heavily interlocked European financial markets came to reflect the Bundesbank's decision to tighten monetary and credit reins.

Currency disparities were a reflection of national economic ones. The mark provided investors with a financial safe haven and protection under the wing of the infamous Bundesbank obsession with maintaining low inflation. Following the Mexican crisis and the collapse of the Barings Bank in March 1995, the mark reached its highest post-war value in relation to the U.S. dollar, thereby further straining other European currencies forced to keep up with the mark.

Corporate interests demanded greater harmony and cooperation from the national monetary authorities, but politicians were also forced to respond to recession-stricken industrial and agricultural sectors as well as to organized labor. Closer integration of monetary and fiscal policies as called for under EC agreements became all the more difficult to achieve: Europeans complained that the single currency goal and unity itself were hostage to the Bundesbank and the imperatives of German unification.

Germany's own tight money fight against inflation translated into a European-wide slump. In 1992 and 1993 speculators began to bet that other European countries would be forced to break free from the monetary and fiscal coordination scheme anchored on the Bundesbank's credit and interest policy. The result was that one European currency after another collapsed, forcing the German government to intervene massively to uphold the French franc and indeed the Franco-German alliance which stood at the heart of the European integration scheme.[21]

In short, the European Monetary System appeared to be floundering on the rocks of the costs of German reunification. Characteristically, German and European capitalists blamed trade unions for refusing to accept wage and benefits "constraints." But the reality was that noncorporate sectors in the European Union as a whole paid the costs of recession, provoking widespread social unrest. Not that the Bundesbank and the German government could be held exclusively responsible — corporate leadership throughout Western Europe continued to back the single currency notion, despite the price paid in social terms. Germany's financial decision-makers became Europe's de facto central bankers. This was less a matter of choice than of accepting the reality that financial markets and interests in Western Europe were transnationalized to the point of limiting the scope for governmental maneuvering to deal with recessionary tendencies.

Herein lay one reason for the diminished faith in the European Union's efforts toward economic and monetary union (EMU) before the end of the century. If only a few member countries met the required preconditions for the common currency and decided to go ahead, observers predicted it could be the beginning of the "two-tier" Europe.[22] Three monetary crises between 1993 and early 1995 convinced some that monetary unity was simply impractical. The British prime minister insisted that economic conditions in Europe were not yet ripe for such a dramatic step and that "it would tear the European Union apart."[23] Specialists increasingly claimed that deep differences among the economies, and the recurring need for particular countries to bend to internal pressures to devalue, made it nearly impossible to stabilize and align major European currencies as the prelude to the creation of a single currency by 1997.

Many of the same financial institutions clamoring for a single currency were also engaged in foreign exchange speculations. They hammered at perceived weaker European currencies, provoking periodic national monetary crises which further undermined the credibility of the rigid transition framework established for monetary unity. European markets were not immune to the repercussions of the 1994-95 Mexican financial crisis or the collapse of particular banking houses, which led investors to seek safe havens, such as German marks, while speculators bet other currencies down.

Traders "thought" European, but at times of market turmoil, fled the weaker currencies and stocked up on German marks. Bankers blamed politicians. According to one prominent financier, the global market was splitting Europe into two ranks of countries: those that adapted to the open global economy and those whose internal policies made them less attractive to investors. The social message was clear, in the words of the chief economist of one major bank in Brussels: "What the market is telling European governments, and what is not understood, is that it wants the welfare state reformed."[24] "Foolish promises of equal wages in less productive eastern Germany have to be cast aside," sentenced the *Economist*.[25]

The political difficulty in "converging" highly disparate economies was also in evidence on commercial questions. The European Commission in Brussels argued that article 113 of the Maastricht Treaty gave it the right to be the EU's sole negotiating body on trade issues. Most of the EU's individual governments disagreed, anxious to retain sovereignty and resist the Commission's claim. France, in particular, stubbornly resisted making national concessions over agricultural subsidies during the GATT negotiations, and even came to suspect that Germany was on the side of the United States on this issue.[26] Such stalemates weakened European bloc positions.

Larger forces were also at work. Cozy interlocking banking-industry ties in Germany and across Europe were being steadily undermined by technology and capital markets often dominated by United States corporations. In many cases it was European corporate capital itself which demanded the breaking down of barriers that would affect transatlantic links. One example was telecommunications. The U.S. government insisted on the opening of Germany's corporate telecommunication sectors, along with those of other European nations, demanding an end to monopolies. Yet the U.S. demand for speedy deregulation was supported by Deutsche Telekom, France Telecom, and the U.S. Sprint corporation, eager to jointly carry out a $4.2 billion cross investment, acquiring shares in each other's companies, in order to construct thousands of miles of fiber-optic cable in Europe and worldwide.

AT&T and MCI were busy forming alliances with foreign telephone companies to provide the same global voice and data fiber-optic communication services to multinational companies. The Clinton administration was fully behind the drive, even if it meant also allowing foreign companies to own networks inside the United States in association with U.S. partners. Sprint, however, was being forced to seek a waiver to Federal Communications Commission restrictions on foreign ownership. AT&T campaigned against the exception, claiming that French and German telephone markets remained closed to competition.[27] In the race among the big three corporations to spin alliances to capture the international corporate telecom business, regulations in each country held back the process.

In Frankfurt as well as London, U.S. banks were already strongly entrenched. As local exchange markets, traditional sources of capital, could not keep up with corporate demand, U.S. banks pressured European companies, forcing them into the U.S.-dominated equity markets. In Britain, U.S. investors thus came to hold some 20 percent of all securities. Important banking firms in Britain, such as Warburg, sought mergers with top U.S. firms such as Morgan Stanley in order to better tap into the U.S. markets.[28] Beginning in the late 1980s, New York investment banks with underwriting experience expanded their operations in Frankfurt, becoming a major force in the German bond market, overtaking most of their European rivals.

At issue was the size of United States capital markets and U.S. expertise in tapping capital markets abroad. Thus the greater the sum required, the stronger the possibility that a U.S. institution would act as co-lender. A large amount of the capital used to rebuild the economic infrastructure of East Germany and to expand eastward came from the United States or was channeled through U.S. investment firms. U.S. banks held three of the top ten rankings on the Frankfurt bond market, taking advantage of the boom in public borrowing.[29] There could be no regionalist or national escape from a U.S.-dominated globalization process.

Notes

1. "A Wider European Union," *New York Times*, November 11, 1994.
2. "Major Is Taking a Tougher Line on Britain's Links with the European Union," *New York Times*, February 2, 1995.
3. "Western Europeans Cast a Cautious Line Eastward," *New York Times*, December 9, 1994.
4. "Portugal Seeks Place in Another New World: The Global Economy," *Wall Street Journal Europe,* June 28, 1995.
5. See the editorials "Convergencia bis" and "Europa con Santer" in *El País*, July 17, 1994.
6. "European Summit," *Economist*, December 10, 1994.
7. *Economist*, January 8, 1994.

8. "European Federalism: À la Carte or Prix Fixe," *New York Times,* December 4, 1994.

9. "Europe's Diminished Leaders," *Economist,* January 21, 1995.

10. "Commentary," *Z Magazine,* February 1994, p. 10.

11. Interview in *El País,* February 19, 1994.

12. "Kohl's Heir-Apparent Offers Tougher Style," *Wall Street Journal Europe,* June 29, 1995.

13. *Economist,* January 15, 1994.

14. 1991 International Monetary Fund survey of 100 leading funds, quoted in *Far Eastern Economic Review,* January 1, 1995.

15. "Germans Finally Hop the Orient Express," *Business Week,* January 30, 1995.

16. "In Europe, Touches of Leanness and Meanness," *New York Times,* January 1, 1995.

17. See for example, "The Struggle to Keep Iberia Aloft," *New York Times,* January 14, 1995.

18. "Culture Shock for Europe's Boards," *Business Week,* January 30, 1995.

19. Daniel Singer, "The Triumph of Euroamericanism," *The Nation,* December 12, 1994.

20. George Ross, "Confronting the New Europe," *New Left Review,* no. 191 (January/February 1992), pp. 55-57.

21. "If the Franc Falls, So Will Europe's Dream of a Common Currency," *Business Week,* March 29, 1993.

22. See the opinions of the Austrian chancellor in the *Financial Times,* July 16-17, 1994.

23. "Major Is Taking a Tougher Line."

24. "The Financial Vigilantes Closing In," *Business Week,* January 30, 1995.

25. "Kohl or Scharping," *Economist,* October 8, 1994.

26. "The EU and Trade," *Economist,* October 1, 1994.

27. "F.C.C. Foreign-Deals Rules," *New York Times,* February 8, 1995; "Bonn's Telecom Bombshell," *Business Week,* February 13, 1995; "Telecom's 'Supercarrier, Deals Bureaucrats," *Financial Times,* June 28, 1995.

28. "Culture Shock for Europe's Boards."

29. "U.S. Banks Gain Ground in Germany's Markets," *New York Times,* November 25, 1994.

8

Building the Hemispheric Order

Until late 1994, Mexico was held up as the shining gem of neo-liberal market virtue in the Third World. The North American Free Trade Agreement was Washington's most celebrated step toward the creation of a new hemispheric and world order. Coming into effect on January 1, 1994, NAFTA was described by U.S. officials as the "benchmark" for free trade initiatives everywhere, beginning with the Americas. Little wonder: it was made to order for corporate capital, eliminating distinctions between national and foreign owned corporations, creating new corporate property rights, and overhauling an entire economic and legal structure especially so as to insure a regime that apparently fitted big capital like a glove.

In essence, NAFTA represents one of the first efforts to constitutionalize the neo-liberal new order. A "bill of rights" for capital designed to protect and insure corporate investment, expansion, and profit repatriation, coupled with the promise of governments and societies reorganizing themselves to fit the corporate mold.

The United States corporations secured more bilateral concessions from Mexico through NAFTA than it could ever have through any other legal instrument in any other period. The old order was unable to rein in so-called non-tariff barriers and subsidies for national production which, according to the United States authorities, kept many products out. Nor had instruments such as GATT or structural adjustment programs given much consideration to the trade in services — a United States specialty — or the protection of intellectual property.

NAFTA was therefore the extreme manifestation of the general GATT/WTO thrust toward transferring more power away from governments and toward investors and huge transnational corporations and financial institutions: a first step on the globalization bandwagon.

"We can't push the rest of the world to do what we believe is correct, but we can push the hemisphere to do so," stated Carla Hills, U.S. trade representative under the Bush administration.[1] "Correct" meant a peculiar mix of liberalization and protectionism measures designed to open Mexican markets to corporations and close U.S. markets to Mexican products competing with politically sensitive industries in the U.S.

Herein lay the best example of how "reforms" could be locked in to the benefit of U.S. capital and its Mexican partners, and in a way that gave U.S.-based corporations an advantage over their European and Japanese competitors, while guarding those same investments against possible reprisals from future democratic governments in Mexico.

For example, the property rights charter granted up to 20-year copyright protection to a vast array of trademarks, patents, semiconductor and industrial designs, and other trade secrets; the monopoly and state enterprises chapter required public bodies to operate "solely in accordance with commercial considerations," to refrain from using "anti-competitive practices," and to minimize or eliminate any nullification or impairment of investor benefits. According to one analysis, NAFTA in effect redesigned Mexican, Canadian, and even United States law in relation to capital, guaranteeing property rights that went well beyond those recognized nationally in each country. To judge by the ferocious effort of governments in each of the three countries to insure its passage, NAFTA highlighted the merging of bureaucratic and corporate interests on a transnational scale.[2]

In pre-NAFTA Mexico, social and economic polarization had worsened as a result of the economic crisis provoked by the end of the oil boom in the seventies. The fall in agricultural prices, the drastic cuts in government social spending, the destruction of collective contracts, the flight of capital and technological backwardness created a crisis for the entire Mexican corporate and one-party political structure. All of this heightened fear in the U.S. of waves of economic refugees.

But the Mexican governing elite thereupon initiated radical policy changes as part of a calculated strategy to obtain a new, and hopefully irreversible, link to the U.S. power structure that would shore up their domestic grip on power. Tariff barriers and financial restrictions came down quickly and unilaterally, making Mexico overnight one of the most open economies in the world. A delighted United States administration cheered the process and dusted off an old integration scheme designed to reward the Mexican elite, while locking in liberalization and the new orientation of the Mexican state. By that time, U.S. corporations were less concerned about trade (already considerably freed), than about lingering restrictions on foreign investment.[3]

It was also in Washington's interest to shore up and hopefully modernize an obsolete and isolated governing structure, beginning with the liberalization of the Mexican economy, accompanied by some political decentralization designed also to ward off long-standing skepticism in different U.S. circles. The gamble was massive on both sides: outright mortgaging of the country's economy while keeping political restructuring to the absolute minimum on the Mexican side: for the United States administration, this meant staking huge amounts of political and financial capital on the regime's ostensible capacity to "modernize." Both sides seemed determined to make Mexico the neo-liberal showcase of the modern world.

After all, Mexico was not to be confused with the rest of Latin America. The immigration question factored heavily in Mexico's relations with the U.S., especially since it was the chief concern in electorally sensitive states such as California and Texas. In the early 1980s, official U.S. analysts concluded that Mexico's internal situation represented the greatest potential threat to U.S. national security. As William Colby, former director of the CIA, stated: "The Free Trade Treaty is part of the new American security strategy."[4]

The Mexican corporate and governing elite conceived the free trade agreement as a hook to attract U.S. capital and technology. Mexico's government and corporations gambled that the drastic reduction in trade barriers — initiated in 1986 — and an official seal of approval from Washington would bring in desperately needed U.S. dollars to reverse the crisis and create dozens of millionaires in the process.

In the light of Western Europe's new focus on Eastern Europe and Japanese concentration in the East Asian countries, the Salinas administration concluded that the world was dividing into trade blocs, and Mexico climbing on board spelled full economic integration with the United States. Mexico was to enhance and institutionalize the rewards provided to U.S. investors by meeting virtually every conceivable demand of U.S. investors as well as the U.S. government. In effect, Mexico was to represent through NAFTA a new platform for global expansion.

One big reason for corporate confidence was that NAFTA provided a "more secure home base," more profitable and less subject to competition. A little-noticed mechanism in the agreement upholds high local content rules that favor companies operating within North American borders, that is to say the principal U.S. business interests. The mechanism in effect created a continent-wide industrial policy preventing Asian and European entities from competing on equal terms, unless they set up plants of their own and buy locally. Nissan plants operating in Mexico, for example, would have to secure at least 62.5 percent of their components from North American sources in order to be able to sell their cars in the U.S. or Canada. And the same holds true for a Mercedes Benz plant in South Carolina or Alabama wishing to send its products to Mexico or Canada duty-free. U.S.-based Zenith could look forward to a $4 million boost in demand for its TV picture tubes now that NAFTA would impose a 15 percent penalty on imports of these items, boosting U.S. demand by an estimated 4 million tubes per year.[5]

This protective, or "industrial policy," local content clause was deeply resented by Japanese and European (and local Mexican) automobile suppliers as well as consumer electronic companies. Mexicans would be driven out of business, while non-North American competitors would be forced to set up shop in Mexico. Established foreign manufacturers in the U.S. or Canada now had to purchase their components in North America in order to enter Mexico or Canada duty-free. Critics charged that the content rules amounted to a "Fortress America" attitude, but corporate circles responded that it was merely a replay of prevailing procedures in much of Europe and Asia. Said one U.S. executive: "If there are countries that want to protect their borders, at least we have a very large free trade zone of our own."[6]

Restrictions on foreign ownership of insurance companies, banks, and security firms were to be phased out. Critics charged that this would enable U.S. banks, through holding companies, to operate such firms in Mexico and then to offer these services back to the U.S., thereby evading regulatory legislation. Beyond the privileged access to the Mexican market, a more important gain for U.S. corporations was the ability to send lower-tech operations to Mexico — also undermining laws and standards in all three countries while keeping the higher-end jobs at home. The goal was to increase profits and gain an edge over foreign rivals. The edge, however, can only be temporary. Many Japanese and European producers made plans to shift operations to Mexico in order also to benefit from NAFTA.

Controlling Mexican politics was also on Washington's integration agenda. In a confidential memorandum from the U.S. ambassador in Mexico to the State Department, dated April 1991, Washington's policy expectations were openly expressed. According to the memorandum, the treaty signing was to be a form of consolidating and guaranteeing "continuity in the economic policies" of President Carlos Salinas, even after his term of office was over. It was to be an instrument "for continued pressure, in order that the opening to foreign investment extend even more," and it would become a manner of "institutionalizing acceptance of a U.S. orientation in Mexico's foreign policy."[7]

For the Mexican business elite, turning their country into a virtual protectorate of the United States was a small price to pay for becoming a privileged haven for U.S. investors and a first-class export base to that country. There were millions to be made in business propositions, speculations, rigged bidding in privatization schemes, brokerage commissions, as well as outright influence peddling. Then too there was the implicit U.S. commitment to upholding the authoritarian one-party rule. On both sides, therefore, NAFTA appeared as an unbeatable proposition, correctly gauging the strategic character of the U.S. government's new commitment to Mexican economic "stability" and market reforms, reinforced — as in the case of Canada — with "anti-dumping" or "subsidy" clauses allowing U.S. industries to cry foul if competition was too acute.

Mexico and NAFTA, in turn, were the models for the rest of Latin America to follow — at least until the near collapse of the Mexican financial system at the end of 1994. Most other Latin American governments and technocratic elites were also devout followers of the "reform" school, clinging to the belief the NAFTA was the first U.S. step toward liberalizing access to its commercial and financial markets.

The logic was simple: the United States needed markets and Latin America needed investors. Free market and trading reforms ostensibly would be the key to meeting both requirements. "The United States needs 450 million guys [sic] down there with credit cards," said the president of Bolivia.[8] Latin America was the only major region in the world with which the United States could show a steady surplus — some $5 billion alone with Mexico, where U.S. firms already controlled some 70 percent of that country's imports and absorbed 76 percent of its exports.

Mexican tariffs on U.S. goods fell from 100 percent in 1981 to 10 percent in 1994. For nearly half a century, Mexico had resisted U.S. pressure to "liberalize" its economy. Integration began in 1967 when Mexico allowed U.S. companies to assemble components across the border for exclusive re-shipment to the United States. Taking advantage of the 1982 debt crisis, the U.S. obtained further concessions, pushing Mexico to sign GATT in 1986 to further lower barriers, to be followed by the market-opening frenzy and finally NAFTA, sponsored by the Salinas administration. U.S. corporations — joined by their Mexican and Canadian associates — were now legally and politically set to enter alliances, tap a larger market and enjoy lower costs, particularly in highly profitable and growing fields such as tele-

communications, financial services, insurance, and possibly oil interests — all previously restricted to Mexican nationals. As for industrial
firms, integration spelled transplanting lower-tech operations to Mexico while keeping higher-end components at home. The objective in
all cases was to move in fast, reduce costs and gain an edge over rivals, not only in Mexico but in the U.S. and global markets.[9]

Business enthusiasts dreamed of a huge Latin American sponge,
following Mexico's example of soaking up U.S. goods and capital by
way of U.S. financiers and intermediaries, which could also steadily tap
into new local capital markets."Free traders" North and South proudly
pointed to the tripling of private U.S. investment in Latin America
over the course of the 1980s. Indeed, on the subject of free trade and
integration the Latin American pupils seemed to be racing ahead of
their traditional teacher, as salesmen-presidents across the continent
were all hustling business and promoting their own sub-regional integration agreements.

Prevailing logic among governing technocrats was that Latin
America confronted trading blocs in Europe and Asia, with another
in the making in the form of NAFTA. All of this heightened the urge
to cave in to U.S. demands in order not to be left out. Heads of state
meeting in Colombia in June 1994 promised more privatization of
state companies, improved "legal security for investors" and the promotion of Ibero-American countries "as attractive places for foreign
investment," calling on the United States to adopt policies of "open
regionalism" which would not preclude other continental nations
from joining NAFTA.[10] For the United States, however, structural
adjustment programs, including liberalization of capital movement
and protection of foreign investment and intellectual property rights,
were also preconditions for eventual integration into the NAFTA
family, the so-called "NAFTA readiness" criteria.

More than simply providing immediate security and advantage to
U.S. capital, NAFTA was the staging post for the U.S.'s global "market enlargement" strategy. Mexico needed to be presented as the
country which proved that capitalism worked, where state-controlled
or directed economies had failed.

NAFTA, moreover, was employed by the Clinton administration
as an effective bargaining weapon against Asian, European, and other
Latin American countries to win further capital-friendly concessions.
Washington's message was clear: further "market reforms" were the
precondition for other countries wishing to join NAFTA or negotiate
a similar trade accord, to maintain equitable access to the U.S. market, or to avoid the diversion of investment flows to Mexico.

Concerns over NAFTA induced a number of Asian countries to push their own free trade zone including the U.S. The EU in turn became more accommodating toward the United States to prevent U.S.-led trade blocs from becoming stronger and exclusive. At the APEC summit in December 1994, the U.S. further drove home the point, virtually pushing environmental and debt concerns off the agenda.

"The Europeans will be encouraged, to use a delicate word, to be more open in a number of areas we have been concerned about," said the U.S. trade representative. "And the Asians will also be encouraged to go in this direction, or they too will be left behind."[11]

Washington's stated assumption was that full conversion to free market order in other continents would also turn trade deficits into trade surpluses. Exports to Latin America had gone from $30 billion in 1985 to $79 billion in 1993, supposedly creating some 900,000 jobs in the United States. U.S. officials predicted that "full liberalization" would allow the U.S. to triple the level of exports, reaching some $290 billion. In this way the western hemisphere was to become the most important market for U.S. products, absorbing some $12 billion of the $20 billion in new exports generated between 1993 and 1994, 38 percent of all sales and representing 44 percent of all Latin American imports. To boot, Latin America was the only region in the world with which the United States had a trade surplus, including the lucrative high-tech category, allowing U.S. corporations to further entrench their competitive advantage. As for U.S. direct investments, the increase was 400 percent between 1983 and 1993, from $24 to $102 billion.[12]

A crucial component of the new liberalization drive was to establish a single international investment code along the lines of those "free market gems" such as Mexico and Chile. For Washington, free trade pacts were less a matter of commerce than of investment and protection of corporate rights, including guarantees on the country's capacity and obligation to service its debts. Economic and legal structures were thus overhauled unilaterally as local regimes and business leaders staked their political and personal fortunes on the free market reforms expecting a matching duty-free integration into the U.S. market along with favorable ratings from Moody's and Standard & Poor to attract big time investment.

By 1995 the United States government promises of guaranteed market access to Latin America became as hollow as earlier ones about substantive debt relief. The November 1994 congressional elections reinforced doubts as to the administration's political capacity to deliver, particularly as legislators reflected increasing constituent insecurities with regard to free trade. U.S. corporations continued to benefit from the new political and investment climate, but the only visible rush was on the part of Wall Street in the form of portfolio short-term "hot money" searching for quick profits.

GATT potentially covered the globe, but in the U.S. view did not sufficiently dismantle national investment and trade barriers, while in other clauses it could make certain U.S. practices liable to penalization. Pet U.S. formulas could best be pursued on a regional basis, playing on one region's fear of being excluded from the vast U.S.-NAFTA market. Under U.S. prodding, for example, APEC went further than GATT, because at the Asia Pacific summit meeting in November 1994 member countries proclaimed a "commitment" to achieve "free and open trade and investment" in the region by the year 2010 while the industrial nations were to do so no later than 2020.

For all the talk of community and democracy, Washington's essential purpose at regional gatherings was to break down barriers that prevented U.S. companies from selling and investing more in the "emerging economies." Because most Latin American governments had already dismantled most barriers, U.S. officials proudly exhibited the hemispheric "open market" example and NAFTA's privileged access to the U.S. market as its logical reward. Washington warned the Asians that their investment liberalization codes did not go far enough in the NAFTA direction, and that as a result they could not count on open markets in North America unless they followed the Latin American example of abandoning long-standing "discriminatory" schemes, including government incentives and protection to domestic industries competing with U.S. ones.[13]

Such multi-continental cajoling went hand in glove with corporate industrial strategy of lowered costs and increased profits through dismembering production processes among diverse "market reform" countries. That is, making different parts in different countries, then supplying all others, taking advantage of the strengths (or weaknesses) of each one, making particular regions and the world at large a more attractive place for doing business.

The full weight of U.S. governmental and corporate power could more easily be brought to bear when negotiating bilateral or regional economic agreements. This meant that vague (GATT) or non-binding (APEC) declarations could be made binding and specific, covering an array of items — particularly services and intellectual property — so dear to U.S. interests. U.S. officials calculated that NAFTA-

Latin America could initiate a global momentum whose pace would accelerate as corporations and governments abroad signed on out of fear of being shut out or simply beckoned by new capital-friendly norms to make NAFTA and not the European Union the building bloc model of a new pro-U.S. world order.

The point was to make free trade (and free investment) a global reality, something GATT was supposed to have accomplished but had not after 45 years of existence. The Asia Pacific region plan was to achieve that goal in 25 years and in the Americas in ten. Sub-regional and regional blocs would then begin merging, bringing the world (and a skeptical U.S. domestic constituency) closer to meeting the corporate nirvana. Thus toward the end of 1994, the administration could claim having reached vague free trade understandings with both regions, without having to make a great many concessions in either case. In this way the U.S. corporate elite was to gain an edge over its European competitors and further pressure Japan and others to recast their economic models.

In principle, the sub-regional trading organizations — Mercosur, the Andean Group, the Central American Common Market, the Caribbean Community, the Group of Three (Colombia, Venezuela, Mexico) — committed themselves to liberalization. According to World Bank and Washington reports, sub-regional blocs in Latin America, Asia, or Africa could become catalysts for the dismantling of trade and investment barriers. But in Latin America as elsewhere common elite ideological adjerence to "free market" principles did not entail political harmony. There were always internal social pressures, competing economic interests, and political rivalries. Peru and Ecuador fought a border war. Argentina and Brazil competed for regional influence.

Mexico for its part was not eager to share its special access to the U.S. market, otherwise it would cease to be special. Caribbean and Central American nations complained that NAFTA made their exports less attractive than similar ones from Mexico in the U.S. market. And practically all grumbled that U.S. portfolio investors now preferred Mexico over the rest of the region, unleashing a feverish competition as one country vied with the other in order to offer capital the highest possible benefits at the smallest possible gain for labor. The story was somewhat different in regard to corporate direct investments. There top U.S. corporations went in for the long run and invested hundreds of millions, chiefly in Mexico and Brazil, to take advantage of opening internal markets and sub-regional breaking down of trade barriers.

U.S. negotiators bluffed that if others wished to play the regional bloc game, they did so at their own risk. Regional and global strategies were one and the same: the enlargement of the global market was possible because the U.S. has its own bloc.

The objective is to lower barriers to capital by raising barriers to government action, to renounce the regulatory power of the State, transfer decision-making to the private sector, both domestic and foreign, so that no major economic decision could be taken without consulting Wall Street and Washington, thus setting limits on any present or future government's capacity to promote non-capitalist or nationalist schemes. Instead, nations and regions are forced to adopt new "economic constitutions" institutionalizing market reforms, especially the holy trinity of privatization, deregulation, and liberalization of trade. Here again Latin America excelled. The removal of virtually all restrictions on capital flows in the region attracted huge amounts of private capital — $170 billion alone between 1990 and 1993, most of which went to Mexico and Argentina — helping to finance an import boom which in turn chiefly benefited U.S. firms. U.S. exports to Mexico grew three times faster than U.S. exports to the rest of the world, jumping 20 percent between 1993 and 1994, and allowing Mexico to surpass Japan as the second largest consumer of U.S. products (after Canada). Overall, NAFTA gains in trade were more than double the gains with Europe and Asia. Two-thirds of Canada's imports came from the U.S., while U.S. purchases accounted for 25 percent of Canada's gross domestic product.[14]

Despite higher exports, however, the trade deficits and balance of payments problem continued to afflict most of the region. As the result of "reform," the rich got richer, but at the end of the decade there was little evidence that the poor had benefited from "integration." Canada's inclusion in NAFTA was due to its fear that a treaty between Mexico and the United States would have negative effects on U.S. investment in Canada and, in the medium term, could negatively affect interchange with the United States.

As the result of an earlier agreement with the United States, numerous Canadian agricultural enterprises had gone into bankruptcy, 150,000 Canadian workers were made jobless, while U.S. control grew over energy resources and the banks, and a prohibition on subsidies by the Canadian government devastated cultural sectors and public media.[15] One leader of Canada's New Democratic Party emphatically declared in 1991: "The experience of two years of free trade with the United States has led us to understand that only one country will come out of this trilateral accord victorious: the United States."[16]

Canadian exporters and investors sang the praises of the trade agreement and spoke warmly of U.S. efforts to expand the pact. But with an economy one-tenth the size of the United States', there was a lingering feeling even among Canadian government officials that the expanded level of dependence on the United States was not in Canada's long-term interests, particularly when U.S. corporations still accused Canada of "unfair" trading practices, dumping, and cultural protectionism. By 1994 the United States had come to absorb 84 percent of Canadian exports, as the two countries came to share the largest two-way trade in the world, some $300 billion in 1994, or 20 percent more than the business the United States did with Japan, its second largest trading partner.

Prime Minister Jean Chrétien, whose party had earlier opposed the free trade pact, proposed in December 1994 the negotiation of a free trade agreement with the European Union in order to achieve what the trade minister described as "a more balanced negotiation framework."[17] Canadian suspicions were that the U.S. wished to make itself the hub of a broader economic network and would proceed to cut free trade deals with major South American countries inimical to Canadian interests.

In the United States, the social costs of NAFTA became apparent even before the collapse of the peso in December 1994. High-tech companies in the U.S. had increased profits and exports without hiring new employees. Imports from Mexico, including from U.S. companies based in that country, had also displaced jobs. According to a U.S. congressional committee, NAFTA had caused a net loss of 10,000 jobs and more than 36,000 workers filed claims of job losses on account of the trade accord.[18]

In Mexico, the local elite insisted that larger markets and the increased competition resulting from trade liberalization would create strong incentives in favor of investment, modernization of production, and technological innovation. Massive portfolio investment, however, chiefly produced profits and opportunities for local stockbrokers and intermediaries. And new direct investment tended to concentrate in the larger countries and industries already enjoying some level of development and a sizeable market. Moreover, many Mexican products were still denied full and free access to the U.S. market, including textiles, clothing, sugar, beef, and steel.

In the United States, labor organizations and certain business sectors became concerned that unregulated trade and investment flows, especially between the U.S. and Mexico, meant job losses, relocation of industries to Mexico, and a downward pressure of wages in the

U.S. For their part, environmentalists and consumer advocates feel that the health, conservation, and safety standards that have been won through decades of struggle will be endangered by NAFTA. The fear is that the lowest common denominator — downward standardization — would apply across the entire region because the agreements emphasize capital over living standards. Mexican workers received lower wages than their U.S. or Canadian counterparts, but also did not enjoy the benefit of effective laws to insure health and safety standards. Nor did NAFTA contain mechanisms allowing Mexican workers to resist repressive, low-wage corporate strategy. At the same time, there was a fear that U.S. investment would also seek pollution havens in order to take advantage of the absence or lax enforcement of environmental laws.

Free trade policies went beyond commercial questions in order to undermine the legal and democratic capacities to regulate investment and the profit repatriation process. In NAFTA's case, power is transferred to unelected institutions such as the North American Trade Commission, heavily influenced by corporate financial interests, with the power to make decisions that can extend the scope of the free trade agreement in areas that infringe on the nominal powers of elected governments.

Some purists asked whether NAFTA did not undermine free trade principles. There was no such confusion among corporate leaders, tired of unenforceable global commitments to liberalized markets while countries shut out entry through non-tariff protective devices and violated intellectual property rights. None of this was tolerated in NAFTA, which is why the president of the Pharmaceutical Manufacturers Association believed that "NAFTA — not GATT — sets the standard for future international intellectual property agreements."[19]

Technocratic U.S.-trained elites in the South, ideologically committed to the free market, and beholden to the U.S., did not have to be convinced of the "need" for market reform measures that are not, as some of the literature would have it, "imposed" from the outside. What was actually negotiated with international financial institutions (under Washington's watchful eye) were the terms and timetables of reform implementation, not its fundamentals. Promises of balanced budgets, cheap and disempowered labor, bargain prices on state property, etc. were all means of luring U.S. investors, obtaining needed loans as well as making the nation as a whole a worthy prospective for a bilateral trade arrangement.

Governments continued to be necessary, not as a counterweight to capital but rather as a subordinate partner and enforcer. Privatization took the form of allowing politically-connected interests to acquire assets at artificially deflated prices. Moreover, the acquisitions could be financed with World Bank or AID funds. But what goes around comes around. To be eligible for the pay-offs, governments must show adequate compliance with structural adjustment programs as dictated by the IMF or the World Bank, and subscribe to debt payment agreements with commercial creditors. Rigorous compliance, including tight spending on social programs, also helps assure early preferential access to the U.S. market.

All one had to do is follow the example of Mexico (until the default crisis of December 1994) or Chile, with its "exemplary" restructuring changes in its legal and economic system, faithfully initiated under the murderous regime of Augusto Pinochet, to see the potential. Yet the U.S. administration is fully aware that there is no acceptance in Congress of an unending chain of bilateral trade accords, particularly after the sharp battle waged over NAFTA. Nor is it the intention of the U.S. government to subscribe to agreements indiscriminately, but rather to maintain the illusory carrot of free entry into the U.S. market to "stimulate" the adoption of adjustment plans in the nations of the region, insisting on "framework accords" that allow Washington to dictate control over the organization of the "liberalization" process.

In fact, the United States offers very little in return. The reality is that the administration cannot guarantee approval of any treaty, as long as protectionist pressures carry weight in Congress, such as the fear that unemployment will rise. Approval requires that the U.S. administration decide to invest political capital, not always within its reach, particularly in times of recession and, above all, elections. Toward the end of 1994, Congress effectively denied "fast-track" negotiating authority to the president. This further underscored the lack of a level playing field and the enormous disparities in power. What became apparent then was that most Latin American and Caribbean governments would simply compete with each other to offer U.S. and foreign investors the most attractive, that is to say lowest, labor and environmental standards for them to do business.

The only binding commitments in regard to Latin America are those which have been signed with Mexico in the form of the NAFTA treaty. Under its terms, all tariffs and import quotas would be eliminated within fifteen years. Non-tariff barriers to free trade, including product safety standards, would be subject to a tri-national panel of judges. Lip service was paid to labor rights, workplace safety, and consumer protection, while environmental ones, after much pressure, became loosely accountable but not enforceable. Not so with regard to commercial and investment matters, for which automatic transnational legal oversight and appeal is assured in cases of corporate protests.[20] In this way these corporations are given new and permanent rights and securities, sometimes more favorable than those provided to domestic capital. In a word, NAFTA amounted to a bill of rights for U.S. corporations, a clear example of U.S. determination to sustain hegemony as a state in a world increasingly shaped by the forces of global integration of finance and production.

Assuring U.S. corporations and capital a permanent opening was one thing, but being able to guarantee that Mexico could sustain sharp increases in imports and debt repayment was quite another, particularly if foreign investment tapered off. Yet the technocratic assumption was that the same capital attracted by integration would pay for it, and brokers on both sides of the border went to work selling paper to that effect and earning handsome commissions in the process. No rate of interest seemed too high to meet, just so long as the buying spree continued. Problems of mounting debt and trade imbalances would simply be met by competing for more capital, offering higher rates to portfolio investors, and low cost working conditions and minimal regulations to direct investors.

A Financial Bosnia

The liberalization model presupposes that export markets and foreign investment would materialize in such a way as to offset social costs while promoting rapid economic growth. Once again, Mexico was cited as the "how to do it" private sector-led model. Instead, or as a result, after ten years of structural adjustment programs, Latin America attained the distinction of having the widest income gap between rich and poor of any region in the world.[21] A massive infusion of private funds and hyper-liberalization took the Mexican system to the breaking point, provoking campesino rebellions in the south of the country, panic in Washington, and chaos on Wall Street.

U.S. political pressures to reform the system only served to create further internal fissures, some of which took the form of high-level political assassinations. Rebellions and murders provoked a capital flight. With vast amounts of short-term dollar debt falling due and virtually no reserves, the peso was devalued in a bungled manner in December 1994. Panicky private investing agencies jumped out as fast and as massively as they had jumped in, their confidence shaken not only in Mexico, but in all "emerging countries." The result was a financial crisis of global proportions, unprecedented international bail-out schemes, and an attack on the dollar itself, underscoring the dangers of the Mexican model in an era of global capital markets.

For ordinary Mexicans, the tearing down of tariff barriers was followed by a 30 percent drop in per capita consumption of basic grains, the result of shrinking real wages and increased unemployment. Small and medium scale business bankruptcies, the squandering of foreign currency on luxury imports, and the multiplication in the numbers of millionaires in Mexico were also by-products of "free trade." Dependence on food imports increased while the national agricultural sector suffered irreparable losses, unable to compete with large, U.S. agribusinesses which, unlike their Mexican counterparts, had continuing access to handsome government subsidies. The same held true with regard to hundreds of small and medium scale businesses.

Much more than economics was involved: "integration" spelled acceptance of new norms in regard to production, culture, education, and even language, along with ecological standards, union practices, and the organization of the military. In the countryside it spelled the uprooting of traditional ways of life, and the overturning of the already meager means of agricultural subsistence. It was the straw that broke the camel's back.

In late 1994, the massive devaluation of the peso brought the country to the brink of insolvency and default. Although the U.S. political, corporate, and ideological investment in NAFTA was such that it launched immediate efforts to bail the country out, the same treaty provisions barred the Mexican government from taking measures to protect itself. Its response to the crisis rather was to further hock the country by speeding up the sell-off of transportation, communications, and financial services to foreign investors, turning over oil export earnings directly to the U.S. Treasury, and taking up massive new borrowing at high commission rates, forcing domestic credit rates up to 75 percent a year, provoking massive unemployment and widespread bankruptcies.

According to bankers and bureaucrats on both sides, the economy would have to contract brutally in order to be saved, wiping out savings, sending hundreds of thousands onto the streets, in order to qualify for a bail-out package to pay-off short-term bonds sold recklessly over the course of the preceding months.

Many wondered whether the cure was not worse than the illness. But this was part of the logic of the Washington-IMF plan to reassure short-term investors that Mexico could repay them, that tighter U.S. supervision was at hand and therefore money could safely be kept in that country. The U.S. government provided the dollars for the Mexican government to pay back foreign bond holders who, instead of re-investing, simply left Mexico altogether and took their funds back across the Rio Grande.

On the other hand, the large corporations, not new at this sort of game and having long learned how to shelter and even enhance earnings during currency upheavals, benefited from reduced production and labor costs. Some even stepped up investment, taking advantage of cheap peso prices and the desperate sell-off of Mexican state holdings as well as the bankruptcy of many Mexican businesses.[22]

Precisely because cheap labor constituted Mexico's chief comparative advantage, wages could not be allowed to keep up with spiraling prices. Real wage levels had steadily diminished in Mexico since 1984, and with the collapse of the peso, they took another sharp plunge. Mexican authorities did not need to be reminded by the U.S. government and foreign investors that workers' demands for higher wages were incompatible with low inflation and tight monetary policy. Inexpensive labor continued to be Mexico's permanent and humiliating contribution to the North American bloc.

After the peso crash, the U.S. government, reflecting Wall Street anxiety and acting on its behalf, assumed direct control of Mexican monetary and fiscal policy. Officers from J.P. Morgan virtually dictated the negotiating terms for the bail-out package to the Mexican government. As *Business Week* stated, "Mexico has reverted to its traditional role as a ward of the United States."[23]

But enhanced Washington control over the Mexican government did little to stabilize the situation in that country or on world markets. Neither the U.S. Congress nor most U.S. allies responded to the Clinton administration's call to close ranks and provide funds. The call itself was confusing: on the one hand, panicky bureaucrats practiced what one legislator called "economic blackmail," warning that not only Mexico but stock markets around the world would crumble in the absence of a bail-out, a domino or tequila effect that could bring down the entire international financial network. Panicky investors, on the other hand, also attempting to salvage what they could, portrayed the peso crisis as a mere bump in the road, an irrational overreaction by market forces.

Business journals joined the clamor that all the fundamentals were "right," it was simply the market which was jumpy. The reality was that bureaucrats, brokers, and many economists had all become part of a market network geared to sustaining Mexican profit-generating capacity and political stability; in short, the entire NAFTA scheme. Objectivity therefore was suspect in virtually every case.[24]

From the U.S. administration's standpoint, NAFTA was necessary for strategic reasons, specifically to prevent a violent breakdown in the Mexican power structure that could have sent millions of Mexicans pouring over the border. Some Mexicans wondered what would happen if indeed the rescue plan did "work" — whether the terms demanded of the Mexican government and people could still provoke even greater social and economic dislocation, severely damaging the neo-liberal model it was designed to save.

The Mexican textbook economic restructuring, so copied and praised as a success story among other Latin American corporate and bureaucratic elites, did after all offer lessons as to the fragility of free market modernization. When the indigenous rebels of the Zapatista National Liberation Army fired a few shots and threatened to resume hostilities against the Mexican government, stock investors began retreating, trading in their pesos for dollars, losing all faith in the Mexican regime. The largest bail-out packages ever assembled for any country were barely able to stem that retreat. The day that the Zapatista leader announced that his rebels had occupied 38 municipalities in Chiapas the peso plummeted to levels practically unknown in the history of the Mexican stock market, shaking confidence in the dollar and in all other emerging markets.

The U.S. government was determined not to allow Mexico to collapse. The border was too close and NAFTA too vital to important U.S. corporations; non-private funds and non-market instruments were marshaled to prevent further losses.

The market could not be trusted but neither could the myth be allowed to prove itself wrong. For the administration the danger was more strategic than monetary. At risk was the neo-liberal global corporate order from which other countries could deviate only at the expense of the United States, its corporations, and their hegemonic aspirations. Even within a capitalist framework, the Mexican debacle raised doubts about the wisdom of a model of unbridled financial liberalization and abrupt deregulation which the U.S. and its Bretton Woods institutions had chosen for the South and East. Other emerging markets, particularly in East Asia, could be tempted to back away from the neo-liberal model, retaining restrictions on investors. One immediately apparent lesson was for governments to place stricter controls over the inflow of foreign capital, especially hot venture money.

Top bankers and officials recognized that they were dealing with a systemic crisis and not simply a single-country one. One unnamed IMF official admitted that a withdrawal of foreign funds from all emerging countries would also shake up indebted industrial countries like Sweden, Italy, and Canada. Other countries could try to insulate themselves and turn their back on financial orthodoxy in gross violation of Washington's new world order ground rules.

Governments could be tempted to reverse economic "reforms," move back toward greater state intervention, attempt independent development, suspend debt payments, restrict corporate profit remittances, and reassume state control over national budgets. Such a scenario would make a shambles not only of U.S. global market leadership, but indeed (and intimately related to the former) risk systemic havoc by blocking private corporate capital from roaming the world freely in search of profits. Given the fact that the flow of private capital to the South had more than quadrupled between 1989 and 1994 — from almost $42 billion to $172 billion — even a partial shut-down could spell world corporate and banking disaster.[25]

It was in this light that the United States government justified (at least to itself) unprecedented action, resorting to extraordinary measures to raise the funds for the Mexican bail-out, ordering the IMF to break its own lending rules to offer Mexico $17.5 billion, more than six times the normal limit and one-fifth of that institution's liquid resources. The immediate objective was to prevent default, a capitalist's worst fear: "a true world catastrophe," according to the IMF chief who termed the episode "the first financial crisis of the twenty-first century" and who claimed to hold a list of ten potential Mexicos in similar predicaments.[26]

The triumphant post-Cold War model for the free world had hit a brick wall. NAFTA, the crown jewel of neo-liberal achievement, now proved a tremendous drain on U.S. resources. According to one report, Japanese financiers now claimed that Mexican events had repudiated the go-fast approach of the "Berkeley mafia" and the free market purists who had been advising many Asian governments. The same technocrats who all too eagerly opened or built up stock exchanges in the hope of tapping in directly to Northern capital markets, passing up traditional bankers and corporations, now came to realize that "hot" money not only could leave as quickly as it came in, but that it would take much local capital with it, leaving the economy in a state of virtual insolvency.

Officials in India and in other countries were making greater distinctions between "hot," destabilizing, short-term portfolio investments and direct investment, reducing the amount of shares foreigners could hold in domestic companies. In South Africa, officials reopened the debate over foreign exchange controls: "The fact is that we don't have a big brother like Mexico does," said the president of the Johannesburg Stock Exchange.[27]

Under these conditions, closed, inward-oriented, state-directed economies, so vilified in the past, began to look attractive, raising the fear in Washington of closed Asian economies feeding off never-ending trade surpluses with the United States, rupturing the United States' attempt to impose its own self-serving rules on the global economic system.

The Chinese government, then in the midst of deciding what type of capitalism it wanted, virtually halted foreign purchases of stock issues, claiming that "hot money" was feeding inflation. The Mexican collapse represented a huge blow to Washington's campaign to impose its economic prescriptions on China and to force an end to Beijing's disregard for intellectual property rights and its restriction on foreign participation in key sectors sought out by Western capital, such as the automobile industry, power generation, and telecommunications.

As capital markets became more interconnected and many countries in the South developed a dependency on uncontrollable private sources of finances, the risk of a chain reaction loomed as strong as the once apparently unbeatable tide of "market reforms." If government officials could not trust the market, why would the market trust them, their currencies, or their policies? The answer was that the "market" was simply not rational; it attacked countries and currencies even when "economic fundamentals" were "sound." The dollar itself came under fire, dropping to new lows against the German mark and the Japanese yen. Financiers quipped that the dollar was now part of the peso bloc, with Mexico a drain on the United States economy as a whole. Mexico revealed just how fragile and reckless the new world order really was, and how easily it could spin out of control.

How to prevent the worst? Corporate and political leaders answered that a new international mechanism was needed in order to prevent, contain, or reverse Mexican-style fiascos. Once again, governments came to the rescue of their capitalists and capitalism, acting to prevent sudden "failures of confidence." But there was no consensus on procedures. The German central bank's president warned that more Mexican-style bail-outs would only encourage developing countries to follow "unwise" policies and investors to take "unwarranted" risks. Business journals felt the same way, insisting that bail-outs were simply a bad idea and that the irresponsible managers in Mexico were the principal culprits.[28]

Yet the system has never been run by purists. Politicians found it difficult to accept the prescription that if each country simply adhered to "market discipline" and kept its economic indicators healthy and available to investor scrutiny, then good times for all would prevail. The question on the minds of the world's chief politicians and financiers was not whether, but who would be the international guarantor of last resort, a role once assigned to the IMF but never put into practice, and now clearly beyond the IMF's limited political and financial resources. The IMF and the global financial system as a whole were simply not equipped to tame the new capitalism.

In short, the volume and nature of capital, along with the speed of its movements, made it questionable whether any "official" non-market institution was up to the task of guarantor or lender of last resort. Investments were too large to be bailed out but also too large to be politically ignored.

Some politicians, North and South, felt it was possible to go back to the days when a handful of powerful firms and persons, in conjunction with top officials in Washington, could dictate the terms of lender repayment and recovery, taking advantage of their considerable experience and operational expertise in markets worldwide. After all, multinational corporations were in for the long run, with hundreds of billions of dollars in overseas investment, with enormous capacity to survive and even profit from economic downturns and foreign exchange turmoil. Having invested so heavily abroad, they had no choice but to think for the long run and attempt to impose greater control.

But the question remained whether august corporations and their financial pilots could bring order into the ranks of the global money traders, particularly when the big investment houses were not above making sizeable profits on currency speculation. The centralization of capital lagged behind its concentration, meaning that the international financial markets were now dominated by U.S. mutual and hedge fund investors, controlling perhaps $2 trillion in assets. There was no structure in place to control such trading, a far cry from the world in which a group of representatives from government, big banks, and multilateral agencies could sit around a table and manage the flow of international capital. With new technology, independently generated funds could be concentrated and moved faster than ever before, forcing virtually any government to its knees.

As hot money managers stampeded out of Mexico, the hope in Washington was that the giant banking firms would plow ahead with new investments. German capitalists had viewed the Mexican crisis as a U.S.

problem. They pointed to the billions of marks invested in Central Europe and the absence of a backlash. One German Economics Ministry official boasted, "We invest in real factories there, not in bonds."[29]

In fact, the wealthy European governments only reluctantly and under pressure took part in the Mexican bail-out: six governments, including Germany and Britain, refused to support the IMF, and Paris went along only to avoid embarrassing the IMF's French executive director.

Was Europe backing away from global "cooperation" in favor of a system of regional solutions to local problems? Should each country in the South find a rich patron to sustain them? But not every country in the South (or East) had a rich neighbor on its border ever ready to "save" it from the furious drives of the market and market speculators. Even countries such as Spain, France, and Portugal felt they were getting less than required support from Germany when speculators drove down the value of their currencies. Were the lenders of last resort to be found within the boundaries of redrawn or traditional spheres of influence?

The new reality was that most countries in the South were simply not deemed sufficiently important to the global market economy, or to the national interest of any one of the members of the Group of Seven. Market economic orthodoxy was expected of each and all, but if trouble arose this was still a task for the IMF. Some suspected that financial crisis of Mexican magnitude, like war itself, would force nations to declare where their true interests lay. For some of the economic powers it was a matter of protecting borders, and they would have no choice. But even if the choice was open, were the U.S. and its G-7 allies really willing to transfer new billions and surveillance powers to the IMF, turning that institution into a central bank for the world? And unlike most central banks, would this one be independent? Would it truly have the muscle to pressure middle and upper income countries into permitting strong supervision and even control? And would the powerful countries not interfere in such supervision and control?

The G-7 leaders discussed these questions but came to no decisions. They too were lost in the unknown territory of late-twentieth-century capitalism. Could financial markets be re-regionalized to better respond or give priority to regional problems, and if such segmentation was possible, could sufficient resources be marshaled to deal with several Mexicos without affecting the stability of the whole? And if there were a trend toward re-regionalization of financial markets, then what would happen to the dollar, whose value possibly had more to do with the sizeable political weight of the U.S. in the world than with the global importance of the U.S. economy? After all, was not the United States drawing on other countries' savings as well as its own in order to help Mexico cope with its situation, and in the process drawing down the value of the dollar and adding inflationary pressure to its own domestic economy?

In the post-Cold War world, investors might be looking to economics more than politics when seeking a safe haven in a tumultuous financial scenario. The U.S. greenback still accounts for more than 60 percent of foreign exchange reserves and roughly half of total world private financial wealth, while two-thirds of world trade is invoiced in dollars.[30] Still, if the dollar remains the world's dominant currency it is because foreigners have opted to hold on to more dollars than any other currency — which in effect amounts to a greater capacity to borrow without worrying unduly about inflation and costs.

A stampede on the dollar could end that privilege, forcing up interest rates in the U.S. as governments, bankers, and corporations shift to buy up marks and yen. While U.S. corporate and government leaders debated the pros and cons of a cheaper dollar value, some investors were turning their pesos into dollars but then into marks or yen out of concern of the cost of an open-ended U.S. obligation to Mexico, claiming that the dollar has now become part of the peso bloc.

The crisis of confidencs extended to the United States, as the Mexican crisis provoked a wave of doubts over the durability of NAFTA and even of the U.S. dollar as the premier world currency. Just as the dollar value of Mexican holdings took a plunge after the peso collapse, many Japanese also felt "burned" by the fall of the yen value of their U.S. investments. In addition to being less eager to sink their excess dollars into long-term U.S. assets, Japanese investors also had to face the $200 billion repair bill after the Kobe earthquake. The result has been a contraction in the flow of Japanese cash to finance the U.S. deficit. Some predicted the collapse of the dollar and began to prepare for it.[31]

U.S. strategists prefer not to discuss these matters, publicly repeating the message that Mexico was "unique," a one-time deal. Bankers insisted that the solution to the problem of breaching "market discipline" was more market discipline, even though a top J.P. Morgan official admitted that the price was "much more painful than anyone ever expected."[32] But if excesses of debt were cause for market discipline and pain, then no nation deserved being taken to the woodshed more than the United States. The irony was that NAFTA, instead of uplifting its weaker partner for a while, was dragging them both down together. There seemed no end in sight to the Mexican problem: even $58 billion in guarantees did not stem the capital flight.

And more Mexicos are in the making. The IMF clearly cannot cope, not only for financial reasons but also for political ones. Other core nations have their own Mexicos demanding relief. But the United States requires an open global economy, less out of a "national" dependence, than a corporate one. According to Goldman Sachs, at the beginning of 1995 the 30 largest banks in the United States had some $32 billion in capital available for profitable squandering, over and above the minimum legal reserve requirements. Merrill Lynch could boast it managed $560 billion in assets from clients all over the world, "because we know that an investor in Asia can profit from the efforts of businesspeople in Brazil and vice versa."[33] There was no stepping back.

Capital demanded more privatization, more investment, greater trading and speculation, and dollar recycling in general. $60 billion in privatized state properties worldwide placed on the auction bloc in 1994 alone was not enough, with an anticipation of an even greater forecast for 1995. A new cycle was already in the making and even the OECD warned in early 1995 that the sheer volume of new privatization share issues could exceed the capacity of international capital markets to absorb them.[34]

The future of banks and corporations depends on finding markets for capital, that is on the expansion and multiplication of market-access regimes, on fueling privatization, pumping up foreign stock exchanges and bond markets, forcing market reforms in order to make way for torrential flows of cash demanding a hefty return, acquiring values totally out of proportion to "market fundamentals" and leaving governments and local capitalists praying the money will not flee en masse. No sympathy could be expected from rich uncles. "It is a whole new set of priorities," said a Clinton administration official. "Forget everything you learned about how to help developing nations. Now it is Fidelity [a prominent investment trust] first."[35]

But capitalism has always placed the interests of capital first, and the role of capital's enforcers is to help set patterns of foreign consumption, production, and commerce, as well as of social development congenial to big business. Bail-outs alone could not do the job; what capitalism required was a new intervention mechanism to enforce political changes in the South, and in the emerging markets in particular, so as to insure full adherence to market "discipline."

Yet who would discipline the bond traders and currency markets that increasingly seemed to be driving policy and shaping events? It was foolish to pin the blame on a few Mexican bureaucrats and sloppy bookkeepers. The signs had been there, but investors had preferred not to look because they were too busy making money. Foreign reserves were being depleted, but an election was at hand, a small cosmetic effort to make it fair and free would bring rich rewards to the regime in the way of renewed investor confidence, and as long as short-term money kept coming in, then the problem was minor.

There was nothing therefore strictly irrational in Mexican management, it merely played up to the irrationality of the market itself. It went as far as investors allowed and even beyond, backed by the steady flow of blessings from official Washington and the IMF. Nobody wanted to push the escape button for fear of losing money and credibility. President Clinton lauded Mexico's economic reforms at a hemispheric summit just a few weeks before the bubble exploded. What did prove shocking to one and all was the massive nature and the speed of the reaction by investors to the first public admissions of problems, turning the problem into a crisis, and the crisis into a panic which shook markets the world over.

The Vietnam of the economic age was Mexico, warned one observer, and the insurgents brandishing "hot money" were moving billions in and out of countries in minutes: "Suddenly the task of trying to direct or at least contain that flow before it topples the next domino is remaking the conduct of American foreign policy."[36]

If the United States could not afford to be the lender of the last resort for the new Vietnams, then who could? Only purists continued to argue that the market itself would pick out winners and losers, rewarding the efficient and well-managed and punishing those who were not. This was an urgent matter for the chief executives of the G-7. They of course paid lip service to the free market and market discipline as the keys to everyone's prosperity and the system's stability, but the reality was that the system required new norms and mechanisms for intervention in order to bring both the market and political regimes in line.

All were agreed, for the sake of corporate glory and profit, that "developing" economies should not be allowed to return to governmental control. This injunction was even more important in the dozen or so "big emerging markets" whose size and growth prospects made them the prime targets for multinational firms avid for massive infrastructure contracts paying handsome underwriting commissions.

But that was about as far as the consensus went. Common global concerns did not translate into coordinated national strategies and resource pooling in order to deal with particular problems. Under close-the-deal neo-mercantilist capitalism, corporate and government elites could not be expected to agree on the sharing of business contracts and lucrative deals which preceded, accompanied, and could even follow the bail-outs. Mexico was the top item on the U.S. foreign policy agenda, but its allies had other worries, especially if the perception was that each nation, and the United States more than others, identified national security with commercial advantage, or economic competitiveness with bidding wars and government assistance to exporters.

If economic security was so intertwined with national security, then there was little room left for economic multilateralism. If the United States had built favoritism into NAFTA, then why should the Japanese or the Germans come to Mexico's rescue? In their minds, it was up to the United States to pay the cost of having secured that "extra edge" in the Mexican market. Not that the European or Japanese governments had much moral authority to denounce violations of free market norms, when in all G-7 countries the agricultural sectors, among others, counted on hefty protective barriers.

And if the CIA was spying on French industry, and blowing the whistle on French bribes to Brazilian officials purchasing advanced radar equipment, then why would Paris go out on a limb for the Mexican peso? The United States could not invoke free market multilateral theology one day, and the next procure deals for guaranteed market shares for U.S. exports. In regard to multiplying competitive frictions over commercial ties to Asia and Latin America, French presidential candidate Jacques Chirac complained, "The United States has reacted by seeking to establish renewed ties with these regions, and wishes to remain their privileged and even dominant partner."[37]

Assuming, however, that a minimal consensus could be reached among governments and bankers, was this still sufficient to deal with the manic-depressive conduct and cowboy nature of the forces now dominant in international financial markets? As much as it tried, the United States could not entirely dictate the pace and scope of economic globalization.

But if the process could not be controlled, then at least it could be influenced, and no power center was in a better position to do so than the United States bureaucracy and the major corporate and financial powers that it chiefly represented. Here lay the challenge of the century, taming the traders, inventing new mechanisms or assuming new authorities that would allow the United States government to return to the scenario of the 1980s debt crisis, when lenders and multilateral banks could be gathered into an office to hammer out individual country austerity and bail-out packages. So the theory went, at any rate.

Wall Street and Washington went to work on the problem, undoubtedly guided by the objective of seeking to bring hot money under the control of more "responsible" money managers. The result in part was the U.S. Treasury's announcement that it would press for the revision of the Glass-Seagall Act to allow commercial banks to merge with investment banking houses and with other financial service firms, including insurance companies, so as to expand their ability to do business on each other's turf. This long-standing demand on the part of big banks gave the impression of transforming the United States and global financial landscape, whereas in reality most of the large banks had already been pursuing securities operations.[38]

Already, U.S. firms held an enormous advantage over their foreign counterparts, first on account of enjoying the wealthiest home customer base in the world, and secondly because deregulation had come early, in 1975, when brokerage commissions were unfrozen. The big Wall Street firms had put computers and mathematicians to work to develop new security products, including futures and derivatives (instruments whose return was tied to the performance of stocks or currencies), ostensibly designed to lessen risks for investors and to generate huge profit margins for brokers. Soon they represented up to 20 percent of the utilities of financial brokerage houses. Managing huge assets with fast traders and a worldwide privatizing boom allowed U.S. firms such as Merrill Lynch, Morgan Stanley, Solomon Bros., and Goldman Sachs to dominate European and foreign markets within a few years. They conducted a decade-long drive to become global investment banks in which foreigners, without access to the U.S. capital market, found competition difficult, and merger with U.S. entities a necessity.[39]

A highly competitive business developed, principally among Wall Street-based global finance powerhouses, where each required more capital in order to meet the growing demand by governments and corporations for advice and underwriting, hedging investments with derivatives and selling them worldwide for the best price. The sharper the competition, the greater the global outreach where profit margins were greater and the more volatile the nature of the operations with potential downfalls, which were virtually incalculable and unaccountable.

J.P. Morgan himself once stated that willingness to pay was at least as important as the capacity to do so. The task was sustaining both capacity and willingness, keeping countries and bankers from losing their bearings. The U.S. power structure could not derive its strategy from an abstract reading of a global market, much less from a multinational state-corporate consensus; its first worries were its own particular strategic corporate and political interests, including those of its own protectionists, the world's most powerful.

The interaction between global process and political power took the form of a corporate globalization strategy. But the agenda proved easier to impose on governments than on people. From the jungles of southern Mexico to the Los Angeles ghettos and the streets of Paris, frontal attacks were made against the neo-liberal order. At times they were quite successful: capital markets the world over, and the value of the dollar itself, were shaken to the core when an ambush in Chiapas took aim not only against an army and a landlord, but against the entire national and global regime which had mortgaged the world's future to neo-liberalism.

Security for capital could not be purchased at the price of destitution and inequality. Neither markets, bureaucrats, nor bankers seemed to understand that economic liberalization spelled social backlashes. Authoritarian regimes could and were modernized economically, while their worst, most repressive, political traits remained untouched or indeed reinforced. There was no excuse, then, for those same bankers and bureaucrats in the North to be surprised, when their loyal English-speaking government technocrats in a country such as Mexico were proven to be thieves, extortionists, and even assassins.

Notes

1. *Excelsior* (Mexico), July 2, 1991.
2. Analysis by Ian Robinson cited by Leo Panitch, "Globalization and the State," *Socialist Register 1994* (New York: Monthly Review, 1994), pp. 74-75.
3. See the interview with Jesús Silva-Herzog, minister of finance between 1982 and 1986, in "Why the Rush to Free Trade," *New Perspectives Quarterly*, vol. 8, no. 1 (Winter 1991), p. 29.
4. *El Financiero* (Mexico), May 9, 1991.
5. *Business Week*, November 22, 1993.
6. "Border Crossings," *Business Week*, November 22, 1993; "The Japanese Have a Yen for Mexico Again," *Business Week*, November 28, 1994.
7. *Proceso*, May 13, 1991.
8. "The Hemisphere Summit: Strictly Business," *New York Times*, December 12, 1994.
9. "Border Crossings," *Business Week*, November 22, 1993.
10. "Latins Envision a Single Trade Zone," *New York Times*, June 17, 1994.
11. "Chile is Admitted as North American Free Trade Partner," *New York Times*, December 12, 1994.

12. "Miami Mambo," *Newsweek*, December 12, 1994; "Cumbre de Miami: Sólo ventajas para USA," *Revista Envío* (Managua), no. 156 (January-February 1995), pp. 156-157.

13. "Asian Nations Wary on Pacific Trade Zones," *New York Times*, November 11, 1994; and "Opening Asia's Door," *New York Times*, November 16, 1994.

14. "What Has Nafta Wrought?" *Business Week*, November 21, 1994.

15. Bruce Campbell, "Las Duras lecciones de vivir en el mercado libre" (unpublished).

16. *Excelsior*, February 28, 1991.

17. "In Canada, Doubts Fade Quickly About Trade Accord," *New York Times*, February 12, 1995.

18. See Sarah Anderson and John Cavanagh, "NAFTA's Unhappy Anniversary," *New York Times*, February 7, 1995.

19. Gerald J. Mossinghoff, quoted in "GATT and Intellectual Property," *New York Times*, April 15, 1994.

20. William A. Orme, Jr, "The Sunbelt Moves South," *NACLA Report on the Americas*, vol. 24, no. 6 (May 1991), pp. 18-19.

21. "Reforming Latin America," *Economist*, November 26, 1994.

22. "Strategies on Mexico Cast Aside," *New York Times*, February 14, 1995.

23. "Washington to the Rescue," *Business Week*, January 30, 1995; "The Mexican Rescue is Dangling From a Cliff," *Business Week*, March 20, 1995.

24. "The $20 Billion Inquiry," *New York Times*, February 10, 1995.

25. "Socializing Risk to Foster Free Markets," *New York Times*, February 12, 1995.

26. Ibid.

27. "Second Thoughts on Going Global," *Business Week*, March 13, 1995; "Rich Uncles Are Rare," *Newsweek*, February 13, 1995.

28. "Socializing Risk to Foster Free Markets," *New York Times*, February 12, 1995; "Hazardous Morals," *Economist*, February 11, 1995.

29. "Second Thoughts on Going Global."

30. "That Damned Dollar," *Economist*, February 25, 1995.

31. "Hot Money," *Business Week*, March 20, 1995.

32. Ibid.

33. Advertisement in *Business Week*, March 6, 1995.

34. "Loan Arrangers Ride Again," *Economist*, February 25, 1995; "How to Privatize," *Economist*, March 11, 1995.

35. "Do Fickle Markets Now Make Policy?" *New York Times*, February 19, 1995.

36. Ibid.

37. "On Hustings, Paris vs. Anglo-Saxons," *New York Times*, March 20, 1995.

38. "American Financial Reform," *Economist*, March 4, 1995,

39. "An Audacious Alpine Assault," *Business Week*, March 6, 1995.

9

Political Engagement and Military Enlargement

According to an official strategy document signed by the Clinton White House, United States "national security strategy is based on enlarging the community of market democracies while deterring and containing a range of threats to our nation, our allies, and our interests. The more that democracy and political and economic liberalization take hold in the world, particularly in countries of geostrategic importance to us, the safer our nation is likely to prosper .... As the world's premier economic and military power, and its premier practitioner of democratic values, the U.S. is indispensable to the forging of stable political relations and open trade."[1]

Much the same logic, with perhaps less democratic rhetoric, shaped imperial British global policy until 1914. Open markets abroad insured prosperity at home, particularly if home was also the world's preeminent financial, commercial, and military power. Now the century-old struggle to succeed Britain as *the* world power has been won. Following two bungled bids by the Germans, also known as World Wars I and II, and the flawed challenge by the Soviet Union known as the Cold War, the United States stands as the sole undisputed "superpower."

Following the Nazi collapse, the U.S. made strenuous efforts to exploit Soviet and Eastern European devastation in order to force them back into the capitalist world. Soviet leaders understood U.S. motives, rejected offers of assistance with strings attached, and proceeded to create an independent bloc. After forty years of economic competition, manifested chiefly in the arms race, U.S.-led Western capitalism won a critical battle to penetrate the major part of the world that had been partially closed.

Although the United States lacks the relative economic clout it wielded in the immediate post-WWII years, when every other competitor was in ruins, today U.S. global political and military influence is uncontested. In this sense, the absence of rival superpowers leads the United States' corporate elite to believe it must seize a unique historical opportunity to shape a new global order for a new century.

The belief is further reinforced by economic trends and the sense that the marketplace itself is forcing greater convergence of "national" economies, so that globalization, with or without United States leadership, is on the horizon. Thus the United States is said to have inherited a "burden." Yet because political and economic conflicts persist and there is no true global army or banker, globalization spells greater "leadership" for the United States, as principal "peacekeeper" and chief economic locomotive of an increasingly integrated system.

Economics aside, the post-Cold War order was not a scenario of mutually balanced or perfectly coordinated national economic aid and military apparatus. During critical junctures, burdens tended to fall more on some than on others. Thus the utilization of national governmental resources (military or financial) was subject to "national interest" interpretations of the broader crisis and the course of globalization itself.

The presumption in Washington was that no other country could or should act globally. "It is not in our interest, nor in that of other democracies, to return to the past times of multiple military powers .... We will retain the preeminent responsibility for addressing selectively those wrongs which threaten not only our interests but those of our allies, or which could seriously unsettle international relations," concluded the Pentagon's Planning Guide for Defense issued in March 1992.[2] The blueprint could not have been clearer in presenting Washington's vision of a world led by a single superpower, bent on exercising intervention against foes and blocking the emergence of other superpowers in Asia or Europe.

Would European and Japanese governing elites submit to this imperial vision? And did this include allowing U.S.-based corporations to gain an upper hand over their competitors? Could military hegemony be separated from economic hegemony? If not, were military counter-reactions to be expected? There is plenty of room for speculation, but the eventual answers may in no small measure depend on how the United States interprets and implements its self-assigned task of managing global security and global markets. It is not that other major capitalist nations do not have a counter-insurgency capacity, yet for the foreseeable future they are dwarfed in comparison to the United States military-industrial complex, its string of bases and facilities and its near singular logistical capacity to project military force massively in a matter of hours over huge distances.

If the United States could steer world politics toward unending harmony, peaceful resolutions of conflicts, healthy free market economies, and equal market access, then perhaps corporate rulers in Japan and Europe might not feel inclined to attain military parity. Indeed there would be no need for extraordinary military apparatuses. After all, democracies were not supposed to fight each other and national self-interest would become a notion of the past. Less optimistically, perhaps, the "West" would arrive at a single foreign policy upholding the interests of transnational capital with a single coercive strategy and a common means to implement it. This hypothesis was quickly put to a test.

"ROGUE" STATES

Senior Clinton administration advisers refer to "recalcitrant and outlaw states" as those who do not accept market democratic frameworks. Cuba, North Korea, Iran, Iraq, and Libya are usually singled out as countries whose governments seek to "thwart or quarantine themselves from a global trend to which they seem incapable of adapting."[3] Unwillingness to become a "market democracy" becomes a basis for external intervention. But, to judge by the number of non-democratic regimes with which Western government and corporations carry out business, the accent is on "market" more than "democracy."

The vocabulary underscores the increased attention given to North-South confrontation as part of a continuing drive to expand capitalism's boundaries. It also features the development of high-tech conventional weaponry designed to be *used*, not just held up for deterrence, to discipline the new dissenters. Of course, deference also continues: the U.S. has reiterated its right, along with a selected few, to maintain nuclear weaponry while all other nations should refrain from developing their own. According to the Republican Party's "Contract with America," the multi-billion dollar space-based Strategic Defense Initiative system is to guard against "accidental launches and Third World attacks."[4]

Even among the five acknowledged nuclear powers, U.S.-led efforts to maintain supremacy continued. Washington used economic bribes to win nuclear disarmament concessions from impoverished post-Soviet Russia, who also controlled arrangements for disarming nuclear arsenals left over in Ukraine and other newly-independent republics. New nations, on the other hand, were barred from acquiring them. Friendly governments by U.S. definition, South Korea and especially Israel were allowed to pursue covert strategies to attain nuclear weapons capabilities abetted by U.S. high-tech corporations; far less advanced efforts by India and Pakistan faced punitive sanctions.

Control of "non-military" nuclear technology was also part of a multi-billion dollar business. U.S. firms were banned from exporting nuclear power plants to China; North Korea was menaced with destruction if it advanced with its own independent program, but South Korea alone had nine Western-designed nuclear plants in operation and five more on order in 1995, while Taiwan, Japan, and Indonesia were also considering building their own. Washington raised no objection to Japanese mass procurement of plutonium. With U.S. assistance, South Korea and Japan succeeded in amassing a nuclear arsenal larger than anything North Korea was capable of achieving, but to avert a stand-off that country received billions worth of nuclear reactors in exchange for freezing its independent program and not exporting high-tech weaponry to other "rogue" states.[5]

Central Intelligence Agency officials dismissed assertions that the world had changed so radically as to diminish the need for a powerful military. Washington strategists spoke of remaining "core threats," ranging from the rise of nationalism in Russia and China's military build-up to attempts by certain nations to develop weapons of mass destruction. According to the head of the CIA, the Soviet dragon might have been slain, but the United States confronted a world full of poisonous snakes.[6]

A White House national security strategy document, appropriately titled "engagement and enlargement," called for maintaining the capacity to wage two wars simultaneously. "As a nation with global interests, it is important that the United States maintain forces with aggregate capacity on this scale .... Our forces must be able to help offset the military power of regional states with interests opposed to those of the United States and its allies .... Projecting and sustaining U.S. power in more than one region is necessary."[7]

According to a former assistant secretary of defense under the Reagan administration, in 1995 the Clinton administration budgeted nearly $30 billion more on defense, in constant dollars, that the Nixon government had in its time. Since defense spending in 1994 was about 85 percent of its average Cold War level, this led to the absurd conclusion that North Korea and Iraq — which perhaps spent some $20 billion between them on defense — equaled 85 percent of the military might of the old Soviet Union.[8]

Yet National Security Adviser Anthony Lake insisted that the U.S. as the "sole superpower" had the "special responsibility" to develop a strategy to "neutralize, contain and, through selective pressure, perhaps eventually transform these backlash states." As for the rest of the international community, U.S. policy is not to request authorization but rather to "encourage" them to "join us in concerted action."[9] According to Lake, "This is not a crusade, but a genuine and responsible effort, over time, to protect American strategic interests, stabilize the international system and enlarge the community of nations committed to democracy, free markets, and peace."[10]

Free markets and democracy were supposed to be inextricable. In a September 1993 public address, Lake was even blunter in defending the policy of "enlargement," which encompassed military unilateralism, free market dogmatism, and imperial self-justification. According to Lake, "We should expect the advance of democracy and markets to trigger forceful reactions from those whose power is not popularly derived." The assumption here was that opposition to the free market was synonymous with authoritarian government and threats to world peace. "Our policy toward such states so long as they act as they do must seek to isolate them diplomatically, militarily, economically, and technologically. When the actions of such states directly threaten our people, our forces, or our vital national interests, we must strike back unilaterally ... "[11]

The goal: to fashion a comprehensive framework of systemic strategic engagement and economic enlargement responsive primarily but not exclusively to United States geopolitical and corporate interests. This was easier proclaimed than practiced. When it came to dealing with the "backlash states," sometimes corporate enlargement and political hegemonism did not coincide. A case in point was that of Du Pont-owned Conoco Oil Corporation, which in March 1995 announced its intention to sign a $1 billion oil development contract with the government of Iran. The announcement precipitated a furious debate within the administration over Conoco's alleged undermining of the policy of isolating Iran due to its "unacceptable behavior," depriving it of revenue which could be used to pursue independent regional and internal policies, including the development of a nuclear industry. Invoking the International Emergency Economic Powers Act, which allows the government to block commerce for national security reasons, the White House ultimately sided with the State Department in acting to block the contract. Administration officials defended this decision, claiming that the agreement to start would have invited Russia, China, and the European allies to proceed with nuclear and commercial accords with Iran, something the U.S. government was unwilling to tolerate. Most important, the administration claimed it was sending a signal to Russia, which had recently agreed to complete construction of two nuclear reactors for Iran. "We're giving up something for the greater good," said one administration official. Secretary of State Warren Christopher insisted on the containment policy, but he withdrew from the discussions because his former law firm represented Conoco.

Commerce Department objections were overruled. Taking the side of the companies, these officials insisted that if Conoco did not get the contract, then foreign competitors would. In reality, there were a number of loopholes designed to permit U.S. oil companies to buy oil and to resell it to third countries, a practice that accounted for one-fourth of the oil sold by Iran. Conoco complained that suddenly the administration was changing the rules of the game which for years had permitted U.S. companies to buy, refine, and sell Iranian oil as long as they did so off U.S. shores and through subsidiaries. It was also a fact that once the oil was refined it was impossible to determine its original source, which therefore meant that at least some portion was being sold at U.S. gas pumps.[12]

The chief argument, however, was political. "We need to send a clear and unequivocal message," said the White House spokesman. "There cannot be normal relations until Iran's unacceptable behavior changes." Giving Iran a "substantial new capacity" to increase oil production would, said the White House, "dangerously add to their economic capacity to do the things that we find objectionable in the world community."[13] Supposedly, the president was trying to send a clear message to other U.S. corporations as well as the U.S. allies as to the need to keep in step with official U.S. guidelines.[14] Senior administration officials met with the Conoco board of directors and virtually forced them to suspend the deal.

Public disputes of this nature were a rare occurrence. But many felt that the administration itself contributed to the confusion, unable to make up its mind over whether business took precedence over strategic hegemonic imperatives. The administration's own export-oriented strategy called for providing aggressive support of U.S. companies seeking to win foreign government contracts and greater access for U.S. investment and exports. Supposedly, such a process wins over regimes to the virtues of market economies and pro-U.S. policies, while beating out non-U.S. competitors. The market and the empire — capital and the State — operated on two different frequencies of expansion, however much headed in the same direction.

Much the same confusion prevailed in regard to North Korea and Vietnam, where U.S. corporations were busy drumming up business while official Washington dragged its feet. There was no consistency. Corporate engagement was right in China, yet wrong in Iran and Cuba. In regard to China, business measures forced the administration in 1994 to separate human rights questions from the issue of trade preferences. A corporate lobby also went to bat on behalf of Vietnam, then still being punished for defeating the U.S. on the battlefield. U.S. companies were after a new source of well-educated, well-disciplined, and inexpensive labor in Southeast Asia. On Cuba, the administration refused to budge, and threatened to sanction any company or government that proposed investing in that country. "We draw the line in countries with policies that are beyond the pale," said the administration.[15] "Beyond the pale" meant regimes where U.S. corporate and political influence had not forced sufficient internal "reforms" to suit the global neo-liberal market agenda.

The U.S. government, however, was not strong enough to impose politically-correct behavior on global capitalism. Other governments, also active in securing business for their corporations, often refused to toe the line, although it would have been rarer to confront the U.S. outright. This posed a serious problem for Washington, whose unilateral capacity to wage effective economic war was less than its ability to wage military war. If, indeed, imposing embargoes and prohibiting investment were the strongest non-military weapons available in Washington's arsenal, it was sometimes only as effective as Washington's political capacity to impose the same policies on other potential suppliers. The Japanese and French governments officially professed much the same preoccupations with respect to Iran, but business was business: Japan remained Iran's biggest oil market and the French companies Elf Aquitaine and Total were delighted at the prospect of inheriting the deal that Conoco, after three years of negotiation, was forced to drop.[16]

MULTILATERAL MASQUERADES

Following the Soviet collapse, and in the absence of any serious challenge to the United States from the other four member powers, the United States decided that the United Nations Security Council should play its part in putting together the new world order. This was not unexpected, except by those critics and defenders of the UN who tended to forget that this international organization had been originally designed to institutionalize, and not challenge, great power prerogatives. The Security Council, by virtue of its power and composition, was the reflection of the undemocratic reality of big power politics. Power disequilibriums were dutifully carried over into the United Nations, notwithstanding the principle of equality of states.

It followed that Security Council military operations either reflected a consensus among the five permanent members, or did not materialize at all on account of big five veto power. In the absence of a revision of the Charter itself making the Council accountable to the General Assembly, it was superfluous to ask whether an undemocratic instrument could act in democratic fashion. Almost as superfluous as asking whether United States unilateralism was capable of being contained by the other capital-hungry members.

In some minds, however, Security Council peacekeeping interventions were viable, legal, and democratic following the demise of the Soviet Union. But the Security Council was no freer to act in the post-Cold War world than it had been before. It was now for the United States to decide the if, when, and how of multilateral operations. Peacekeeping thrived as long as Washington remained enthusiastic. In 1994 there were 17 peacekeeping operations underway, as compared to five in 1988, and some 67,000 UN-mandated soldiers were in the field, incurring costs of approximately $3.5 billion per year, as compared to 10,000 soldiers and an annual budget of $233 million deployed and spent in 1987 peacekeeping operations.[17] Best of all, most of the money and almost all of the troops were provided by others; of the 67,000 troops deployed in early 1993 only 963 were U.S. soldiers.[18]

This left the UN in a no-win situation, criticized for either attempting to do too much or too little, for being unprepared for or unable to deal with the complications which spring from intervention or humanitarian need. The reality was that the UN field operations derived from Security Council mandates drawn up by the big five, particularly the United States. Without U.S. money and U.S. logistics, few major operations went beyond the drawing board. Thus, UN operations become hostage to internal U.S. politics, often to the despair of the Pentagon and the State Department. The supreme case of cold feet came in the wake of the Somalia operations. U.S. public opinion revolted in 1993 when the Pentagon-directed "get Aideed" campaign failed, following the well-publicized killing of several U.S. soldiers. The U.S. pulled out of Somalia, while scolding the UN that in the future it would have to "learn to say no."

Following Somalia, the Clinton administration insisted on even greater United States control over UN operations. The UN became the scapegoat, even though operations in Somalia were directed by the White House and the Pentagon. Ignoring the overwhelming fact that the UN responded chiefly to U.S. power, Republican Party stalwarts opposed participation in the UN force which took over control of Haiti from U.S. forces, even though it was to be commanded by a U.S. officer and, more importantly, responded primarily to the U.S. demand to be in control of its own "sphere of influence." This time the UN mission contained about 40 percent U.S. troops, a U.S. commander, and Green Beret training for the entire international staff. The administration itself opposed congressional demands to cut off funding to the UN because this would mean keeping the UN from dealing with situations where the U.S. itself did not otherwise wish to risk U.S. lives or spend too much money.

There were, however, operational problems. Enforcement missions which combined several major powers or several smaller nations had trouble with communication and equipment compatibility, in addition to quarrels over command and budget apportionments. A tendency appeared in 1994 to scale down mandates, size, and numbers of peacekeeping operations, reversing a five-year trend. The Security Council even gave its blessing to unilateralism, as in the case of France in Rwanda, the United States in Haiti, or Russia in Georgia and in other ex-Soviet republics.

On a few rare occasions, the U.S. was unable to hammer out a consensus in favor of punitive action. Sometimes big four rebellion came in reaction to U.S. high-handedness. Why would the Russians or France abide by UN sanctions on Iraq, if the United States ignored UN resolutions on Bosnia? The United States government found it could not always afford to damage, through its own behavior, the credibility of the same instruments it hoped could serve U.S. interests elsewhere. This explained why the administration opposed congressional moves to unilaterally lift the UN embargo against Bosnia, arguing that such a move would give other countries the green light to ignore UN resolutions designed to give a multilateral underpinning to the new order.

UN enforcement actions, including sanctions, were as effective as the willingness of the big powers — historically the principal sanctions violators — to uphold these. After much debate, U.S. official circles finally came to the obvious conclusion by mid-1994 that "the United States views [UN] peace operations as a means to support our national security strategy, not as a strategy unto itself .... The primary mission of our Armed Forces is not peace operations; it is to deter and, if necessary, to fight and win conflicts in which our most important interests are threatened."[19]

Yet there was a cost to be paid if UN peacekeeping was scaled back too radically. As the *New York Times* reminded the Republican UN-haters, "peacekeeping is a cost-efficient deal for the U.S. If the UN were so financially hobbled that it could no longer mount operations in support of policies Washington favors, American forces might have to act alone, at far greater human and financial cost to the U.S."[20] Trying to secure the best of both possible worlds, U.S. officials then took to micro-managing peacekeeping operations through the Security Council, chiefly at the expense of the authority of the secretary-general and of ground commanders.[21]

The secretary-general expressed particular irritation that one of his main tasks should be keeping Washington happy: "We must avoid projecting the image that the United Nations is a subcontractor of the State Department."[22] Somalia as well as Bosnia served as examples of how the United Nations could be used by the United States either as a cover for its operations or failures, or as an excuse for inaction. The choice seemed to be between injecting U.S. force overwhelmingly and under full U.S. command, or not at all. In each case the crude fact was that the UN accomplished as little or as much as the U.S. desired, and in cases of U.S. flip-flopping on particular issues, the UN also appeared incoherent. Failures, however, were blamed on the UN, while successes were the product of U.S. policy genius.

Blaming the UN reduced the scope for any genuinely multilateral or humanitarian intervention. Some believed that what was needed was to define tighter guidelines for U.S. participation in UN operations, but the reality was that recurring crises in the world did not follow the neat scenarios contemplated by creative strategists. New "mistakes" were followed by new guidelines, at least until domestic public opinion could be manipulated to support military intervention, on the one hand, and until Congress provided the necessary funding, on the other. In the final analysis, paying others to police the U.S. world order was less politically costly than sending U.S. troops. And so the U.S. government strived to have its world cake, eat it too, and have someone else pick up the tab.

INTERVENTION: NEW AND OLD

Absolute non-intervention, like absolute sovereignty, if it exists at all is subject to moral and juridical questioning. Just as there can be no tolerance anywhere for genocide or forced migration, nor can we accept failure or refusal to assist the victims. These are or should be everyone's moral, legal, and practical concern. But rescue operations are one thing, and power-centered approaches by Western policy-makers laden with ideological, economic, and cultural biases, even if short-term, quite another. And they are not to be confused.

Gone was the original vision of a reinvigorated United Nations freed from Cold War restraints, able to bring peace and stability to troubled nations on behalf of the international community. Some ventures, as in Mozambique or Cambodia, were judged in the North to have been successful, but this was a matter of perspective. In the South, many believed that the United Nations Security Council had gone considerably beyond the letter and spirit of its Charter, assuming the "white man's burden" and stepping in to reorganize both governance and the governed.

How compatible indeed were the principles of self-determination and non-intervention with new-found UN assumption of duties once considered the exclusive prerogative of states? And even if interference was warranted and legal from the juridical standpoint in regards to human rights, what guarantees were given that human rights were not interpreted and enforced as synonymous with Western free market values and practices?

If peace-building was deemed a worthy objective, who defined the character of the peace? Where was the dividing line between humanitarian intervention and peace enforcement, nation-building or re-colonization? Was it simply a matter of imposing power-sharing agreements among leaders of the different parties? Could enforced reconciliation come at the expense of social justice and economic redistribution, giving war criminals amnesty and a clean bill of health?

Were horror images and the media's selective criteria for projecting humanitarian tragedies to be the trigger for international action? Could or should UN or other humanitarian actions be "neutral" to the point of protecting the ethnic-cleansers and perpetuators of genocide, in the name of achieving peace and reconciliation or of not getting bogged down?

Part of the problem was that the urgency to act often did not permit non-governmental sectors a full consideration of the issues involved. Worse yet, the humanitarian dimension provided certain governments with a justification to intervene for more than simply humanitarian matters, particularly those who conceived that peace-building and free market fundamentalism went hand in hand.

There is a long-standing tension inherent in the UN Charter between peace and justice, between human rights and sovereignty. The Charter justifies collective intervention in the face of a "threat to international peace and security," but threats are now taken to include socio-political national breakdowns and mass displacements. Were events in Haiti leading to the U.S. and UN intervention a "threat to international peace"? Some Latin American governments suspected that Washington was less concerned with peace in Haiti than with stability for Florida in the face of Haitian immigrants. In ominous fashion, the Security Council's heads of state session in January 1992 proclaimed that peace and security were not simply matters of war and military conflicts: "The non-military sources of instability in the economic, social, humanitarian, and ecological fields have become threats to peace and security." By the same token, the expansion of the range of "threats to international peace and security" entailed the radical reduction of the domestic jurisdiction of states contemplated in the Charter.[23] What convenient dove-tailing with the philosophy of privatization and the administrative incapacity of states!

If great power interventions are claimed to serve the larger economic or political interests, this must be proven, not simply asserted. This is particularly important in the context of real humanitarian emergencies, where the moral compulsion to "do something" cannot blind everyone to the self-interests of the intervenors. There must always be an analysis of intentions, of alternative options, and the tendency to propose new adventures in attempts to disguise past or ongoing failures.[24]

The fact is that United Nations intervention is no guarantee against illegality, unaccountability, and superpower manipulation. Indeed, the UN Security Council is widely seen in the South as a tool employed by the U.S. to impose sanctions or interventions on a preselected few. Sanctions against the North or friends of the North are virtually unimaginable. Thus Security Council endorsement of sanctions is less the product of an international consensus than of the power plays and national decisions of one or two of its most powerful members.

As a result, the willingness of the Council to intervene is thoroughly bound up with great power interests, and specifically the willingness of the U.S. to tolerate, within boundaries, the inclinations of permanent members to resurrect spheres of influence: the French in Central Africa, the Russians in the former Soviet republics, not to mention the U.S. in Latin America and the Caribbean. More ominously, however, such reassertion under the watchful eye of a U.S.-dominated Security Council departs from previous peacekeeping modalities of intervening *between countries* to the stationing of troops *within* nations, intervening in internal conflicts usually though unofficially on behalf of one of the parties, invoking the defense of "democracy" and "humanitarian" compulsion. The tragedy is that such behavior undermines the capacity and acceptance of other forms of humanitarian intervention, by affording tyrants the opportunity to invoke anti-imperialist sentiment and state sovereignty arguments.[25]

Claims are made that the UN is too incompetent to carry out such missions; that armies are made to fight wars and not keep peace; that military intervention complicates instead of facilitating relief efforts; that the UN and relief agencies tend to bypass local pro-peace and humanitarian efforts, imposing their own culturally-biased civic structures which are usually unable to survive once the intervenors leave.

The UN and its members share much of the responsibility for what is wrong. But most damaging is Washington's irregular and inconsistent delegation of authority to the UN, denying it a place in matters where the U.S. determines it has no business: for example, in regards to Middle East affairs or on broad debt and trade questions. These are handled by the empire directly, or through the IMF and World Bank, which of late have been moving into the field of social engineering.

By 1994 the Clinton administration had backed off from its earlier defense of "aggressive multilateralism." New strategy planning on peacekeeping, as reflected in an official May 1994 report, indicated a U.S. decision to downplay multilaterial peacekeeping in general in favor of a return to using UN operations only if consistent with U.S. policy and immediate interests. According to the report, the tactical use of the UN insures that the "U.S. benefits from having to bear only a share of the burden. We also benefit by being able to invoke the voice of the community of nations on behalf of a cause we support." Thus the UN would be strengthened but only in its capacity to provide financial, tactical, and juridical support to U.S. objectives. In military as in other important matters, the UN command was to be limited, as much as possible under U.S. operational control or those of a U.S.-dominated NATO.[26] Madeline Albright, U.S. ambassador to the UN, stated that "U.S. troops were more likely to play a logistical rather than military role ... and the longer the peacekeeping operation, the more likely that Americans will be under American commanders."[27]

The U.S. government claimed it could not play the role of "global cop." But neither could the UN be allowed to do so either. Post-Somalia public sentiment, as well as the pressure of the military establishment, had pushed the Clinton administration into the uncomfortable position of having to defend the multilateral order without risking the lives of its soldiers or spending too much money, and yet also determined not to allow the UN to go too far on its own. Much the same logic prevailed in regard to NATO/European intervention in Bosnia.

The UN-bashing reached the point where some in the U.S. began to insist that the U.S. should act independently or not at all in world affairs. Part of the trouble with this rationale was that UN authorization for the United States to take on peace-enforcement in places like Haiti, could also be used to subcontract decisions to others, such as Russia to enforce a "monroski" doctrine of its own in Georgia and other violence-prone ex-Soviet republics, or for France to come to the unilateral rescue of its influence and interests in Franco-phone Africa. The UN, in other words, was simply to abandon the Charter-mandated notion of raising and commanding a force of its own, and instead become a rubber stamp ahead of time, or scapegoat when things went wrong.

The U.S. national security adviser, Anthony Lake, insisted that the UN could not be entirely side-stepped. He reminded inconsistent unilateralists that their critique of international organizations did not extend to NATO, the IMF, or GATT. Still, the United States was powerful enough to have it both ways, he said, because only one over-riding factor could "determine whether the U.S. should act multilaterally or unilaterally, and that is America's interests."[28]

The Pentagon adamantly insists it must continue to count on sufficient combat power, logistical capacity, and political support for its "two-war doctrine," that is the ability to fight and win two major wars at the same time. Although by the end of 1994 the number of U.S. troops had been reduced, the overall arsenal was more potent than ever. In the aftermath of the Gulf War, when 500,000 troops were mobilized, the U.S. air force and navy more than doubled the number of attack planes that could drop laser-guided bombs. In addition to stockpiling massive amounts of equipment in key "forward bases," the navy was buying or converting ships specially designed to load and unload tanks, trucks, and other vehicles quickly.[29]

There could be no peace dividend as long as the Pentagon was entrusted with global peacekeeping. Because it comes to projecting massive force in a matter of hours across the world, the United States has no equal and will not allow one to emerge. With the disappearance of Soviet deterrence, the United States is freer than ever to use military power as a foreign policy instrument. The question is no longer whether, but where and how to intervene, and how to insure the indispensable backup of the public purse and public opinion.

Because the administration could not always deliver the public or Congress, the Pentagon has an interest in other nations' troops and other people's money doing the bidding of the U.S. under the UN flag — more than 90 percent of UN peacekeeping troops have come from other countries and almost 70 percent of that cost was borne by non-U.S. sources. Of course, senior U.S. officials were the first to insist that the U.S. government did not subcontract its foreign policy, retaining the right and capacity for unilateral intervention.

If Saddam Hussein had not existed, he would have had to be invented. In a post-Cold War context, how else was the Pentagon to justify keeping 100 major military bases in 16 countries, and the negotiation with some 30 additional countries (according to a U.S. congressional study) to allow the U.S. military to deploy troops and equipment?

True, some of the more expensive, traditional, and provocative bases were being shut down, yet mainly to be substituted by so-called "access" facilities rights, geared to provide the staging ground for rapid troop military intervention around the world, pre-positioning supplies, equipment, etc. Thirty of the 38 access agreements, signed or under negotiation, were with governments in the South and designed to move in quickly into trouble areas employing highly mobile military units with increased airlift and sea-lift capacity.[30]

JAPAN AND TECHNO-NATIONALISM

Clearly, the United States, in military terms, is in a league of its own. Not simply on account of nuclear weapons, but also because of its unrivaled capacity to make increasingly deadly and precise "conventional" weapons. Would the Japanese and the Europeans spend the extra 2-3 percent of GDP per year that specialists believe would in time bring their armed forces to U.S. levels of computer and satellite technology? If weaponry is tied to technology and technology to economic competetiveness, were today's technological giants to be tomorrow's new superpowers? An often made argument is that the United States has been falling behind in the economic race because it spends too much on defense: some 70 percent of all money spent on research and development in the U.S. is spent on or in the military, as compared to less than 5 percent in Japan.[31] Hence the mistaken conclusion that the powers which lost World War II have won the Cold War on account of a debilitated U.S. economy characterized by a technological base interlocked with the military complex.

Much of the cutting-edge civilian technology in which the U.S has excelled has military origins. "Dual-use" technology cuts both ways: "civilian" technology has potential military use. The implications of such developments for U.S. hegemony must be assessed in the political context of Japanese-U.S. relations more than Euro-North American ones, first because of the superior level of Japanese technological development and second on account of the cultural and economic tension prevailing between these two poles and models of capitalist development. We pose then the question whether the Japanese elite could develop the will to employ technology to acquire strategic independence from the United States.

Operating out of the public eye, the Japanese military-industrial complex generates $20 billion in annual revenue and employs an estimated 160,000 workers, a third of whom are employed by the top 20 contractors. Although conglomerate giants such as Mitsubishi and Kawasaki derive only 15 to 20 percent of their sales from military production, the aircraft industry depends on defense purchases for 80 percent of its business. Thousands of smaller firms act as subcontractors for the larger ones and are even more dependent on government spending. Together they are building pressure on the government to lift a ban on weapons exports in effect since the 1970s.[32]

Japan is a nation whose very survival depends on a peaceful flow of commerce: about 55 percent of its basic foodstuffs are imported, along with much of its industrial raw materials and energy. A blockade of its sea lanes would provoke chaos, yet until recently this nation on its own was barely capable of insuring the free flow of maritime commerce. Today Japan's defense apparatus is quite sophisticated and that military spending is on the increase: the third largest budget in the world in 1990 after the United States and the Soviet Union in absolute terms, the defense budget went from 3.3 trillion yen in 1986 to 4.7 trillion in 1995.[33]

But anti-militarist feeling is also strong in Japan, and increased military spending and deployment are fiercely resisted. The powerful peace lobby claims the build-up violates the spirit if not the letter of the Japanese peace constitution, the three non-nuclear principles (not to produce, not to possess, and not to allow the introduction of nuclear weapons), and the established ceiling (1 percent of GNP) for defense expenditures.

Japanese politicians and bureaucrats have tried to chart a middle course, claiming that the selective upgrading of military capacities is geared to eventual participation in United Nations peacekeeping missions. The trouble with burden sharing, from the nationalist standpoint, is that the United States prefers to share its burdens but not its decisions.

The lesson was driven home to Japan during the Gulf War, when the U.S. pressured the Japanese government to make a symbolic military showing of the flag in the Gulf, and, more importantly, to write a substantive check to the U.S. to help pay for the costs of the operation. The Japanese government, however, was scarcely consulted on the military and strategic decisions: top-level communications from the U.S. came late and bypassed the prime minister's office, going instead to the top party leaders — something that would have caused a diplomatic uproar if perpetrated against a major European ally, said one account.[34]

Perhaps such strategic discrimination is a form of retribution over Japan's unwillingness to curtail its export surplus at home and to restructure its economy in a way that will facilitate the penetration of Western capital and goods. Japanese neo-nationalists pick up on this point to reinforce the argument for greater independence, claiming that intra-capitalist tensions could get out of hand if the U.S. continues to insist on fundamental changes that could threaten Japan's stability.[35] When push comes to shove, Japan Inc. has no military muscle to flex.

In the short term at least there is no contradiction between the neo-nationalists' military agenda and the willingness of the governing elite to fit Japan into the U.S.-dominated international security regime. Upholding global capitalism is not in question. Supporters of military "normalization" can count on the U.S. as an ally, insofar as the Pentagon demands greater Japanese involvement in peacekeeping missions and greater financial contributions to U.S.-controlled "collective security" arrangements. But could involvement in collective security (UN) peacekeeping and more U.S.-led ventures elsewhere create openings that allow right-wing nationalists to push for Japanese military autonomy, lift public skepticism of the Self-Defense Forces, and strengthen independent military production?[36]

Here the United States government assumes that a Japanese entry into the UN Security Council and participation in collective defense missions will harness a post-Cold War Japanese military build-up to the U.S. chariot. Some U.S. intelligence officials place their hope in a new generation of Japanese defense officials, now mapping out a global military role for Japan in line with Pentagon specifications, breaking sharply with earlier notions of domestic and sea-lane defense. The same officials worry that the White House is giving second billing to political-security considerations as opposed to economic and technological transfer issues.[37]

Japanese military "normalization" on these terms, and these terms only, is eminently acceptable to most United States officials, even though it presupposes the effective shelving of Japan's peace constitution and nuclear ban. Japan could develop its military apparatus and defense technology only in the framework of its subservient partnership with the United States. Its military forces and its technology were geared to supplement, but never to substitute, those of their U.S. counterparts.

Independent participation in collective security schemes continues to be ruled out, and even the bilateral security agreement with the U.S. specifies that Japan is not permitted to come to the defense of the United States if the U.S. were to be attacked. In this context, the new Japanese predilection for multilateralism, security or economic in nature, does not entail a weakening of its bilateral subservience to the United States, and in fact may even reinforce it.

Nor can the U.S. afford to allow Japan to escape its bilateral dependence on the U.S. to guarantee access to essential resources, chiefly oil, foodstuffs, protection for Japanese investments in East Asia, and of course access to the North American domestic market. The imperial guardianship or "protection," past and present, has its price. Beginning in the late 1970s, U.S. governments manipulated that dependence to obtain commercial favors as well as financial contribution to the support of U.S. military bases. Such "extra-economic" levers to extract concessions continue to be a central feature of U.S. policy toward Japan, upsetting European competitors as well as the self-esteem of the nationalists.

But can a high-tech industry be as readily harnessed to U.S. security interests, including the demands of the U.S. weapons industry? Japanese nationalists insist on an independent defense and that Japan is financially and technologically capable of achieving it. Indeed, recent studies show that Japan continues to lead the world in crucial technologies with both civilian and military applications. Weapons systems could be assembled by Japanese producers if sufficient investment were secured. Unlike the other advanced industrial powers, Japan is seen as capable of doubling defense spending without a negative impact on growth. Japanese literacy rates are among the highest in the world and the number of economically active engineers is twice as high as in the United States. So it is not a question of money or brains.

Furthermore, there is a strong governmental organizing tradition capable of directing human, financial, and technological resources to precise strategic objectives. If in civilian technologies Japan has shown a proven ability to advance into new sectors, the same could apply in the military field, especially as there is already some experience in military production. The Pentagon itself has supported joint U.S.-Japanese research ventures. A 1989 study concluded that given its technological, human, financial, and organizational resources, Japan could if it wished emerge as a military superpower within the next 10 to 25 years.[38]

In effect, the only limitations seem to be political. Some argue this constraint is also being breached, the sizeable public opposition and constitutional impediments notwithstanding. Ironically, the principal culprit is the United States, the same country which most insisted on the very constraints it now seeks to reverse. The U.S. began to push the development of the Japanese armed forces in the 1950s, when a U.S.-imposed security treaty called on Japan to "increasingly assume responsibility for its own defense against direct and indirect aggression" — a contradiction to the arms renouncing clause (Article IX) of the Japanese constitution.[39]

Another question is whether Japan has the political will to seal off its technological prowess and block the United States access to research in sensitive areas. This does not seem to be the case, because of U.S. government demands for "equal access" to Japanese research, including access for U.S. researchers into Japanese government and private sector laboratories, as stipulated in the 1988 U.S.-Japan Science and Technology Agreement.[40]

The scenario, therefore, of Japan as a military superpower, counterbalancing the U.S., however technically feasible, is politically unrealistic. Minority neo-nationalists would proceed in stages, beginning with participation in UN peacekeeping, as a means of regaining Japan's full military and political sovereignty. The governing elite, however, notwithstanding the cracks in the political system, seems committed to upholding its alliance with the United States, pursuing its high-tech strategy in such a way that the United States can also profit, both commercially and militarily. Above all, do nothing to endanger Japanese access to the United States market seems to be the guiding principle.

The actual Japanese objective is not to displace the United States, but to extract greater political leverage in its bilateral relations by making use of its wealth and technology, and, to a lesser extent, its own defense apparatus. From the U.S. standpoint such "burden sharing" is applauded, in the full confidence that a carefully monitored defense build-up and technological breakthroughs do not translate into decisions to become an independent military, nuclear, and economic power. In this way, the Pentagon continued to realize savings by importing many military components from Japan, while that nation was able to further specialize in important technological fields.

Such an arrangement seemed to work well during the last decades of the Cold War. But since the collapse of the Soviet Union, the Pentagon has been much less accommodating to Japanese requests for access to weapons technology. Japan, for example, lags considerably behind the United States in aerospace, partly on account of the pacifist constitution and also because U.S. officials and U.S. aircraft industries do not want more competitors. What aircraft Japan did develop were principally on the basis of tightly controlled licensed transfers of U.S. technology. Yet there was no stopping the Japanese from further developing techniques originally copied from Boeing, Douglas, or Lockheed, to the point that by the 1980s Japanese companies became large suppliers of parts to Boeing and others.

By this time, the Japan Defense Agency and Mitsubishi Heavy Industries — Japan's largest military contractor — had moved toward designing and developing its own aircraft, spurred by military ambition to develop an all-Japanese-made fighter. The initiative met corporate and government resistance from Washington, as some argued that since Japan depended on the U.S. for its defense, it should buy U.S. aircraft instead of developing its own (and in the process alleviate the trade deficit and employment crisis in the U.S. aircraft industry). A compromise was struck in 1988 under which a new prototype — the FSX jet fighter — would be developed jointly using the U.S. F-16 as a model. The pioneer model would be built in Japan with U.S. companies doing 40 percent of the work. This time, however, instead of providing technology to Japan, as had always been the case, the United States (McDonnell Douglas) would be entitled to get technology back.[41]

In the light of new political developments and Japan's own advances, Washington increasingly insisted on what it calls a "fair exchange" of expertise, seeking to extend the FSX understanding to other programs. The Japanese government, however, is much less acquiescent, trying to cap Washington's demands for free access to dual-use technology. According to an official of the Japanese Defense Agency: "The Americans are very aggressive about this, but dual-use technology is the property of private industry and we can't just tell companies to hand it over." U.S. corporations were part and parcel of Washington's campaign. The manager of Mitsubishi Electric Corporation complained, "Lockheed and other U.S. companies that provide aircraft technology to Japan want civilian know-how in return. But how can you expect us to trade different kinds of technology."[42]

In Washington's view, however, it was the Pentagon that first provided Japan with the technology to develop its own aircraft industry. An argument then broke out over who should build the airplanes and whether Japan would hand over all the technology used in the FSX which the Pentagon claimed was no more than Japanese improvements on U.S. technology entitled to flow back to the U.S. Those who feared Japan's growing industrial competitiveness argued that allowing Japan to produce the prototype would eventually do for Boeing and Lockheed what Toyota and Nissan did to General Motors and Chrysler.[43] At stake were billions of dollars of business for beleaguered military contractors in each nation, as well as the capacity to develop an independent export business in an already tight aerospace market. In all, the episode highlighted the complexities of separating trade, technological, defense, and political issues from each other; although the fundamental cleavages found governments on the side of their respective corporations.

A similar story emerged in the semiconductor industry, only here the worst possible scenario had already begun to materialize. Japanese semiconductor manufacturers were already the Pentagon's principal suppliers. U.S. strategists came to fear that Japanese semiconductor manufacturers could use the threat to halt exports as a lever to attain concessions in other economic or political negotiations. Just as worrisome in Washington was the possibility that Japan could make this sensitive technology freely available to others, including rich "rogue" states, in violation of official agreements.

Some feared that China, equipped with Japanese dual-use technology, could acquire certain levels of military parity with the United States. Or that Japanese manufacturers could one day decide to give greater priority to filling orders for commercial concerns than to supplying the Pentagon specifications. But it was not only semiconductors for the Pentagon, but a host of other products to U.S. industries as well, including liquid crystal displays for ubiquitous laptop computers.

From the military standpoint, there were certain assignments that could not be left to the law of comparative advantage and the free market. If cost-benefit analysis was carried out strictly in financial terms, then it made a great deal of sense for U.S. corporations and the Pentagon itself to purchase abroad what could not be manufactured cheaply at home. According to one expert, the United States' most vaunted weapons, from the AmRam missile to the M-1 tank, could not have been built without commercial Japanese machine tools. Nor could the F-16s employed against Iraq with such destructive force have found their way around the desert without Japanese-developed radar components.[44]

Pure market conditions and free competition would have also dictated that some U.S. military contracting firms be allowed to go under if other companies, foreign or national, could offer more competitive bids for military contracts. But the market logic has its limits in regards to dual-use technologies. Some corporations feared being left out of cutting edge developments which stood to make a crucial difference in military as well as commercial contests. Thus the Pentagon endorsed multi-billion dollar mergers of military contractors — Lockheed and Martin Marietta were joined to create a single aerospace industry giant that would be involved in everything from submarine missiles to cargo planes to spy satellites.[45] If there was no alternative to global competition, governments would insure it had a national basis.

Not everyone was convinced that "techno-nationalism" was achievable or even practical, in the light of limitations and huge research and development costs. Cross-border mergers demanded by profit-minded contractors clashed with the strategic concerns of government officials. They claimed there was nothing wrong with linking U.S. basic research capacities with Japanese applied research skills — or marrying U.S. sophistication with Japanese reliability as they termed it. Nor were there great corporate protests when Rolls-Royce, the British jet engine manufacturer, announced it was buying Allison Engine, a U.S. firm which built the engines for Lockheed's C-130J military transport, a model that U.S. companies and the Pentagon was bent on selling in Europe.[46] Business was business.

"Foreigners" buying up national defense contractors was going too far, cried the techno-nationalists usually to be found more in think tanks than in business. Increasingly U.S. officials chastized U.S.-based corporations for being "overly driven" by cost-efficient criteria, for purchasing massively from Japan and entering into loosely controlled research and development joint ventures. Hence the government's interest in subsidizing national mergers and technology development. Again, military and export market considerations became interwoven in the administration's technology and industrial policy, a practice common in Europe and Japan. Each cited the other's practice as justification for its own. Officials insisted that in the absence of government-assisted product improvement and production innovation, rival government-supported firms would manufacture components so advanced that their complacent counterparts would never be able to catch up.[47]

As defense contracts for a bloated Cold War arms industry diminished and unemployment resulted, alliances became strained and competitive arms production became the subject of new political frictions. The fate of thousands of jobs became intertwined with "national security" concerns. One calculation indicated that some 350,000 defense-related jobs had been lost worldwide in 1993 alone, and that one-fifth of worldwide defense-related employment (three to four million jobs) could be lost by the end of the 1990s. In the U.S., defense jobs dropped from 1.35 million in 1990 to 800,000, and defense expenditures were expected to continue to drop, unless politicians and generals made good on their promise to reverse the trend.[48]

The problems were particularly acute in Europe, where national and regional over-capacity was greatest. Membership in NATO had never precluded national European industrial combines from competing with United States contractors and with each other. The French took the British to task for not "buying European," and the need to protect domestic arms makers was no small factor in the French government's long-standing and recently abandoned goal to build a purely European defense structure to substitute for NATO.

Creating new combines seemed the answer to the problem of excess capacity, and to avoid duplication of overhead, manufacturing lines, and research and development. However, for the defense industry at least, cross-industrial mergers did not always entail cross-border ones. Three types of battle tank and three different fighter plane models were being developed in Western Europe, but in the absence of a common defense policy and a supranational strategic command, governments were unwilling to witness the erosion of jobs and defense capacities. The concentration of sales and production in key industries and technologies could only go as far or become as large as national markets permitted.

This was less of a problem in the U.S. arms industry, all privately owned and able to take advantage of a huge national and international market. Still, the 1990 Pentagon-approved merger of Martin Marietta and Lockheed indicated that U.S. industry was more advanced in the consolidation cycle. The new firm would become the world's largest defense manufacturer, controlling 32 percent of the world market in tactical aircraft alone, followed by McDonnell Douglas (also predicted by experts to be absorbed before too long) with another 25 percent. To have matched the anticipated defense revenues for the new Lockheed Martin Co. ($16.5 billion) would have required the merger of the five biggest defense contractors in Britain, France, Japan, and Italy.[49]

Some cross-border mergers were underway in Europe, but the reality of politically divided markets and competition created barriers that postponed the "restructuring" demanded by industry executives. This was not the case in Japan, where the size of the market and defense budget, as well as the concentration of dual-use technology in few hands, offered further opportunity for expansion and profits. What barriers existed were not national but still political.

Upholding "national defense" capacities was as much a question of markets as of military prowess — an instrument for commanding international influence and import orders. U.S. companies, backed globally by the U.S. military and government, remained the most ruthless and most successful in capturing international markets. In their version of globalization, at least, the national came first.

On account of its size and clout, the U.S. military-industrial complex was bound to prevail over its competition. A further example of the U.S. was setting the strategic standards for the intended global security order. Still, the new arms exports race was intense. In 1994, the U.S. arms industry commanded just under half of total world trade in arms — some $10 billion — as opposed to 19 percent in 1981. Europeans as a whole sold $7 billion that year. East Asia represented the most contested market — one of the few places in the world in which defense budgets were still growing. This was fine with the West, until Asian and other "emerging" countries began manufacturing their own weapons.

The Pentagon was bent on replacing manpower with technological firepower as fast as possible. The technical revolution was as much a threat as a promise to arms makers. But could the United States or any government monopolize critical technologies, heralding the advent of what some termed the "transparent" battlefield, characterized by information technology, most of it U.S.-based? Industry analysts spoke of the coming generation of "brilliant" sensors, including surveillance systems and long-range, self-guiding precision weapons. At that point, traditional manufacturers of ships, tanks, planes, and missiles would become more reliant on computer firms, software producers, and high-tech companies.[50]

To the degree that technological innovation became increasingly dependent on foreign sales, the ban on military exports was a problem for the Japanese. "Dual-use" technology represented only a partial way out. The future of its aerospace industry could not be divorced from generating domestic and international defense contracts. But Japanese proposals to mass produce fighter planes met a cold shoulder in Washington because the military-industrial complex insisted that its own production lines be given priority.

Still, plans proceeded for the construction of Japan's first spy satellite and the joint U.S.-Japanese development of a "theater missile defense" system. This only encouraged right-wing Japanese demands to break with the past, revise the constitution, do away with political inhibitions, and export military components with or without overseas partners. To them the goal was to recover the national pride that once accompanied the building of the infamous Zero fighter of World War II.[51]

Yet until the early nineties at least, Japanese official policy maintained limitations on the development of weapons systems capable of projecting military power over great distances, such as aircraft carriers or in-flight refueling tankers. The 1976 ban held on the export of weapons and pure military technology (except to the United States). A problem would arise, however, if Japanese participation in UN peacekeeping carried with it a need for specialized offensive military equipment. Perhaps the government could then kill two birds with one stone: invoke UN authority to escape U.S.-imposed limitations on military development and at once neutralize Japanese public opinion.

Commercial differences and trade competitions only fed the increasingly bitter character of the techno-nationalist rivalry between Japan and the United States. Some nationalist quarters came to demand a radical revision of the agreements whereby Japan provides the United States with advanced military technology that cannot be used for itself, nor made available to other military powers.[52]

Given the dual-use basis of many of these technologies and their high profitability, some analysts foresee an alliance between Japan's high-tech military complex and the neo-nationalists. European, Chinese, and Russian, as well as some U.S. companies would be ready partners in the technology trade. It may prove impossible to exclude the aerospace sector, which would mark the end of Japan's techno-military isolation and of the weapons export ban.

Will the growth in technological and economic prowess translate into an independent strategic policy capable of mounting a global challenge to the United States? Corporate interdependence, public sentiment, and the make-up of the present pro-U.S. governing elite all combine to make this an unrealistic scenario. Nonetheless, the neo-nationalists may well have some success in exploiting public resentment over U.S. economic pressure. A new generation of politicians may feel less indebted to the U.S. than its predecessors.

Military, technological, and economic power may grow, but a generational turnover does not necessarily signify the political will to employ that power in a way contrary to U.S. hegemonic interests. Thus, as in economic and financial international affairs, Japanese global political and strategic influence is bound to increase. However, in light of present post-Cold War trends it will likely continue in the form of "burden sharing" supportive of U.S. hegemony. Under present political and social circumstances, the growth in Japanese power adds to instead of diminishing the U.S. capacity to impose the new world order. The Japanese elite seems willing to "pay" for its protection, and pay handsomely, matching technological with financial and even token military contributions to the new order.

But the query remains, what happens if the U.S. continues to increase the "ante" to encompass reforms that affect the profit-making basis of the Japanese corporate-bureaucratic structure? Diplomacy alone will not prevent market crisis, which tends to force such issues, and with it a whole new set political and military calculations on both sides. If both Tokyo and Washington contend that corporate well-being depends upon perpetual economic expansion, then a contest may be inevitable, more so in the context of a limited export market; although it is a contest Japan is in a poor position to win.

Perhaps Japanese officials suspect the outcome. Perhaps this is why the "new world order" to them means subservient "burden sharing" or, as the nationalists say, to act as an orderly of the United States in world affairs. The burden is not a small one and seems to be increasing, ranging from higher Japanese subsidies to U.S. military bases and the cost of training exercises, to strategic aid for U.S. client states, the purchase of U.S. military equipment, funding of UN peacekeeping, support to Russia, and increased sharing of military technology. But none of this is enough, nor does it address the central U.S. concern. According to the White House national security strategy directive, "Japan must take measures to open its markets and stimulate its economy, both to benefit its own people and to fulfill its international responsibilities."[53]

Japanese loyalty to U.S. global strategy appears to entail some degree of economic restructuring. Just how much is the subject of recurring diplomatic and trade negotiations. Perhaps this also explains why the corporate-bureaucratic elite, in order to avoid ceding on domestic economic order fundamentals, will give ground on virtually all other issues in what neo-nationalists regard as a continuation of the victor-vanquished relationship of the occupation period.[54]

NATO AND THE NEW EUROPE

Germany's strong economic growth, its territorial unification, and above all the collapse of the Soviet Union created a crisis of identity for Europe, its supranational institutions, and its security alliance with the U.S. The Bush administration — sensitive to the opportunities posed by a new emerging configuration — demanded that the Europeans accept German unification, notwithstanding serious misgivings in London, Paris, and of course Moscow.

The question of NATO and Germany is a crucial one for the United States, as it lies at the core of an emerging security architecture to scaffold the new global market order. Security in this context embraces political and economic considerations, so that any attempt to fracture the model is bound to be resisted by the United States. According to the White House strategy document, "the first and most important element of our strategy in Europe must be security through military strength and cooperation," and to this end U.S. policy toward Europe was to be focused, among other elements, on "helping to confirm NATO's central role in post-Cold War Europe ...." Advancing integration and solving conflicts were immediate priorities, and many European institutions and the UN would play a role, "but NATO, history's greatest political-military alliance, must be central to that process."[55]

The assumption here was that, divided or not, with or without the communist enemy, Europe was not to be allowed to manage its security outside of the framework of U.S. power, chiefly represented by NATO and politically anchored in a traditionally pro-U.S. Germany. Economies and military structures were to become further "atlanticized" and liberalized, that is, open to U.S. corporations and the presence of U.S. troops, under a single security-market umbrella, designed to prevent new wars and hegemonies in Europe. "Vibrant European economies mean more jobs for Americans at home and investment opportunities abroad," said the strategy document.[56]

Washington's most important task was to place strategic limitations on the capacity of Western Europe to develop a single independent military force. Secondly, and not unrelated, the U.S. aimed to expand NATO to encompass Russia and the former Soviet bloc.

Not all European governments were avid about the U.S. embrace. From time to time over the course of the Cold War there were Gaullist attempts to challenge the "Atlanticist" framework, to make Europe more autonomous, draw the British closer to the continent and away from the United States, all under French strategic leadership. A Franco-German axis was supposed to provide a counter-weight to the Anglo-American one, more so if France could dictate politics while Germany simply tended to economics.

With the Soviet demise, new opportunities opened up for Gaullism. In December 1991, France and Germany dropped a political bomb-shell by announcing a joint initiative to form a new military structure, under exclusively European auspices, independent of the North Atlantic Treaty Organization and, therefore, outside U.S. military tutelage.

That France would sponsor the initiative surprised no one, par-ticularly those familiar with Paris's love-hate relationship with Wash-ington dating back to 1944. France's quitting of NATO had more to do with posturing and image than ideological contradictions. It called for independent foreign and defense policies, not only for France but for all of Europe. The new initiative responded to De Gaulle's old as-piration of constituting a "European" Europe on the basis of a Paris-Bonn axis that would secure good relations with the Eastern bloc countries. In the words of the legendary general, the aim was to pre-vent a European Community from being transformed into "a colossal Atlantic Community under American domination and leadership."[57]

But that Germany, historically the most ardent defender of NATO, would also spearhead the project, shocked everyone. This flew in the face of Bonn's historical "Atlanticist" deference to Washington in strategic questions. Coming only a few months after German unifica-tion, the question now was whether a new Germany was embarked on a new foreign policy, assuming the nationalist and "Europe-first" positions of France.

On October 16, 1991, the governments of France and Germany sent a public a letter to the president of the EC, elaborating the de-tails for the creation of a joint force. According to the document, the force would be open to all members of the Western European Union, until then a moribund body dealing with European defense matters that had been marginalized by NATO. Practically all members of the EC were members of the WEU anyway, argued the initiative, in an unsuccessful effort to play down the strategic implications.

According to the French government, the proposal "for the first time and very precisely gives substance to the EC's foreign policy and common security, endowing it with content, form, and structure." Besides, it was also known that many in the United States were de-manding a scale-back of its military presence in Europe and the real-location of the defense budget. And if Europe seemed willing to assume a greater defense burden, did that not coincide with what Washington had been demanding for years?

At the Maastricht Summit, the French and German governments went one step further, insisting on EC approval of their initiative, including the call-up of 50,000 soldiers to form the first contingent. The United States government was furious, and through the British demanded strict adherence to the Atlantic alliance, dismissing the Franco-German plan as "dangerous" to NATO. Although the notion of a European rapid reaction force appealed to most EC members, the British and others insisted that any such body would have to be subordinated to NATO.[58]

Reacting to the Franco-German proposal, the U.S. State Department reminded Europe that European security was the exclusive business of NATO, regarding as "disagreeable and threatening" any attempt to bring the WEU back to life. William Taft, U.S. delegate to NATO, affirmed that any attempt by the Europeans to take charge of their own defense would be viewed with great mistrust. "The people of the United States will not understand any proposal which aims to replace NATO with another mechanism."[59]

Washington, of course, was quick to accuse France as the principal troublemaker putting forth yet another maverick foreign policy initiative. During a visit to Washington, the French foreign minister, Roland Dumas, so exasperated U.S. officials to the point that Secretary of State James Baker inquired, "Are you with us or against us?"[60]

The answer was neither, at this junction in 1991. The predominant fear in Washington was that the economic challenge posed by the EC was now being complemented and reinforced by a strategic one. Theories and theses were posited that a new German-led Europe was bent on transforming itself into a true superpower with global economic and military reach. Indeed, a partnership between France's historically "Euro-first" aspirations and a reunited Germany's economic power could, it was argued, represent an unstoppable combination capable of providing leadership for all of Europe in global affairs.

New strategic thinking in Europe often contained traces of the old geopolitical anxiety of German hegemony. France and other (though not all) continental European governments feared a Washington-Bonn axis giving Germany a hegemonic status and making it less sensitive to its neighbors' concerns. But if German resurgence was unavoidable then the formation of a European Army could neutralize Bonn's unilateral pretensions.

At the Maastricht Summit, the European "Atlanticists" (with the U.S. behind the scenes) were able to dilute the WEU proposal, approving instead an abstract version of the original plan. The heads of state agreed that any new military pact would have to be linked to

NATO — a body which could neither be substituted nor dispensed with. In deference to Paris and Bonn, however, the summit indicated that Europe should "eventually" possess its own military force. The WEU would continue to be a ghost organization, the target of United States suspicion but also the victim of the larger confusion in European Union decision-making.

In strictly military terms, there was not much ground for comparison between the two bodies. The WEU had no integrated military command and no communication system to match the U.S.-supplied NATO. European armies were powerless and humiliated when the U.S. suspended intelligence support during the Bosnian episode. "This proves just how much Europe needs to be autonomous where intelligence-gathering, satellite reconnaissance, and logistical support are concerned," said the British MP who headed legislative efforts on behalf of the WEU.[61]

Alarmed by initial U.S. reticence in the Balkans, the leaders of Britain and France announced the formation of a joint Franco-British air command at their summit meeting in Chartres in November 1994. The four-nation Eurocorps (consisting of units from France, Germany, Belgium, and Spain) came into being, to be assigned, however, to either NATO or the WEU. It was clear that access to U.S. intelligence and airlift capacities would be subject to Washington's approval. According to one calculation, the WEU was at least one decade away from operating on its own two feet, presuming of course European taxpayers could be persuaded to finance the huge costs that upsizing entailed.[62]

Also in Chartres, the heads of state announced the creation of a Franco-British European Air Group to undertake peacekeeping operations "within and outside" the NATO area. As Western Europe's only nuclear powers, both countries had also been advancing in defining common post-Cold War nuclear doctrines, much to the chagrin of U.S. officials, who frowned on sharing too many secrets with the French. President Mitterand hailed this cooperation as the "very foundation" of a future European defense. French officials were under the illusion that the agreement marked a new British acceptance of the need for a separate European "defense identity."

The British, for their part, more than having a change of heart, were signaling their displeasure over the Bonn-Washington axis as well as U.S. government involvement in the Irish conflict. Still, British officials went to great lengths to explain that the initiative in no way weakened their NATO commitment. French officials said the move was interpreted best in the framework of their steady rapprochement with NATO, after more than 25 years of separation.[63] Fanfare aside, London remained more Catholic than the pope in its loyalty to the United States, and France continued to give priority to its relationship with Germany. But in light of the incomprehensible United States policy toward Bosnia, Europeans asked how much value could be placed in the U.S. position, incompatible with NATO "integrated" commands and in violation of UN Security Council resolutions. To many Europeans, Washington seemed all too eager to watch certain conflicts from the sidelines, refusing to send soldiers to join the "peacekeeping" contingent in Bosnia yet insisting on conducting the orchestra.

It seemed that the U.S. was not powerful enough to lead, but had just enough power to prevent others from doing so. For example Russia and other European countries hoped that the Conference (now Organization) on Security and Cooperation in Europe (CSCE/OSCE) could be groomed to take over from NATO as the premier European security institution. The U.S., however, once again made clear its opposition to any measure or mechanism which strengthened European autonomy at its expense.

Also unacceptable was a1994 French effort to place limits on NATO's expansion by having the United Nations Security Council approve all NATO military action in the ex-Yugoslavia. Under this scheme, NATO would become the Security Council's enforcer, allowing the United States to be outvoted by the Europeans, including Russia, establishing a grave precedent for dealing with outbreaks of violence on or near European territory, in effect neutralizing the NATO chain of command.[64]

None of the schemes got very far because each presumed European capacity to attain consensus. France, Britain, and Germany had important differences among themselves on Bosnia and other issues.

As early as September 1993 the U.S. secretary of defense reiterated his government's decision not to "abandon Europe" but to engage it via NATO in the safeguarding of the new global order, particularly toward the restless East. In short, NATO was now expected to help the U.S. fight around the world. "To remain relevant, NATO forces must be able to respond to the challenges of a new era. These include challenges of peacekeeping and enforcement operations. But NATO must also be prepared to deter and defeat aggression against Western interests beyond the NATO boundaries," he said. This would insure military cooperation in areas the U.S. considered critical "to our shared interests" and to "thwart the new dangers we face not only in Europe but elsewhere."[65] Islamic nationalism came to mind.

With French approval, NATO's forces have now been reorganized into "combined joint task-forces," enabling different national contingents to serve under mobile commands for peacekeeping missions. NATO assets are now available to the WEU, the military arm of the European Union. East Europeans supported NATO's eastward expansion and the drawing of "a new line," as President Clinton put it, pledging that at least 100,000 U.S. troops would remained stationed in Europe.[66] Stationing troops, however, did not prove whether the "West" had the will, unity, and means to successfully tackle simmering military conflicts and economic dislocations in Central and Eastern Europe.

THE BOSNIAN FIASCO

Perhaps the German government managed to make a likely war inevitable by forcing Western recognition of Slovenia and Croatia, by demanding the recognition of an independent Bosnian state and thereby precipitating the Bosnian Serb offensive. In an unusual display of diplomatic force, the German government practically dictated policy based on the erroneous premise that a demonstration of diplomatic strength (recognition of the breakaway republics) would be sufficient to force the central Serbian government in Belgrade to abandon expansionist aspirations.

The result was just the opposite. Serbia went to war against Croatia and persisted in maintaining its control over territories and nationalities, beginning with Bosnia-Herzegovina. Nationalists rebelled, stimulated in some part by German diplomatic rhetoric, awaiting Western political and military intervention on their behalf. What they received, however, was more rhetoric, cries of indignation, incoherent governmental responses, and symbolic troop deployments under neutral UN auspices, which all failed to put an end to Serbian aggression.

Official Western enthusiasm for the Bosnian state did not go so far as to be willing to fight for it. Europeans sent thousands of troops under the UN banner, while the United States politely resisted making a commitment, preferring to cheer from the sidelines, sending in airstrikes, insisting that NATO assume greater responsibility, that the UN stop interfering with military operations, and that Washington be allowed to broker a political settlement. Only then were some troops dispatched.

U.S., UN, and NATO credibility were all put to the test. The United States urged an aggressive course but resisted sending soldiers. Pressed by Congress, the administration announced in November 1994 that it would no longer enforce the Security Council embargo on arms shipments to Bosnia. It promised its allies, however, that it would continue to supply intelligence, but later reneged. The Clinton administration pressed Britain and France to maintain their troops, but the Europeans threatened to pull them out because a UN peacekeeping cover alone would not provide security to their forces on the ground; they threatened — hollowly, as it turned out — that unilateral measures from one side would be met in kind.[67]

Both the U.S. and German governments were unhappy that NATO was playing the role of subcontractor to the UN, but the French had insisted and French troops (and not German ones) were on the ground. There was one report that French officials were deliberately accentuating differences with the United States in order to finish off NATO, force a break between Britain and the United States, and clear the way for a purely European defense network. Although the same officials held to the position that there was no incompatibility between two separate defense organizations, their efforts had already failed and the WEU project was eventually abandoned, at least in its original autonomous design.[68]

U.S. preponderance could not stop endless bickering. This was less the result of differences among equals than of internal debates in Washington. It seemed that Washington was more adept at preventing rivals from emerging than at keeping its own house and that of its allies in order. As with the UN, it became clear that "multilateral" organizations such as NATO could function smoothly only when the signals were clearly emitted from Washington. When they were not, chaos was the result. Few commentators were willing to point out the disingenuousness of U.S. hand-wringing over "NATO-UN divisions," when U.S. preeminence was exactly the same in both organizations.

Germany, Holland, and Britain advocated a more active role in the Balkans, but France initially opposed it. The result was the position of lowest common denominator, which is to say doing nothing. As the crisis progressed, the Europeans turned over the diplomatic and backup military responsibilities to the U.S. In the final analysis, the Balkan crisis indicated that the appearance of a European superpower was most unlikely: the Europeans were not capable of defining, much less carrying out, strategic decisions on their own, even where the conflict raged within a few hundred miles of their capitals. For their part, U.S. officials could not hide their own complacency in the face of a humiliating European showing. Referring to the EU's diplomatic setback, a U.S. official commented that "the truth is that these people couldn't even organize a three-vehicle caravan."[69]

Even at the peak of Euro-optimism, few believed that national foreign policy and defense decisions would be delegated to Brussels. Power was too scrambled. Germany had no military Bundesbank able to impose some semblance of hierarchy in the European order. Lack of a nuclear capacity, a permanent seat in the United Nations Security Council, or a military apparatus politically able to move outside its borders without provoking a domestic political row made Germany a power inferior to Britain and France in a global system still characterized by instability and conflict.

NATO AND THE EAST

After Bosnia, no security issue loomed larger than the future of Russia. Common Western wisdom held that acute Russian dependence on trade and capital from the West would force Moscow to relinquish independent posturing. Economic restructuring, however, helped feed an ultra-nationalist and anti-Western sentiment that the Yeltsin regime, on occassion, felt compelled to reflect. At the December 1994 CSCE summit meeting, President Boris Yeltsin admonished the U.S. president that "the destinies of the world community [cannot] be managed from a single capital [i.e., Washington], and that Europe was in danger of plunging into a 'cold peace.'" Clinton retorted that there could be no external vetoes on the expansion of NATO.[70] The reality was that in the absence of a Russian "threat" many believed that NATO had no reason for being. This was not a feeling shared by Washington, which viewed NATO as an instrument of leverage to entrench a free market regime in Russia — an historical objective of U.S. strategy and the surest way of domesticating Russia.

Faced with multiplying conflicts in Eastern Europe and in the former Soviet republics, Washington sought to extend a NATO "security umbrella" to uphold market-oriented allegiances. Economic integration into the European Union was not enough, and certainly was not an immediate prospect for most of the old socialist bloc countries. Fearful of being newly relegated to the South, the Eastern Europeans, including Russia, proclaimed that geography and ideological technocratic affinity with the West warranted a privileged status, with preferential access to Western capital and markets.

The economic became political, however, inasmuch as financial shock treatments were provoking second thoughts among the citizenry with regard to free market fundamentalism. This was reflected in electoral results which threatened the reappearance of "market-closing" regimes. Market access, enlargement of the European Union, and NATO became inseparable issues.

For the most part, NATO's projected expansion to the East was seen in Washington as complementary to the political and economic. The problem was the fear in Moscow that NATO would continue to pursue an anti-Russia strategy, in part to signal its displeasure over the bumbling course of privatization and liberalization in that country.

Most Eastern European governments were keen to form part of any arrangement which would help draw in Western commitments and escape from what Russian rulers felt to be their continuing sphere of influence. Yet European Union members such as Ireland, Sweden, and Austria retained neutralist principles and could object to NATO membership for the countries to the East. More important was the objection posed by the Russian government to any explicit extension of NATO's security umbrella.

Hence the contradictions between Washington's will to expand the NATO umbrella and the desire to secure Russian allegiance to the new order. Moreover, some felt that an overly warm U.S. bilateral relationship with Russia could strain the Atlantic alliance and tempt Germany to seek its own accommodation with Moscow, disrupting the long-standing Franco-German alliance.[71]

Russian authorities demanded a "special agreement with NATO corresponding to the position and role of Russia in world and European affairs, to our country's military might and nuclear status," according to President Yeltsin. By badgering NATO to give it more rights than the other would-be Eastern partners, Russia hoped to bolster its influence in the former Soviet Union, and influence when and how its former associates in Eastern Europe joined the alliance.

Washington, for its part, gambled that Russia's Western-directed economic agenda in the end could force more compliant diplomatic behavior, including submission to the Euro-Atlantic alliance. The assumption seemed to be that Russia's economic restructuring could translate into political as well as social compliance.

Some analysts believed that Russian policy was to reintegrate the components of the old Soviet Union, at least on an economic level. While capital would benefit from a more integrated Eastern economic zone, some conservative strategists fear the re-emergence of a global power which may prove unable or unwilling to transform itself into a "market democracy."[72] Insuring the transition and "market reforms" were crucial and inseparable political and economic objectives common to the Western powers. According to the White House national security strategy document, "the short-term difficulties of taking Central and Eastern Europe into Western economic institutions will be more than rewarded if they succeed and if they are customers for America's and Western Europe's goods and services tomorrow."[73]

But there could be no good customers or market reforms without stability. And imposing stability was a military objective for which Europeans both East and West looked toward NATO and the U.S. The idea of the WEU acting as the "central pillar" of European security had been dashed by the Bosnian episode, but moving the United States' military presence eastward risked isolating and humiliating the Russian regime, thereby placing the neo-liberalization process in danger.

While the overall concern was the nurturing and expansion of capitalist market regimes, geopolitics also figured into the equation. Some of Germany's neighbors demanded the continuation of the United States presence, to them a guarantee against a temptation for Germany to go it alone and nuclear. NATO in turn was to pressure Moscow to reduce its armaments and accelerate capitalist reconstruction. The brutal Russian campaign against Chechnya was evidence that market reforms did not entail friendly democratic behavior. But because Russia was still a nuclear power and its government made market reform pledges, excuses for non-democratic behavior, imperialist reassertion, and even demands for a voice in NATO councils all found considerable acceptance in Washington.

There was some opposition to the inclusion of "have-nots" into a reserved NATO club of "haves." This was a different school altogether, and perhaps the more dangerous. It reflected the thinking of officials in several Western capitals who believed that NATO, if it was to play an effective police force role defending the privileges of the rich countries, should not include countries subject to being policed. Such a line of thought ran parallel to those who opposed bringing in poorer countries into the European Union.

Some Western officials shuddered at the prospect of going to war to defend Hungary against Romania, or the Ukraine or the Baltic countries against Russia; Russia therefore should be included in order to better influence its external and internal behavior. According to NATO's secretary-general, "we do not need security consumers" but countries that could bear the full responsibility, including the risks and financial costs of membership. A more blunt official put it this way: "We don't need any more Frances, Spains, Greeces, or Turkeys."[74] NATO was to be the military arm of the North, led by the United States, in which there was little room for dissidence (France) and none for the non-elite, non-white, or non-Christian.

Money was also tight. Countries such as Greece and Turkey had received enormous amounts of U.S. assistance before being admitted to

NATO. Spain and Portugal received hefty annual sums from an EU compensation fund designed to assist in their integration. Times had changed, however; Cold War imperatives and economic resources were not found to begin a new round of subsidized integration, no matter how worthy the free market objective. A "partnership for peace" in regards to strategic matters, or an "associated" status in regard to economic ones, emerged as compromise schemes that satisfied no one.

Internal Pentagon documents argued that U.S. interests would not be served by the emergence of a European power which could place the continent's massive resources under a single command. Washington is not unaware that the sum of all EC member armies and budgets far exceeds those of the United States. According to the Pentagon, "the United States must convince potential competitors that they do not need to aspire to leadership or adopt more aggressive postures in order to protect their legitimate interests."[75] The Pentagon's worst nightmare entailed Germany going its own way, securing access to nuclear power or influence over former Soviet states with nuclear warheads, with which it could forge an alliance cemented by German capital: highly improbable but not impossible. Both NATO and the WEU, like the governments which composed them, shared the same dilemma of being unprepared to engage in conflicts against non-ideological enemies in which there was little or no Western interest and in which corporations held little stake, independently of the human proportions of the catastrophe. Western agreement was more in evidence when it came to threatening military intervention against "Islamic fundamentalism" — the "rogue" states and peoples, apparently more of a threat than ethnic cleansing advocates in Europe itself.

Vexing situations strained the fabric of the Western alliance that had lost its geopolitical but not its ideological market rudder. Europeans demanded that Washington explain how it could truly value NATO, if it was not willing to place its troops on the line. To which the U.S. would respond, how could the Europeans act in the absence of U.S. political clout and logistical support? For a period, the U.S. exempted itself from standing UN and NATO directives with regard to the Bosnian war, but it was still very much present because an independent pooling of European foreign, financial, and security policies had proved impossible. Some felt that Europe was hopelessly condemned to continue under the U.S. wing, abandoning its hope of becoming a world power, clamoring for U.S. strategic leadership yet sniping about its specific course and cost.

East Europeans for their part complained about overly strict economic and security conditions for joining the EU or NATO, warning this could devastate the "new democracies." But at stake was not so much the possibility of a "new Yalta," in which the West would again recognize Central Europe as part of a Russian zone of influence, or a new North-South divide across Europe to take the place of the iron curtain. Rather how to insure that all of Eurasia remained market-friendly and subservient to Western corporations and multilateral institutions coupled with what the Pentagon termed "interoperability" and the "partners for peace program," which in effect translates into bringing the local military establishments under NATO's wing. None of this required formal and expensive Eastern incorporation into either the EU or NATO.

NATO's survival depended not so much on imposing peace on the ex-Yugoslavia nor on how and when to take on new members, but rather on how the U.S. used it to find new enemies in order to justify its leadership of the "Western" alliance. This meant in part broadening NATO's original purpose — defending member countries' own territory against attack — adding to it the defense of the established corporate order on a global level against new foes. That is, to prepare governments, peoples, and of course military hardware to intervene in foreign conflicts and to deal forcefully with the "rogue" states.

If common agreement could be achieved on such aims, then indeed the development of a European "defense identity" would pose no problem for Washington "in cooperation with NATO rather than in competition with it." Taking stock of the limited European capacity to forge common security policy, and taking into account mounting congressional demands for greater economic burden sharing, the Clinton administration began to take a less suspicious view of the WEU. In order to use NATO assets, the WEU would still require approval from each of NATO's 16 members, including the United States.

In all, for political, financial, and operational reasons, U.S. concerns regarding the emergence of an independent European strategic capacity proved exaggerated. Most governments were not willing to make the massive multi-billion dollar investments for weapons systems, air transport, satellites, communication gear, and aircraft carriers to substitute for the United States contribution to NATO over a 25 year period.

Re-nationalizing Europe's militaries was not viable either. German national defense self-sufficiency, or the independent projection of German military power abroad, were anathema to Germany's neighbors and internal public opinion. As one diplomat explained: "For us Germans, being integrated is part of our whole purpose."[76] Such an attitude and core commitment to NATO and the U.S.-run structures were further guarantees against independent national or regional aspirations. Indeed, even the French governing elite seemed to be coming to the conclusion that the "defense" of Europe could not be left to the Europeans alone. Some French officials warned that it made no sense to talk of a "European identity" unless Europeans could decide to mount their own operations without NATO strings attached, adding that the U.S. Congress could well veto the use of U.S. military equipment in operations the U.S. had no control over.[77]

A more naive view held that the United States would one day pull out of Europe and turn over NATO to the Europeans. Perhaps this assumption explained why by the end of 1995, France rejoined NATO military structures in all but name.

Much to Washington's delight and faced with an asserted rogue or "fundamentalist" threat from the South, the French government came to collaborate in NATO restructuring to allow it to undertake operations outside of Europe. The White House strategy document justified the continued presence of some 100,000 U.S. military personnel assigned to the U.S. European command not simply to "preserve U.S. influence in leadership in NATO" but also to provide the "capability to deter or respond to larger threats in Europe and to support limited NATO operations out of area."[78]

Herein was the new or updated basis for "Western" unity. In early 1994 NATO created "Combined Joint Task Forces," described as "NATO's most radical piece of new thinking in its 45-year history."[79] Under the Pentagon's guidance, NATO was being overhauled to mount military operations outside Western Europe and North America, even allowing troops from non-NATO countries to participate in the task forces.

In effect, this meant further enhancing NATO's range to include non-NATO members of the WEU, as well as NATO's so-called "partners for peace," chiefly from Eastern Europe. The U.S., as any other country, could choose not to contribute soldiers, but this did not mean that Europe could act alone, because indispensable NATO "assets," including transport aircraft, command-and-control systems, and intelligence, could only be used with Washington's approval. In this way, the U.S. could retain control and at the same time not have to contribute U.S. lives, allowing Europeans the privilege of sharing the burden of upholding United States global hegemonic pretensions and taking up possible new interventions against nations of the South.

Notes

1. White House, *A National Security Strategy of Engagement and Enlargement* (July 1994), pp. 2, 5.
2. "U.S. Strategy Plan Calls for Insuring No Rivals Develop," *New York Times*, May 24, 1992.
3. Anthony Lake, "Confronting Backlash States," *Foreign Affairs*, vol. 73, no. 2 (March/April 1994), p. 45.
4. "Star Wars: The Sequel," *New York Times*, February 10, 1995.
5. "Fast Breeding in the East," *Economist*, February 18, 1995; Eric Nadler, "North Korea's Nuclear Neighbors," *Third World Resurgence*, September 1994, no. 49, p. 37; Selig Harrison, "Zero Nuclear Weapons, Zero," *New York Times*, February 15, 1994; "Battle Looms for Treaty to Halt the Spread of Nuclear Weapons," *New York Times*, March 2, 1995.
6. *New York Times*, December 29, 1994.
7. *National Security Strategy*, White House, pp. 6, 7.
8. Lawrence J. Korb, "The Readiness Gap: What Gap?," *New York Times Magazine*, February 26, 1995, pp. 40-41.
9. Lake, "Backlash States," p. 46.
10. Ibid., p. 55.
11. *New York Times*, September 24, 1993.
12. "The Iran Exception," *New York Times*, March 15, 1995.
13. Ibid.
14. "U.S. Oil Company Drops Deal with Iran as Clinton Acts," *New York Times*, March 15, 1995.
15. "The Iran Exception," *New York Times*, March 14, 1995.
16. Ibid.
17. *New York Times*, March 4, 1993.
18. Ibid.
19. White House, *National Security Strategy*, p. 13.
20. "Bipartisan Foreign Policy," *New York Times*, February 2, 1995.
21. See interview with Boutros Boutros-Ghali in the *New York Times*, January 6, 1995.
22. Ibid.
23. Jim Whitman, "If It's Right It's Got to Be Done: A Cautionary Note on Humanitarian Intervention," *Cambridge Review of International Affairs*, vol. 8, no. 1 (Spring 1994), pp. 44-45.
24. See the thoughtful argument made by the editors of *Middle East Report*, vol. 23 no. 2-3 (March-April/May-June, 1994), pp. 1 and 39.
25. Alex de Waal and Rakiya Omaar, "Can Military Intervention Be 'Humanitarian'?" *Middle East Report*, vol. 24, no. 2-3 (March-April/May-June 1994), pp. 3-8.
26. Phyllis Bennis, "Blue Helmets," in Erskine Childers (ed.), *Challenges to the United Nations: Building a Safer World* (London and New York: CIIR/St. Martin's Press), pp. 19-21.
27. Address at the National War College, September 1993, cited in Wayne Robinson, "Japan's Security Debate: Uncovering the Political," *Pacifica Review*, vol. 6, no. 1 (May/June 1994), p. 52.
28. The text of the Lake address is in the *New York Times*, September 24, 1993.
29. "Pentagon's Two-War Doctrine Faces a Challenge of Logistics," *International Herald Tribune*, October 18, 1994.
30. U.S. House of Representatives, Arms Control and Foreign Policy Caucus, *Global Outreach: The U.S. Military Presence Overseas* (September 1992), cited in Daniel B. Schirmer, "Access: Post-Cold War Imperialist Expansion," *Monthly Review* (September 1993), p. 44.
31. Peter F. Drucker, *Post-Capitalist Society* (New York: Harper Business, 1993), pp. 138-139.
32. "New World, Few Orders," *Far Eastern Economic Review*, January 26, 1995.
33. Shegeto Tsuru, *Japan's Capitalism: Creative Defeat and Beyond* (Cambridge, U.K.: Cambridge University Press, 1993), pp. 228-229.
34. Robinson, "Japan's Security Debate," p. 32.

35. Ibid., pp. 34-36.
36. Ibid., p. 35.
37. "Golden Opportunity," *Far Eastern Economic Review,* July 21, 1994.
38. Steven K. Vogel, "Japanese High Technology, Politics, and Power," *Berkeley Roundtable on the International Economy, Research Paper no. 2* (March 1989).
39. Tsuru, *Japan's Capitalism,* p. 63.
40. Vogel, "Japanese High Technology," p. 94.
41. "A New Warplane's Murky Horizon," *New York Times,* January 13, 1995.
42. "New World, Few Orders," p.54.
43. "A New Warplane's Murky Horizon."
44. Jay Stowsky, "From Spin-Off to Spin-On: Redefining the Military's Role in Technological Development," *Berkeley Roundtable on the International Economy, Working Paper 50* (May 1991), p. 3; Vogel, "Japanese High Technology," pp. 3, 103.
45. "Pentagon Backs a Deal for Suppliers," *New York Times,* December 30, 1994.
46. "Defense's Tug of War," *Newsweek,* December 5, 1994.
47. Vogel, "Japanese High Technology," p. 101.
48. "Defense's Tug of War."
49. Ibid.
50. Ibid.
51. "Japan's Aerospace Giants Are Flying Low," *Newsweek,* December 5, 1994.
52. Robinson, "Japan's Security Debate," pp. 57-58.
53. White House, *National Security Strategy,* p. 17.
54. Robinson, "Japan's Security Debate," p. 39.
55. White House, *National Security Strategy,* p. 21.
56. Ibid., p. 22.
57. Quoted in Stephen E. Ambrose, *Rise to Globalism: American Foreign Policy Since 1938* (New York: Penguin, 1991), p. 199.
58. *New York Times,* November 16, 1991.
59. *Wall Street Journal,* October 23, 1991; see also Claire Teran, *Le Monde,* November 13, 1991.
60. *El Pais* (Madrid), June 22, 1992.
61. "Make the World Go Away," *Newsweek,* November 21, 1994.
62. "Playing at Euro-Soldiers," *Economist,* November 26, 1994.
63. "Playing at Euro-Soldiers"; "Make the World Go Away."
64. See interview with Willy Claes, secretary-general of NATO, in *Newsweek,* December 19, 1994.
65. Quoted in Robinson, "Japan's Security Debate," p. 52.
66. *Economist,* January 15, 1994.
67. "The Sly Game of Liar's Poker," *Newsweek,* December 19, 1994.
68. Report from *Time* magazine quoted in *El País,* December 12, 1994.
69. *New York Times,* May 30, 1992.
70. "A Cold Peace," *Newsweek,* December 19, 1994.
71. Zbigniew Brzezinsky, "The Premature Partnership," *Foreign Affairs,* vol. 73, no. 2 (March/April 1993), pp. 77-80.
72. Ibid., pp. 67-82.
73. White House, *National Security Strategy,* p. 23.
74. *New York Times,* February 9, 1995.
75. *New York Times,* May 24, 1991.
76. "The Defense of Europe," *Economist,* February 25, 1995.
77. Ibid.
78. White House, *National Security Strategy,* p. 22.
79. Ibid., p. 20.

10

Conclusion

Market globalization and the global expansion of U.S. power are a single overlapping though not totally coinciding process. Imperial economic and military power have always combined to create dependent markets and subsidiary states, to shape new mentalities and open cheap labor pools, to marginalize or dispose of entire segments of populations.

International power structures are multi-faceted, and in this day and age more integral than ever before. Social and gender structures of domination are distinct from, but not independent of, those which pit capital against labor, rich against poor, and state against state. At the core of oppression lies not the individual, but a pattern of social relations, reproduced internationally, characterized by the domination of capital and the practices of the powerful: the corporate elites of the United States and its principal allies, in both the North and South. The battle for the transformation of human consciousness and social interaction begins with an attempt to understand the application of this principle of material empowerment by the few at the expense of the many.

Not that the concentration of power is coherent or driven by consensus among the powerful. It cannot be stable in the light of outbursts of market forces, political conflict, and social protest, which seem to be part of the "system" itself. Yet there is a general projection of power which, fully articulated or not, seeks and needs to impose by whatever means necessary a stabilizing social, economic, and ideological conformity on the world.

This also imposes a need for greater global political awareness in the South (and East) about the new patterns of domination which supplant or reinforce old ones. This is not so much a question of nations as of classes, which is why more attention must be paid to the dynamics of social struggle in both North and South as it also shapes capitalism and affects the rest of the world.

234

The oligarchies and the system are there, even though they deny being alive, pretending that the power structure is amorphous, God given, and operates on automatic pilot or the law of gravity. And the closer one looks, the more the United States corporate apparatus and ruling elite stares us in the face, directly, immediately, and locally, however much they try to privatize or universalize their projection.

This is not to argue that there is a special state-class in the United States that runs the government for its own "national interests" and no one else's. Capital has a way of linking capitalists across borders and such linkages cannot be divorced from global politics. But corporations, as much as they may pretend to uphold a state-less status, carry political baggage which cannot easily be left behind upon expanding abroad; nor do they necessarily wish to do so.

Rich governments also carry political and particularly electoral baggage. None of the governments in these countries can afford to totally dismiss the social consequences of transnationalization, however much their business cousins may favor or profit from it. In a way, this also constrains the real transnationalization of corporations.

Globalization also forces governments in the North to address non-corporate concerns. Across the industrialized North, societies are hurting. In the U.S. and Europe, unemployment is relatively high and job prospects bleak; in Japan the economy has experienced its worst downturn in decades. Unfairly, many blame immigrants for the loss of jobs and reduced access to social services. Governments are also faulted and punished. Perhaps the pressure has always been there in some degree, but heightened dependence on the world economy and the end of the Cold War have prodded politicians to point to exports as panaceas, claiming that trade is an integral part of creating competitiveness and jobs, and placing commercial concerns at the center of foreign policy, becoming intertwined with security questions and power moves. While preaching free trade, some powerful governments threatened to launch a new era of protectionism and managed trade. In their bureaucratic economic vision, the global was often subordinated to the national. As President Clinton asserted, if the U.S. was going to keep its markets open or even tackle its budget deficit, "the rest of the world has to also make their economic adjustments."[1]

Neither pure geopolitics nor pure macro-economics can, by themselves, explain the terms and thrust of contemporary globalism. Economic illness, however, tends to bring out political surgeons. Thus we witness U.S. government attempts to manipulate markets and finances. The question now posed here is whether U.S. military suzerainty obliges the European and Japanese governing elites to accept the prescriptions laid out by a global Monroe Doctrine, while tolerating cut-throat U.S. trade and currency strategies. Pushed too aggressively, "competitive" commercial and dollar devaluation manipulation could feed on itself, touching off wholesale trade wars along with a run on the dollar with calamitous consequences for the world political economy.

The trends in this direction are undeniable, and individual corporations appear powerless to stop the progressively deeper engagement of rich governments, individually or through regional associations, in resorting to ruthless economic survival tactics restricting access to their own markets, thwarting the efforts of competitors to tap markets in the South, and in general fueling existing sentiment in Europe and Japan for each region to develop independent regional and global projections — military as well as economic.

Upon examining the regionalist phenomena in Europe and East Asia, market integrations and capital's transnationalization do not appear to be accompanied by the formation of a regionally dominant class power apparatus capable of generating common political institutions, supranational authorities, or an independent defense capacity. One is drawn therefore to the conclusion that the United States government-corporate elite continues to provide its counterparts in Japan and Europe — and elsewhere — with a share of profits and of global power they would otherwise lack, particularly in a world which still cannot do without the use of military force to contain the forces of radical change. And it is this deeply conservative common class dimension that helps explain why the "allies" continue to swallow U.S. policies they would otherwise consider unwelcome and counterproductive. Capacities aside, the political and economic will to coherently contest U.S. government "leadership" is not there.

The United States remains the only country in the world that does not need to "consult" any other country before acting. Military factors come to the fore. As an ex-head of the United States Joints Chief of Staff explained in 1992, "No other nation on earth has the power we possess. More important, no other nation on earth has the trusted power we possess. We are obliged to lead .... America must shoulder the responsibility of its own power. The last best hope of earth has no other choice. We must lead. We cannot lead without armed forces. Economic power is essential; political and diplomatic skills are needed, the power of our beliefs and our values is fundamental to any success we might achieve; but the presence of our arms to buttress these other elements of our power is as crucial as the freedom we so adore. Our arms must be second to none ... there are other Saddam

Husseins in the world .... In the Pentagon we believe our military strategy fits the world we see developing like a tight leather glove."[2]

Globalization notwithstanding, at no time has any recent U.S. administration shied away from claiming that major challenges to U.S. interests in the South could if necessary be handled directly and exclusively by the U.S. In Powell's own count, the United States deployed troops on 35 occasions between 1990 and 1993 alone. If multilateralism does appear, in a military or any other context, it is the conscious result of a U.S. decision and directive; otherwise it does not take place at all. "America first" and global duty need not be contradictory.

Right-wingers, however, believe the United States has been much too shy to behave as it should; that is, as the world's only superpower. But this is not always a matter of choice. However powerful, the U.S. government is not strong enough to construct and control supranational structures which could reliably manage divergent interests and conflicts in the consistent interests of the U.S. On the whole, capitalism has proved successful in generating such oversight systems on a national basis. Political and military power has allowed state apparatuses to help organize and enhance economic forces. The question now is whether those same economic forces, globalized with a vengeance, will be accompanied by the formation of a parallel political world apparatus also capable of regulating the supranational economic traffic, presuming those forces are not so powerful as to become unmanageable, as some have argued, actually inhibiting the projection of new regulatory authority. There is no apparent answer, but the United States government is seeking to fill the void, not by creating a new global authority, but by further transforming itself into a megastate or non-territorial empire.

Culturally, the U.S. as a nation has made world headway. The ground rules of the new global order also entail influencing the imagery and content of ordinary communication, coopting mentalities as well as institutions in order to broaden the foundation of a new global order. UNESCO studies indicate that the United States exported seven times more television shows than the next country (Britain) and has the only global network for film distribution. U.S. films account for 6 to 7 percent of all films made, but occupy 50 percent of world screen time. The U.S. was also responsible for 8 percent of worldwide transmission and processing data in 1981. U.S. English is becoming the common language of economics and sciences in the world and U.S. universities dominate research in basic scientific fields. Predominance in the knowledge structure is overwhelming.[3]

Knowledge and commercialism intertwine, becoming ideological constructs designed to demobilize and further disempower people, or worse yet, group them in defense of unethical values under the leadership of the United States.

Given the disunity among and within ruling elites across the Pacific and Atlantic oceans, and the magnitude of the economic world market demanding yet defying taming, conditions are not propitious for the creation of the global mega-state capable of playing the role of world manager. In and of themselves, transnational corporations and the international financial institutions are no substitutes, totally incapable of dealing with "Saddam Husseins" or "tequila effects" in the South or frenzied money markets in the North. While the increasing political assertion of the Group of Seven represents an effort to enforce norms of economic and political behavior in the South (and East), it is not true that the private or multilateral institutions have accumulated more power than governments; over most governments, perhaps, but over the richest not at all. Much the same can be argued in regard to other political superstructures such as the UN Security Council: as Russia becomes more dependent on Western aid and China gives priority to maintaining its economic ties to the West, the Security Council becomes a tool of a U.S.-led West.

Thus global capitalism is still unable to articulate a genuinely multilateral world governance framework, capable of assuring not democracy (which would be too much to expect), but at least to provide for an equitable division of authority and distribution of profits among corporate elites. Economies continue to become integrated but political power remains diffused, thereby distorting any pure market or technological basis of accumulation.

For their part, governing classes in the South meekly stand as interested bystanders competing for junior partner sinecures. In return they rid themselves of notions of sovereignty and accountability, in the same way they banish distinctions between foreign and domestic capital, offering capital concessions which would be unacceptable in the North. There is general agreement in the North on the need to assure the political-juridical market-access environment in the rest of the world for the sake of capital's reproduction. Yet otherwise, the partnership between capital and state, far from harmonious on the national level, is even less so when projected internationally. The pure profit motive is often filtered and even distorted by existing state apparatuses, with the result that global economics continues to be subject to non-economic forces. It may well be that the competitive global scenario, far from contributing to class-class or state-state co-

hesion, actually works against these (reinforcing class-state antago-
nism instead), whereupon the system as a whole enters into new and
more dangerous crisis.

All this spells an even more disorderly global scenario. Can chaos
and North-North global contradictions carry benefits for the South?
If the prevailing order serves the elite partnership North and South,
disorder could concievably, at least in the long run, favor the interests
of the poor or at least force the rich to rethink. Even before the Chiapas uprising and the peso crisis devastated corporate capitalist and
IMF/World Bank claims about Mexico's neo-liberal structural adjustment "success story," some of the global magnates were already beginning to worry that the privatizing revolution had gone too far,
provoking uprisings or fueling financial speculation. The call for political re-regulation was increasingly heard, if for no other reason than
to protect core economies and also the absorption capacity of key importing "emerging" markets.

Such self-critical appreciations do not necessarily signal significant
shifts in Northern policy and power. They do, however, represent a
step toward acknowledgment of social problems long apparent to victims. The question then is whether popular forces can deepen and
capitalize on such shifts in order to push discussions to their logical
political conclusion — including a shift away from structural adjustment policies. Whether awareness and rationality alone can transform
policy is another debate. For now, it is safest to argue in the negative
and ask if the system itself is capable of supporting self-generated
or U.S.-induced shock therapies. The power structure is its own
worst enemy, epitomized perhaps by Washington's penchant for
unilateralism and purposeful disruption as a means of pressuring its
"allies," buttressing its military apparatus, and in general serving its
imperial needs and interests. It may well be the global system's irrational helmsmanship more than its endemic injustice that sparks new
and greater crisis. One and the other are two sides of the same coin or
order, guided by the unbridled greed of a few while failing to provide
for the basic needs of the many.

In the short run, global disorder may inflict hardships on everyone,
but throughout history even beleaguered societies and cultures have
managed to survive and even prosper. People in the South will simply
feel induced to step up passive and active struggles against the amorphous new world order and its various domestic expressions. Mexico
stands as an example of the potential headway which democratic
forces can make as the result of a breakdown in the new world political apparatus, opening similar possibilities for the recuperation of

popular sovereignty in other nations whose governing class rigidly adheres to global neo-liberal rules. But Mexico also poses the question of whether the space is used effectively or not. This depends on other considerations and configurations having more to deal with the strategy and cogency of opposition movements. Until then, technocratic elites may find it necessary to contain their instinct to blindly follow the dictates of foreign capital and foreign governments.

Social or national assertiveness in the South opens up the possibility of massive retaliation from the North, particularly if access to huge markets, cheap labor, investments, resources, or strategic implacements are threatened. Here any disagreement among the powers in the North tends to be more about means than ends. The system's coercive features (without which there can be no system) work with uncanny smoothness against the South, punishing all straying from the path of neo-liberal orthodoxy. There is a remarkable degree of Northern consensus in regards to the upholding of global norms of overall societal and governmental pro-market behavior, seeking to penetrate the very fiber of a community.

The multilateralism which is preached and imposed on the South, however, tends to be ignored at the level of the capitalist big powers. And it is at the level of intra-capitalist disputes where we witness the breakdown of the myth of political globalization. The same model that permits the big powers to practice extortion in the South increasingly entails locking horns against each other in vain attempts to escape globalism's social dislocations. This leads to a situation where the preservation of economic "stability" in one core state may require its weakening in another, inhibiting the capacity for independent political, military, and social organization. The tendency does not stop at the borders of weak nations. But unlike most governments in the South, some in the North throw up resistance, having in some cases the economic and technological capacity to compete.

The United States is currently engaged in an effort to restructure political forms worldwide in order to better reflect, accommodate, and enhance its present position in the global political economy. But as the U.S.'s one-time allies are now discovering, such a drive entails much more than the simple adherence to market capitalism. It entails molding markets and controlling foreign policies according to Washington's drive for total openness to U.S. capital and corporations. Does this mean that the next "rogue" states will be identified and targeted in East Asia or Western Europe? We have argued that the United States government and corporations can only hope to continue exerting minimal, yet not insignificant, influence over a world economy characterized by instantly mobile capital and new divisions of labor — that there is no guarantee. But this is an insufficient basis to postulate the erosion of U.S. hegemony in international capitalism relative to other powers, or that emerging trade and investment blocs will spill over into competing political and military thrusts which can provide an opening for progressive change in the South. It would be naive, therefore, for progressive political forces in the South to stake their strategy on the appearance of new global or even regional powers which could act as geopolitical guarantors and subsidizors of social change in poor countries. At the same time, however, some valuable lessons can be extracted by the South from ongoing efforts in Europe and Japan to resist U.S. efforts to break down political barriers to its further economic empowerment.

Much of "America's" claim to "leadership" derives from its enormous military superiority and capacity to deploy it in a world where the new "threats" come from developing countries and take the form of waves of immigrants, religious fundamentalism, narcotics production, weapons proliferation, arms races, national rivalries and outbreaks of armed conflict, and total economic breakdown. The "need" for military protection cannot and is not set aside during economic summits. It follows that for the U.S., sustaining hegemony entails preserving and asserting for political gain its new-found status as the world's only military superpower. Pentagon strategists have made it clear that competition in the security field is not permissible, while the Commerce Department reminds challengers that foreign markets will be stubbornly contested. The point is to impede the formation of a competitive, integral power bloc in the post-Cold War era on the one hand, and secure more openings for U.S. capital and influence on the other.

Nations of the South must closely observe European and Japanese reactions to the new United States drive. Although the United States governing elite assumes the task of preserving the conditions of world security which permit capitalist expansion, it does so in a way that most benefits its own capital and interests. The sharp turn toward neo-mercantilism and "aggressive unilateralism," reaching new heights and doctrinal dimensions under the Clinton administration, indicates that the United States is in the process of revamping its economic and perhaps even political relationship with its old allies turned sharp competitors, particularly in the contest for the emerging markets.

From the standpoint of the German-centered European Community and Japan, Clinton's "new order" raises new questions. Is Europe not more entitled to greater participation in the rule-making on account of its economic standing? Can alternative regional political and economic integration provide a basis in Europe and Asia for disputing U.S. "leadership"? The questions assume new urgency in the light of the new U.S. stance, and we have tried to reach some tentative answers. What is clear is that because the deterioration of the U.S. economy was part of the price paid for victory in the Cold War, the Clinton administration insists on post-Cold War reparations from its allies.

The United States defends the principle of a liberal, multilateral, capitalist global system, in which the "allies" are called upon to play their assigned role. Regional leadership on the part of Japan and Germany is permissible and even encouraged, as long as the doors remain open to U.S. commerce and capital, and as long as strategic leadership is seen as belonging to Washington. Any concentration of power independent of United States interests is met and will continue to be met with hostility. In reality there is not much reason for the U.S. to fear the emergence of new regional powers: Japan's neighbors grimaced at the notion of a Japanese-led regional military alliance, while the Japanese government obediently followed the U.S. lead in opposing a proposed East Asia Economic Caucus.[4] Discussions about the emergence of an East Asian bloc remained exactly that: talk and speculation.

Europe still lacks a European military arm as such; the closest approximation is NATO, chiefly under U.S. command anyway, and there is not sufficient sentiment to generate a substitute regionalized NATO. And, as seen in the Bosnian war, even NATO tended to get bogged down in the absence of a clear cut U.S. policy. At heart in the EU is the issue of political will or political capacity to agree on the terms of unity. According to one observer, "even those Europeans who most favor European integration, however, depend increasingly on symbolism — sonorous statements issued by their gerontocrats, François Mitterrand and Helmut Kohl — while real policy choices on economics, real movements under the European Union's Maastricht Treaty, and real restructuring of NATO are postponed *sine die*."[5]

National capitalist-bureacratic interests continue to outweigh collective concerns, and in this sense the end of Soviet power made the job of global organizing more difficult, notwithstanding increased dependence on and vulnerability to global markets. Still, the United States elite did not automatically "lead," but rather assumed that others were willing or able to fall in line and assume subordinated military or financial tasks.

Perhaps there is a structural dimension to leadership. U.S. military logistics, U.S. banking firms, U.S. capital and trade markets have been, and still are, vital to European and Japanese corporate stability. But politicians in these countries are also aware that U.S. military and financial power have been utilized without consultation with them — irresponsibly, from the perspective of their own corporate and electoral interests.

Even if the international pecking order were finally set, there would still be specific limits to what any state or group of states, corporations or group of corporations, could accomplish. It may well be that the bulk of world trade is intra-corporate trade, nominally subject to organizational control, but this is not the case with world finance. The global corporate elite, including its bureaucratic spokespersons, cannot disguise their worry over the enormous increase in international financial transactions, which has accentutated the vulnerability of the entire profit-making system to market shocks like the one provoked by the Mexican collapse. Tens of billions of dollars barely sufficed to keep the Mexican economic and political system afloat. There is no governmental and banking capacity to prevent exchange and stock markets from overheating and spinning into frenzies. Over the course of the last decade, bond issues have tripled, securities transactions have increased more than tenfold, and foreign exchange transactions quadrupled to one trillion dollars a day, according to the International Monetary Fund.[6] Yet less than 10 percent of these mind-boggling sums deal with trade in actual goods and services — the rest represent financial speculation.[7]

In this casino economy, speculators appear more powerful than governments, particularly as even illustrious banks are not above making quick profits in the 24-hour-a-day financial markets, inventing the bogus instruments to keep the frenzy and the profit flow growing. Authorities in Tokyo, Bonn, and Washington have difficulty regulating that flow and already have their hands full with the rescue of national financial institutions, blaming each other for the ups and downs of particular currencies. G-7 ministers of finance wishfully reaffirm their faith in the market and guided political action, claiming that exchange rates are "out of sync with fundamentals" and calling for "an orderly reversal of exchange rate movements."[8]

Neither global markets nor exchange rates are subject to "order." And governments are largely not free to ignore the socio-economic dislocations created in their own countries and the mounting vulnerability to market shock waves. This may translate into aggressive commercial policies and political posturing which can upset corporate

networks and further rattle markets. Yet as multinational cross investment multiplies and production separates from territoriality, the loyalty between capital and nation-state becomes strained, however
much governments and corporations propagate the public need to
defend national companies. With new technologies permitting
stepped up corporate tapping of cheap labor — so-called global sour-
cing — as workers lose jobs and a sense of security, "national" social
cohesion itself threatens to fall apart.

As in previous historical periods, the combination of social insecurity, international economic rivalry, and overproduction spells international strategic instability. Export imperatives take the form of
cut-throat North-North competition in the South. In theory, successful globalization and liberalization enhances the purchasing power of
countries and peoples everywhere. In practice, creeping protectionism in the North and limited purchasing power in the South reduce
the possibility of generalized economic expansion and overall stability.

Social cleavages developed over centuries are too deep to be easily
bridged. Most of the South's population will not become potential
customers overnight, on account of the legacies of colonial underde-
velopment. The trickle down that did not materialize earlier, does not
materialize later, because the same structures of inequality leave the
majority too poor to exercise effective demand. Local elites and more
privileged segments of the populations in the "emerging countries"
do have new wealth to spend, and corporate capital backed by their
respective governments have gone after them with a vengeance.

In this way, a rather reduced global economy has created shared interests and shared conflicts between elites in the South and their
counterparts in the North, divorcing both of them in many senses
from their own peoples. While more than 80 percent of world trade
was controlled by the richest 20 percent of the population, the rest of
the debt-strapped world could not play a meaningful role in globalization schemes, other than to hasten the "race to the bottom," trying
to further drop wages to attract capital and implementing increasingly drastic "reform" processes to gain IMF/World Bank approvals.
The only significant binding link seemed to be between long-standing
economic crisis in most of the South and the new social crisis in parts
of the North. Herein lay the new North-South divide.

State-applied remedies to this situation could prove deadlier than
the global economic disease ailing the world. The lack of global political authority to manage global corporate expansion remains a source
of instability, but the world will not become trouble-free when and if
global centralization of political power catches up with the global

concentration of economic might. In a market context, more turmoil will lead to the reappearance of a nationally-minded trigger-happy sheriff. From the perspective of the South, and sectors of the South in the North, the results could be further oppression.

How to address global instability? The United States governing elite had one answer: more intervention. At the same time, right-wing ideologues continue to hold that the answer to the problems of the free market was even greater freedom for capital and markets.

Among those less concerned about the health of the elite than with its victims, two camps appeared. Each placed primacy on the role of individual human beings and social movements. One approach focused on civil society, or on building or restructuring supranational bodies to secure global democratic governance. Another camp, particularly in the South, upheld the importance of the State. For them, the potential rewards of a humanitarian multinationalist order are not within the grasp of that overwhelming portion of global citizens living in misery. Transnational solidarity is not denied, but preserved in essence, which means supporting and accepting, instead of trying to redirect, the character of national struggles waged by peoples in particular countries.

In our effort to organize global constituencies we must be careful not to allow a utopian vision of transnational struggle to substitute for the even more arduous task of resistance within existing temporal, national, or spatial parameters. This does not mean embracing, in the name of local community development, individualistic solutions or escapes from the global responsibility. For some time to come popular struggles, particularly in the South, will be waged primarily within the framework of nation-states, perhaps less obsessed with the "capture" of state power, but certainly the product of specific national histories and social formations.

How will humanity best avoid self-destruction in the face of predatory global capital increasingly successful in overcoming the specific constraints attempted by non-imperial states? The transnationalization of popular struggles is a goal which is first approached by battles waged at home, even if there are no short-term "domestic" solutions in sight. Socializing local economies to develop human resources may be a starting point, remembering that the method of building power defines the eventual nature and potential of that power. Method is critical because alternative forms of power (popular movements) and global governance will not be defined only by economic criteria, but primarily by the nature of the local relations, between genders, and between people and authorities.

We can and must always be conscious of common problems that plague different nations, but the magnitude of those ills and of the mobilization required to remedy them may appear overwhelming to many — and a sense of hopelessness is neo-liberalism's best ally.

Long-term global proposals are still in the process of articulation, and some of their exponents will have difficulty in signing up recruits, particularly if these proposals do not look to people's struggles to discover the actual contours of alternative courses of life. A failure to understand the social and transnational content of national struggles, along with the national reality of transnational and social struggles, in present-day conditions, can only retard the advancement of the democratic transformations so desperately required and sought by a majority of the world's peoples.

Notes

1. "U.S. and Japan Edge Forward," *Wall Street Journal,* June 28, 1995.
2. Colin Powell, "United States Forces: Challenges Ahead," *Foreign Affairs,* vol. 71, no. 5 (Winter 1992-1993), pp. 33, 35.
3. Cited in Joseph S. Nye, Jr., *Bound to Lead: The Changing Nature of American Power* (New York: Basic Books, 1991), pp. 193-194.
4. Sanen Marshall, "Japan Surrendering Economic and Political Independence," *Just World Trust* (Malaysia), April 6, 1995.
5. Robert A. Levine, "France and the World," *Foreign Policy,* no. 95 (Summer 1994), p. 196.
6. "Bagpipes and Bailouts as Leaders Meet," *New York Times,* June 15, 1995.
7. Richard J. Barnet and John Cavanagh, *Global Dreams, Imperial Corporations and the New World Order* (New York: Simon & Schuster, 1994), p. 17.
8. "Bagpipes and Bailouts as Leaders Meet," *New York Times,* June 15, 1995.

INDEX

247